Feminisms
and
Critical
Pedagogy

Feminisms
and
Critical
Pedagogy

Edited by Carmen Luke and Jennifer Gore

ROUTLEDGE   NEW YORK   LONDON

Published in 1992 by

Routledge
An imprint of Routledge, Chapman and Hall, Inc.
29 West 35 Street
New York, NY 10001

Published in Great Britain by

Routledge
11 New Fetter Lane
London EC4P 4EE

Printed in the United States of America on acid free paper

The illustration on page 19 first appeared in *The Works of Jeremy Bentham,* vol. 4 (1843), edited by Bowring.

Library of Congress Cataloging in Publication Data

Feminisms and critical pedagogy / edited by Carmen Luke and Jennifer Gore.
     p.   cm.
   Includes bibliographical references and index.
   ISBN 0-415-90533-8 (hb)   ISBN 0-415-90534-6 (pbk.)
   1. Critical pedagogy.   2. Feminist theory.   3. Feminism.
I. Luke, Carmen.   II. Gore, Jennifer, 1959—
LC196.F46   1992
305.42—dc20   91-43568
                                                                    CIP

British Library cataloguing in publication data also available

Contents

Acknowledgments

We express our appreciation for permission to reprint the following:

Elizabeth Ellsworth. "Why Doesn't this Feel Empowering? Working Through the Repressive Myths of Critical Pedagogy," *Harvard Educational Review,* 1989, *59*(3), 297–324. Copyright © 1989 by the President and Fellows of Harvard College. All rights reserved.

Jennifer Gore, "What Can We Do For You! What *Can* We Do For You? Struggling over Empowerment in Critical and Feminist Pedagogy," *Educational Foundations,* 1990, *4*(3), 5–26.

Jane Kenway and Helen Modra, "Feminist Pedagogy and Emancipatory Possibilities," *Critical Pedagogy Networker,* 1989, *2*(2&3).

Patti Lather, "Post-Critical Pedagogies: A Feminist Reading," *Education and Society,* 1991, *9*(1–2).

Magda Lewis, "Interrupting Patriarchy: Politics, Resistance and Transformation in the Feminist Classroom," *Harvard Educational Review,* 1990, *60*(4), 467–488. Copyright © 1990 by the President and Fellows of Harvard College. All rights reserved.

Valerie Walkerdine, "Progressive Pedagogy and Political Struggle," *Screen,* 1986, *27*(5), 54–60.

We thank an anonymous reviewer for insightful readings and constructive suggestions, and Jayne Fargnoli, our Routledge editor, without whose support this book would not have been possible.

Importantly, we are indebted to the women in this volume who have raised many theoretical and practical issues of political significance to all of us. Our dialogues in print and in person have created friendships that connect some of us located in isolated institutional contexts in alliance across continents and oceans. We must also acknowledge that we have experienced a qualitatively different tempo and commitment among the women working together on this text. When we asked for text edits, they were dealt with promptly and meticulously, without lengthy disputations. In the context of this group of women, collaborative scholarship within non-combative working relationships has been a rewarding experience.

Finally, some personal acknowledgments:

I wish to thank Pam Nilan, Terry Lovat and Jenny Allen for their support of my work during my first year at Newcastle University. I am especially grateful to James Ladwig, Alison Dewar and Annette Corrigan whose enduring friendships, and political insights, have provided much of the support and challenge to sustain my academic work.

Jennifer Gore
Newcastle, Australia

The preparation of this book was partially supported by a James Cook University Merit Research Grant. My appreciation to Richard Smith for his continuing support of my work and provision of institutional support to enable me to keep writing. Many thanks to Dianne Cooper for the hours of proofreading, typing and checking of references. Most of all, thanks go to Allan, Haida, and Rhonda for years of conversation and friendship.

Carmen Luke
Townsville, Australia

Foreword

Passion, acerbity, and spurts of brilliance mark the "uneasy" discourse in the chapters to come. In the context of an anthology focusing on diverse feminisms and critical theories of various sorts, a range of women writers enter into a multilogue among themselves. Most of them deliberately resist temptations of harmonious agreement, although they surely come together in a concern for authentic liberatory teaching and for the rejection of patriarchy. Demonstrating at every step that there exists no "essence" of radical feminism, they are drawn to shifting viewpoints, interruptions, the idea of multiple identities. And yet, as they make clear their refusals and resistances, they identify some of the most crucial and unsettled issues confronting teachers in search of emancipatory pedagogies today.

The tone of the book is poststructural (verging on what is called postmodern in the United States). That means that there is a focal interest in signification, in power/knowledge relationships, in the harm done by master-narratives, and in the way institutional structures are controlled. The editors, emphasizing the centrality of subjectivity, identity and knowledge in the work of schooling, say that their book should be read "as a re-thinking and re-vision of subjectivity, identity politics and formation, and knowledge from the standpoint of feminist educators."

Perhaps most interesting, and bound to engage all but the most complacent readers, is the effort to break with the kinds of discourse and theory-building that have remained under the control of men. It is well known that the most well-known and widely used radical pedagogies have been devised by males. Men, particularly in the academy, still claim discursive authority; women are still expected to identify their positions with theoretical signifiers that are fundamentally paternal. In the different chapters of this book, the writers declare their responsibility to alter this: to clarify the meanings of gender; to redefine the masculinist "subject" and to rediscover the significance of embodied subjectivity; and to develop, as women, a pedagogy of possibility.

These writers are seriously attentive to the diffusion of power and to the ambiguities of "empowerment." Whether they are addressing themselves to the normalizing impacts of the motherly teacher in the early primary grades, or the blunted emancipatory efforts in undergraduate education, they probe such notions as the kind of "vanguardism" that (contrary to the intention of the teacher) renders students passive and deprives them of a sense of agency. Some find the insights of deconstruction helpful in problematizing the exaggerated conceptions of the powers of human reason. Others find Paulo Freire's idea of conscientization helpful in stimulating the self-reflexivity characteristic of feminist critique. Still others turn their attention most of all to Michel Foucault, especially when he challenges the notion of power as a possession rather than as something that only exists in action.

All, committed as they are to identifying an emancipatory feminist praxis, cannot but work to clarify what it signifies to "empower" and what, given the institutions in which feminist teaching must take place, empowerment may imply in specific contexts. Teachers who care about provoking students to some sense of agency often become concerned about making those students "other," and thereby demeaning as well as distancing them. But how are they to launch a critique of dominant discourses (racist, perhaps sexist, classist) those students have never questioned? How, on the other hand, are they to move to self-definition students whose lived experiences are entirely different from their own? How are they to deal with what *they* choose to identify as oppression, especially when the voices in the classroom become defiant, rather than expressing eagerness to understand, to share? One difficulty with the theory and the general literature available is, these writers say, that these remain laden with masculinist assumptions about oppositions, hierarchies, and justifications for neglecting contradictions and unknowability.

Feminist pedagogies, therefore, demand critical examination of what lies below the surface. They demand confrontations with discontinuities, particularities, and the narratives that embody actual life stories. At once, they require renewed attentiveness to the construction of knowledge and the life of meaning. Relational, practice-centered, contextualized, open-ended: this anthology has been developed in accord with the feminist practice the writers here are reaching towards. It offers an opportunity to readers, female and male, to go in search of new emancipatory modes of teaching that refute the old authorities and undermine old institutional controls.

An adventure in self-reflection and discourse lies ahead. There will be occasions to come in touch with some of the great questioners and demystifiers of our troubled time: Jacques Derrida, Michel Foucault, Jacques Lacan, Gayatri Spivak, Cornel West, and a number of others. More important, however, will be the opportunity to perceive a feminist pedagogy in the making—a pedagogy actually defined by activist women teachers, forged out of the palpitant stuff of their own classroom practice and the material of their own embodied lives. This book is a sign of something happening, something that has never happened in this manner before.

Maxine Greene
Teachers College
Columbia University

1

Introduction

Carmen Luke and Jennifer Gore

The circumstances that brought us together in this book are different from those usually associated with anthologies. We did not send out invitations for chapters to fit with a topic that we defined. Rather, we decided to center an emergent feminist discourse by bringing together various recently published or presented papers that reflected on personal encounters with critical pedagogical practice. Some of us had expressed skepticism of the theoretical bases which informed what had become known as "critical pedagogy." Others had related unsatisfactory classroom attempts at implementing strategies prescribed by critical pedagogy discourse. This book positions collectively these different, but connected, readings of critical pedagogy discourse.

As feminist educators, we all attempt on a daily basis to create pedagogical situations which "empower" students, demystify canonical knowledges, and clarify how relations of domination subordinate subjects marked by gender, ethnicity, race, class, sexuality, and many other markers of difference. But in the process of trying to create "emancipatory" classrooms, we have come up against "uneasy" readings: our own readings of the texts of emancipatory pedagogy, our readings of our students' reactions to us and to each other, and our readings of where feminist educational work stands in relation to male-authored critical pedagogy.

In different ways and at different times, each of us began to write about these "uneasy" experiences with, and understandings of, the works associated with the discourse of post–New Sociology critical pedagogy. As the first of these feminist critiques of critical pedagogy were published (some with considerable difficulty), many of us recognized that something was on the move; that our personal reactions weren't that personal and unique. Indeed, women in other universities, in other classroom contexts, and other countries were experiencing similar theoretical, political and pedagogical "dissonance" with what the "founding fathers" had conceptualized as a pedagogy for self- and social empowerment and for freedom from oppression.

The production of this book is a political move—as well as a philosophical

1

and social endeavor—to distinguish this ongoing work in and through pedagogy from a generalized critical pedagogy. Our texts were already being circulated, cited by each other, by female and male colleagues, and added to reading lists as another important point of view that students should read. It seemed to us that bringing these texts together in a book would contribute to the wider political struggle to get women authors and feminist perspectives on reading lists (in any discipline), one of many struggles in disrupting the "Masculine/feminine regime" (Cocks, 1989). Moreover, given the text-centered logos of all institutionalized pedagogy—whether in public schools or the university—a book still signifies "manifest discourse" and discursive authority, more so than tattered photocopies of journal articles. While we don't want to suggest a seamless (analytic) epistemological unity here, we do want to highlight the unity of our task as feminist educators, and the unity of collective voices marked by resistance to many unexamined assumptions underlying the discourse of critical pedagogy. Foucault taught us that disciplinary power (e.g., via the text[book] of social science) is both negative and positive: both disabling/coercive and enabling/productive. Some might read this book as a disabling betrayal of the critical pedagogy discourse which many of us at one moment (however brief and tenuous) found appealing. We see our text instead as a productive and enabling intervention towards a re-visioning of pedagogical relations as these are structured by institutional discourse and by embodied subjects.

Learning the masters inside-out—from the outside

Institutional discourses define the classroom, the teacher and the student. For instance, we are inscribed as either student or professor: students take exams, teachers don't; students are graded, teachers grade. Such inscriptions are key in the production of subjectivity, identity, and knowledge in pedagogical encounters. In short, we might argue, subjectivity, identity and knowledge *are* the work of schooling. Yet, such institutional inscriptions, as well as numerous other (some contradictory) discourses of identity, are embodied by real women and men. Our efforts in this book are directed towards a re-thinking and re-visioning of subjectivity, identity politics and formation, and knowledge from the standpoint of feminist educators. As feminist educators, we are also women who stand hip-deep in cultures saturated with phallocentric knowledges, in institutional structures ruled epistemologically and procedurally by men and masculinist signifiers, and in a discipline which, despite its historical terrain as "women's work"—a caring profession—remains the theoretical and administrative custody of men.

Unlike women in many other disciplines, we have all invested substantial life time coming up through the ranks of education: all of us as girls in school, some of us later as teachers; all of us as students and then teachers in undergraduate and graduate university programs. We all have learned well the lessons of dutiful daughters in reciting the fathers. We learned the Greeks, we learned Hegel and Marx, we "did" Dewey, we did Freire. We agonized over Piaget or Kohlberg, Foucault or Derrida. We managed to learn their discourses inside out in order to frame our theses in the master discourses. In most cases, we did this well, knowing that we had to over-achieve in order to get at least equal praise and recognition in relation to the men we were going through school with. After the proverbial "well done" slap on the back at the end of (often lonely) orals or final comprehensive exams, we were on our own. Armed to the teeth with credentialled knowledge and a newly certified identity, we headed out in search of work.

Our apprenticeships completed, our theoretical positions professed in print and in body at the confessional oral, where *did* we stand? After years of uneasy readings of the fathers, our various responses to the discourse of critical pedagogy were not "critical" choices, conscious moves in a moment of avant-garde leftist leaning toward a culturalist or continental "theory" of the subject. Rather, our readings of critical pedagogy have been arrived at out of our positioning, location, and identity as women in education: as women within a patriarchal system of knowledge, scholarship, and pedagogical relations. We may not have "spoken" subversively all those years as students, as research and teaching assistants. But a language of critique, with which we began to understand our absences in the master texts—including those of critical pedagogy—and began to read "critically" their writings of us as others, developed as a condition of being other: of being written to the margins, of being someone else's representation and fantasy. The acuity of this double-vision derived precisely from our experience of being within and constituted by the master discourses, and from the years of "close readings" (and reproductions) of the masters. As Irigaray (1985) points out so eloquently, the years of looking straight into a straight mirror have reflected back clearly only the spectacle and rule of the father. We know it well. But we also know our otherness by virtue of being in the dark and on the outside of those refractions: knowing ourselves in the hidden and oblique spaces accessible through the curved specular mirror.

Ours is not a studiously acquired posture of skepticism and critique. It is not "critique" as a designer add-on to leftist post–Marxist or Frankfurt School thought. Rather, it *is* skepticism and critique as subjectivity, as perhaps the only position in (the master) discourse available to us by which we learned to know and read the world. Our essays stem from that skepticism and reflect a shared epistemology, socially shaped through our long educational apprenticeships, that is intrinsic to our subjectivities as women in education. These essays are written by women whose identities are written for them from the center and who live those identities both inside and outside the center. Our self/other, insider/outsider dual positioning is not ambiguous but real, inscribed as it is on material bodies and in lived (not studied, not assumed) subjectivity. This is our standpoint here.

Identity papers: poststructural feminisms

To give this standpoint a name, we situate the essays in this volume within poststructuralist feminisms. That is, texts, classrooms, and identities are read as discursive inscriptions on material bodies/subjectivities. Pedagogical encounters and pedagogical texts are read both as a politics of signification and as historically contingent cultural practice. And, with a politics of reading that takes seriously Foucault's (1980) notion of power-knowledge, assumed meanings deployed in critical pedagogy discourse are examined as we trace how those meanings correspond to specific practices and embodied relations in classrooms. Meanings associated with concepts of, for instance, "power", "citizenship", "voice"—signs of considerable significance in critical pedagogy texts—are not only a point of struggle for many feminists but they are a source of struggle for a variety of embodied differences among students and teachers in classrooms. As teachers with all good intentions rush into classrooms ready to emancipate, to liberate, to grant space and time for silenced voices, few would question the importance of "giving" students voice, or empowering the marginalized, and of democratizing classroom discourse. But a poststructuralist feminist position takes issue with the technology of control, the silent regulation, deployed by signifiers such as "power", "voice", "democratic freedoms" and the "class, race, gender" triplet.

The confessional impulse of fronting up with one's position is as important to feminism's commitment to standpoint as it is to masculinist claims to discursive authority across disciplines in the academy. For academic women, however, the pressure to identify their feminist position with a paternal signifier of "real theory" is quite different. Cixous (1981) puts it well: "the moment women open their mouths—women more often than men—they are immediately asked whose name and from what theoretical standpoint they are speaking, who is their master and where they are coming from: they have, in short, to salute . . . and to show their identity papers" (p. 51). Our identity papers are dog-eared passports, marked by entry and exit stamps among foreign discourses and languages in which we have travelled as tourists. We speak here at a moment in history, in a language and textual terrain not of our making. We may claim affinity with poststructuralism, but we do not owe a debt of gratitude. Instead, we salute feminists past and present. After all, it is the voluminous feminist literature of the last two decades that has made the most powerful contribution to re-thinking the subject, to questioning theory in all disciplines, and to the debates on difference.

We take seriously, however, Elspeth Probyn's (1990) point that the postmodernist epistemological metaphor of travel and nomadic subjectivity threatens to remove the ground from feminist theory. As outsiders, we have travelled in foreign territory: some of us through dialectics, Marxism, existentialism, and critical theory onwards to liberal pragmatism, structuralism, poststructuralism, and probably through various territories in feminisms. These treks have taught us that there are no finite answers, no certainties in any one position. Even feminisms have found that they cannot arrive at finite certainties about feminine subjectivity, identity or location. Trajectories of difference cannot be subsumed under a generalized other.

Thus, while tentatively proffering identity papers we have marked with poststructuralist feminisms, we refuse to align with, or pay homage to, what others totalize as "postmodern [or poststructural] feminism", a feminism that "rejects all forms of essentialism" (Giroux, 1991, p. 44). Through our engendered thinking and situated knowledges (de Lauretis, 1990), as women in education, our positions are feminist. Poststructuralist or postmodernist theoretical tenets have been helpful to the extent that they fit with our feminist political project(s) and our attempts to construct pedagogies. Through the naming of our feminisms as primary, especially in the project that is this book, we adamantly resist the hidden agenda of erasure that drives much of current postmodernist theory and analysis—one that drives attempts to parcel off work such as ours under yet another label that has been thrust upon us.

Feminist foundations and poststructuralist thought?

Central to poststructuralism and postmodernism is an anti-foundational epistemology. This epistemology rejects foundational truths located in disciplinary knowledges and rejects the unitary rationalist subject as foundational to all knowledge. The poststructuralist agenda focuses on the deconstruction of taken-for-granted historical structures of socio-cultural organizations within which various versions of the "individual" have been inserted and, importantly, on the language and theoretical structures with which the individual and the social have been written. Deconstruction under the poststructuralist banner is most commonly referred to as archaeology of knowledge and has characterized much Australian, British, and Canadian work. In the United States, by contrast, deconstruction tends to claim allegiance with what has been named postmodernism. Influenced largely by the American importation of both Derrida and Lyotard and their discourses, the postmodernist signifier has had much greater currency in the United States than elsewhere (Husseyn, 1984). Yet both poststructuralism and postmodernism take issue with the centuries-long rule of Enlightenment epistemology and the fictions of the individual that it spawned. Both reject the self-certain subject, the truth of science and fixity of language, and the functionalist order imputed to the social and to theories of the social.

Feminist theories, likewise, reject the universal subject, theories of that subject and its other, and the social structures and theories that contain the masculine and feminine subject. Grounded in a politics of embodied identities, differences, and historical location, these theories do not give up their foundations in attempts to alter the gender regime. The historical contingency of feminine subjectivity is central to feminist theories, and therefore the refusal of identity is not part of the feminist theoretical or political project. Moreover, we are not at all convinced that men are giving up their identity and authority, even as they speak a good postmodernist game of "multiple narratives" and "border crossings". As bell hooks (1990) point out, "It's easy to give up identity, when you got one" (p. 28). In this context, feminist theories are far from ready to give up feminist struggles for identities of our own making.

So, despite some similarities between poststructuralist/postmodernist and feminist theories, the historically necessary feminist politics of our standpoints require a cautious and careful embrace of these "new" discourses. As bell hooks (1990), Nancy Hartsock (1990) and Carmen Luke (Chapter 3) point out, the abandonment of the subject and, by extension, the rejection of (grand) theory may have serious political consequences for all marginalized groups which attempt, at this historical juncture, to redefine their subjectivities and identities, and theorize self/other relations from their standpoint. Why are claims about "the end of man" most vocal at this particular historical moment when colonized others struggle for and begin to acquire small spaces in which to write themselves (e.g., women in some spaces in the academy)? How, then, do the poststructuralist feminist standpoints of many of the essays here fit in (or not fit in) with poststructuralist and postmodernist skepticism, deconstruction, and valorization of difference? And how might feminist educators theorize their theoretical foundations and assumptions, and their visions of practice, within such a framework?

Foucault's work, more so than the works of postmodernist theorists such as Derrida, Lyotard or Baudrillard, has shown the historical contingency of "the individual", and of systems of knowledge. He argues that it is the representation of subjects in language organized in particular discursive systems (such as science, schooling, the clinic, or the army) that positions subjects in relations of control, discipline, and moral regulation. If we look at, for instance, the discourses of psychology, sociology, or progressive pedagogy, we find the organization of race, and feminine and masculine gender, in specific representational systems. For instance, race has a long history associated with deviance, dysfunction, and remediation in psychology and sociology. And these representations of race, along with feminine gender, circulate in social science disciplines constructed as subjects of difference in compensatory or "at risk" discourses. Pedagogic discourse is a good case in point. Children of color and girls have long held a prominent place in "compensatory" discourses which write their differences as at risk and in need of recovery, remediation, special inquiries and policies.

Hence, our poststructuralist feminist task is to go beyond the deconstruction of the normative masculine subject valorized as the benchmark against which all others are measured, and to examine how and where the feminine is positioned in contemporary emancipatory discourses (including feminist discourses). The high visibility of "gender" in social justice and equity programs and policies, and its status in almost all progressive pedagogical tracts, easily obscures the fact that equal space and representation in curriculum, policy or the conference agenda does not in itself necessarily alter the status of the feminine as an add-on category or compensatory gesture. As such, the poststructuralist feminist agenda remains focused on challenging incorporation and marginalization, even and especially in liberal progressive discourses that make vocal claims to social justice on behalf of marginalized groups while denying their own technologies of power.

Unlike the postmodernist "vanishing act" (Thiele, 1986), a poststructuralist feminism acknowledges its own position in discourse and in history, and therefore remains critical of its own complicity in writing gender and writing others. Contrary to the anti-foundationalism espoused by poststructuralist and postmodernist theorists, a poststructuralist feminism does not give up its theoretical foundations. Feminists disagree on many theoretical and political issues but they do agree on the rejection of the masculinist subject in history as foundational to all truth and knowledge. Poststructuralist feminisms do not float uncommitted on a sea of postmodernist theoretical indeterminacy. In line with the feminist project of standpoint—standing firm on a politics of location and identity—poststructuralist feminisms do not disclaim foundation. Instead, they ground their epistemology on the foundation of difference. A construct of difference that extends beyond the sociological trinity of class, race, gender (usually in that order), and makes conceptual space for difference in subject location, identity and knowledges, renders such a foundation anti-essentialist and indeterminate. This kind of indeterminacy is not the same as the postmodernist deferment. Rather, it is an indeterminacy that lies in its rejection of certainty promised by modernist discourses, a rejection of a self-certain and singular subject, and a rejection of knowledges that promise answers which lead to closure.

A poststructuralist feminist epistemology accepts that knowledge is always provisional, open-ended and relational. Our treks through language and master narratives on the way to this kind of knowing are located in historical and cultural context. This contextual character of all knowledge and knowing suggests that there can be no finite and unitary truths. So, for instance, while we might claim that male rule oppresses women in a near seamless historical and global patriarchal regime, the specificity of women's oppression as it intersects with class, color, nationality, history and culture implies that one theory, one method of analysis, or one concept of the subject cannot unproblematically be applied to all women in all contexts. Our poststructuralist feminist standpoints are grounded in the specific, emergent and conflictual history of the female-embodied subject (de Lauretis, 1990) and, especially, in our histories as academic women in education (see Chapter 10).

Feminist poststructuralist discourse and constructions of pedagogy

In relation to pedagogical discourse, a poststructuralist feminist position suggests that we cannot claim single-strategy pedagogies of empowerment, emancipation, and liberation. The essays here claim no finite truths and fail-proof answers. Rather, we believe these contributions to be part of an ongoing and provisional debate that challenges the liberal complacency settling in around questions of gender and pedagogy, and that challenges the assumptions and political effects generated by critical pedagogy. Poststructuralist feminist challenges to and interventions in both feminist and masculinist knowledges are provisional and ongoing because of the historical specificity within which feminisms and adjacent discourses map their trajectories. The emergence of poststructuralist feminist discourse on pedagogy has its own historical legacy and momentum to which we now turn.

Much of the feminist work in education throughout the 1970s and early 1980s can be characterized as "gender and education" research (see Kenway and Modra, Chapter 9). Analysis tended predominantly to expose classroom and curricular gender inequalities in efforts to equalize decidedly imbalanced classroom practice and curricular representation. Throughout that period, the results of gender and education research filtered through to state and federal commissions and inquiries into girls and schooling, and subsequently into educational policies and curricula. Policy texts prescribed the need for gender-inclusive curricula and for girls' greater access to and participation in maths and sciences, sports and physical education. Curricular texts began to give girls equal representational space. More textual illustrations of and references to girls became evident, although girls in math and science texts were still counting buttons or washing beakers. Equal classroom time, equal numerical participation, and equal curricular presence were the main aims and outcomes of the 1970s and 1980s gender and education research.

Other feminist educational work done during the same period (primarily in the United States) concerned itself with the construction of "feminist pedagogy" (Gore, 1992). This work emerged from a growing discontent with the patriarchy of schooling and pointed to the absence of gender as a category of interest or analysis in most pedagogical theory, including those discourses which proclaimed themselves as progressive and critical. Attempts were made to argue for, and practice, a pedagogy that would be more inclusive of the experiences of girls and women (e.g., Greenberg, 1982; Maher, 1985, 1987). This work aligned itself with the feminist pedagogy discourse that emerged within Women's Studies, much of which was collected in the anthologies by Charlotte Bunch and Sandra Pollack (1983), Margo Culley and Catherine Portuges (1985), and Nancy Schniedewind and Frinde Maher (1987). Reflecting the separatist move of much feminism of that period, the construction of feminist pedagogy in Women's Studies gave limited attention to male-authored constructions of pedagogy, with Paulo Freire's work the only significant exception. Constructions of feminist pedagogy within the field of education engaged most directly with the emergent pedagogical discourse within Women's Studies and left male-authored pedagogical theories largely unchallenged.

Unlike feminist work in other social science disciplines, then, educational feminist research concerned itself more with the pragmatics of school policy and practice, or with feminist accounts of university classrooms, than with theorizing gendered subjectivity. Those of us who began to investigate theories of the subject as they pertained to pedagogy had to look elsewhere, particularly to psychology (e.g., Gilligan, 1982; Walkerdine, 1984), where we also learned much about Kohlberg's and Piaget's heresies that have informed so much of educational practice.

The discourse of critical pedagogy, grounded more self-consciously in histories and theories of education and social thought generally, seemed to provide better theoretical grounding for the construction of alternative pedagogies which could be sensitive to multiple sites of pedagogical practice. Some of us began trying to practice critical pedagogy, attempting to construct the "emancipatory classrooms" we had come to believe were both desirable and possible.

As the work of Foucault became available in English translations, applications of his analyses of power and discourse emerged in reworkings of educational practice, theory, and history (e.g., Beechey & Donald, 1985; Cherryholmes, 1988; Gore, 1992; Grumet, 1988; Hunter, 1988; Jones & Williamson, 1979; Lather, 1991; Luke, 1989; Walkerdine, 1984). These reworkings marked a subtle turn in critical educational studies, from latter-day "new" sociology research to what has been named poststructuralism. The works in this volume are positioned in the midst of this turn to poststructuralism. It is a turn which highlights the complicity of all discourses in disciplinary power, and so shatters any illusions of innocence held by self-proclaimed emancipatory discourses. Moreover, the early poststructuralist educational work points out that modernist and structuralist discourses, including some feminist discourses, have failed to achieve their goals, in part because of their dogmatic insistence on global and unitary projects and subjects.

Our poststructuralist feminist readings of critical pedagogy discourse emerge in this volume at a time when some critical pedagogy theorists are themselves beginning to explore the implications of postmodernist and poststructuralist theories (e.g., Giroux, 1991). Like all discourses, critical pedagogy produces and is produced by "situated knowledges" (Haraway, 1988). The readings of critical pedagogy contained in this volume, most of which were written in the latter half of the 1980s, generally take as their major object critical pedagogy discourse as it was at that time, situated comfortably within modernist enlightenment epistemologies.

Despite recent efforts by critical pedagogy theorists to incorporate poststructuralism/postmodernism, our poststructuralist feminist standpoints, situated as they are within feminist knowledges as well as poststructuralist ones, continue to distinguish our work from critical pedagogy discourse. The strength of our perspective lies, in part, in the feminist theory and politics which ground our poststructuralist theorizing and pedagogic practice. With this foundation there is greater specificity about our pedagogical goals than currently exists for what is still an abstract, generalized discourse of critical pedagogy, even as it now turns to postmodernist discourse. By locating our work in particular sites and with attention to specific practices, the possibilities for genuinely reshaping discursive and embodied relations in pedagogy seem within reach. The critiques of critical pedagogy discourse in many of the essays which follow constitute one part of the larger project to re-vision pedagogy through poststructuralist feminisms.

Situating texts

After agonizing over the myriad ways to position the various essays of this volume, and wanting to avoid the textual politics of hierarchy and status that inhere or are read into any author list, we have arranged the essays in a way which we feel provides a narrowing toward such a re-visioning of pedagogical practice and theory. Although all of the essays are concerned with pedagogical practice and derive from the authors' experiences in classroom encounters, some writers have framed their experiences in more theoretical terms, whereas others draw more specifically on classroom experience to illustrate theoretical issues. The grouping of the essays according to their different style of voice and different perspectives on similar issues, therefore, reflects our judgements of a textual arrangement that would make the volume most "reader friendly." The early chapters by Valerie Walkerdine, Carmen Luke, Jennifer Gore, Mimi Orner, Elizabeth Ellsworth and Patti Lather map poststructuralist feminist theoretical concerns with some of the key assumptions underlying progressive and radical pedagogy discourse. The latter chapters by Magda Lewis, and by Jane Kenway and Helen Modra, turn to feminist educational work in classrooms and in research. Our closing chapter extends this analysis to reflect on different conditions, experiences, and possibilities in a situated history of feminists' political and theoretical work in the university.

Valerie Walkerdine, in Chapter 2, explores some of the problems and possibilities for and with progressivism as a pedagogic mode and political strategy. She argues that concepts of power and liberation are intimately connected to the radical bourgeois project, the formation of the modern state, and the modern concept of democratic government. Forms of pedagogy demand a self-regulating individual and a notion of freedom as freedom from overt control. Second, Walkerdine suggests that the position of women as teachers is vital to the notion of freedom and liberation implied in such a pedagogy. Women teachers, it is argued, historically have been trapped within a concept of nurturance which held them responsible for the freeing of individuals and therefore for the management of an idealist dream.

In Chapter 3, Carmen Luke argues that gender add-on tactics to patriarchal metanarratives are insufficient theoretical grounds on which to build a distinctly feminist pedagogy. Specifically, she traces the concept of the subject in critical pedagogy to its roots in Frankfurt School social theory. The subject in that discourse, and its transposition to critical pedagogy, is a distinctly Anglo-European male subject which, Luke argues, is theoretically and practically untenable for a feminist pedagogy. The chapter concludes with a call to look beyond the "gender and schooling" literature in attempts to come to terms with feminine subjectivity. Current developments in philosophical and cultural postmodernisms over attempts to re-theorize the subject are discussed as one area of particular concern to feminist educators.

The central argument of Jennifer Gore's essay in Chapter 4 is that the language of "empowerment" so popular in critical pedagogy literature, and also employed in some feminist literature, should be used more cautiously and reflexively. Gore examines the conception of power as property, the particular relationship between the agent of empowerment and those who are to be empowered, and the visions of empowerment implied in much of this discourse. Drawing on Foucault's analyses of power-knowledge, she illustrates how even these liberatory discourses can function as regimes of truth. With a focus on the discursive continuities between empowerment and pedagogy, Gore concludes with a call for greater humility and reflexivity in attempts at empowerment through radical pedagogy.

In Chapter 5, Mimi Orner takes on the specific notion of student voice, a central concept in critical pedagogy discourse, and offers a critique of its structural assumptions about silence and speaking. By deconstructing the concept of voice as it relates to classroom practice, Orner demonstrates the repressive potentials of teacher demands for students to speak in radical classrooms. She concludes with a discussion of alternative perspectives on the meanings and practices of student silence.

In Chapter 6, Elizabeth Ellsworth draws on her attempts to teach and practice "anti-racist" pedagogy in the university classroom. On Ellsworth's reading, the class found the discourse of critical pedagogy not only unhelpful, but disruptive of its attempts. Ellsworth argues that if assumptions, goals, implicit power dynamics, and issues of who produces valid knowledge remain untheorized and untouched, critical pedagogues will continue to perpetuate relations of domination in their classrooms. She provides a critique of "empowerment", "student voice", "dialogue", and "critical reflection", and raises issues about action for social change and knowledge.

Patti Lather, in Chapter 7, addresses the question of how our efforts to liberate perpetuate relations of dominance. Lather applies Foucauldian discourse analysis to examine several conflicting readings of Elizabeth Ellsworth's 1989 essay "Why doesn't this feel empowering?" (which appears here as Chapter 6). This juxtaposition and analysis of conflicting positions within the discourse of critical pedagogy shows that even emancipatory education is a site of struggle and contestation, wherein relations of dominance re-emerge. Turning to "post-critical" pedagogies, Lather focuses on the difficulties of a position that seeks to use postmodernism to both problematize and advance emancipatory pedagogies.

In Chapter 8, Magda Lewis draws on her attempts to formulate a viable feminist pedagogy of transformation out of student resistance to feminist politics. In taking up the psychological, social and sexual dynamics of the feminist classroom, Lewis examines a violence/negotiation dichotomy as a feature of women's educational experience. Teaching strategies used to subvert the gendered status quo of classroom interaction between men and women are outlined and discussed. Lewis concludes by suggesting a specific framework that articulates the terms of feminist teaching.

Chapter 9 outlines a critical analysis of various strands of feminist pedagogy. Jane Kenway and Helen Modra review a broad range of feminist pedagogies and identify a "women's studies" and "gender and schooling" strand. Within the former strand, Freirian, essentialist, and consciousness-raising models tend to guide feminist pedagogy. Within the latter strand, analysis of gender tends to be dominated by more "central" sociological focuses, such as the curriculum, the teacher and learner. Kenway and Modra analyze and discuss the theoretical and practical differences between the two strands and the various positions within them. The chapter concludes with a postscript in which the authors re-examine their essay in light of historical and intellectual developments.

In the closing chapter, we consider the specific struggles of academic life shared by the contributors to this volume and by women in universities elsewhere. This chapter demonstrates how the politics of academic knowledge production enable and contain feminist women's research, writing and pedagogies. We discuss the experiences of feminist academics within academia's power-knowledge regime as contestations against sexist, patriarchal, and phallocentric knowledges.

Anthologies, by definition, are a collection of different positions and modes of expression on a topic or theme. Editors of anthologies are typically charged with the task of unifying the text and glossing over differences in attempts to circumvent the standard criticisms of "unevenness", of ruptures or discontinuities. Such criticisms are based on assumptions about unity and sameness of the disciplinary corpus or canon. We make no totalizing claims to unity here, but acknowledge the differences of position and voice among the women in this volume. These very differences are what unite us across local sites in a shared theoretical and political re-visioning towards pedagogies that are consistent with our poststructuralist feminist standpoints.

References

Beechey, V. & Donald, J. (eds.) (1985). *Subjectivity and social relations*. London: Open University Press.

Bunch, C. & Pollack, S. (eds.) (1983). *Learning our way: Essays in feminist education*. Trumansburg, NY: The Crossing Press.

Cherryholmes, C. (1988). *Power and criticism: Poststructural investigations in education.* New York: Teachers College Press.

Cixous (1981). Castration or decapitation? *Signs, 7*(1), 41–55.

Cocks, J. (1989). *The oppositional imagination: Feminism, critique and political theory.* New York: Routledge.

Culley, M. & Portuges, C. (eds.) (1985). *Gendered subjects: The dynamics of feminist teaching.* Boston & London: Routledge & Kegan Paul.

de Lauretis, T. (1990). Upping the anti (sic) in feminist theory. In *Conflicts in feminism,* M. Hirsch & E. F. Keller (eds.), 255–270. New York: Routledge.

Foucault, M. (1980). *Power/knowledge: Selected interviews and other writings 1972–1977,* C. Gordon (ed.). New York: Pantheon Books.

Gilligan, C. (1982). *In a different voice: Psychological theory and women's development.* Cambridge, MA: Harvard University Press.

Giroux, H. A. (ed.) (1991). *Postmodernism, feminism and cultural politics.* Albany, NY: State University of New York Press.

Gore, J. (1992). *The struggle for pedagogies.* New York: Routledge.

Greenberg, S. (1982). The women's movement: Putting educational theory into practice. *Journal of Curriculum Theorizing, 4*(2), 193–198.

Grumet, M. (1988). *Bitter milk.* Amherst, MA: The University of Massachusetts Press.

Haraway, D. (1988). Situated knowledges: the science question in feminism and the privilege of partial perspective. *Feminist Studies, 14*(3), 575–99.

Hartsock, N. (1990). Foucault on power: A theory for women? In *Feminism/postmodernism,* L. J. Nicholson (ed.) 157–175. New York: Routledge.

hooks, b. (1990). *Yearning: Race, gender, and cultural politics.* Boston, MA: South End Press.

Hunter, I. (1988). *Culture and government: The emergence of literary education.* London: Macmillan Press.

Husseyn, A. (1984). Mapping the postmodern. *New German Critique, 33,* 5–52.

Irigaray, L. (1985). *Speculum of the other woman.* Trans. Gillian C. Gill. Ithaca, NY: Cornell University Press.

Jones, K. & Williamson, K. (1979). The birth of the schoolroom: A study of the transformation in the discursive conditions of English popular education in the first half of the Nineteenth Century. *Ideology and Consciousness, 5*(1), 59–110.

Lather, P. (1991). *Getting smart: Feminist research and pedagogy with/in the postmodern.* New York: Routledge.

Luke, C. (1989). *Pedagogy, printing and Protestantism: The discourse on childhood.* Albany, NY: State University of New York Press.

Maher, F. A. (1985). Classroom pedagogy and the new scholarship on women. In *Gendered subjects: The dynamics of feminist teaching,* M. Culley & C. Portuges (eds.), 29–48. Boston & London: Routledge & Kegan Paul.

Maher, F. A. (1987). Inquiry teaching and feminist pedagogy. *Social Education, 51*(3), 186–192.

Probyn, E. (1990). Travels in the postmodern: Making sense of the local. In *Feminism/postmodernism,* L. J. Nicholson (ed.), 176–189. New York: Routledge.

Schniedewind, N. & Maher, F. (eds.) (1987). Special feature: Feminist pedagogy. *Women's Studies Quarterly, 15* (3, 4).

Thiele, B. (1986). Vanishing acts in social and political thought: Tricks of the trade. In *Feminist challenges: Social and political theory,* C. Pateman & E. Grosz (eds.), Sydney: Allen & Unwin.

Walkerdine, V. (1984). Developmental psychology and the child-centred pedagogy: The insertion of Piaget in early education. In *Changing the subject: Psychology, social regulation and subjectivity,* J. Henriques, W. Holloway, C. Urwin, C. Venn & V. Walkerdine (eds.), 153–202. London & New York: Methuen.

2

Progressive Pedagogy and Political Struggle

Valerie Walkerdine

An idealist dream, an impossible fiction, or something to hope and struggle for? I would like to explore some of the problems and possibilities for and with progressivism as a pedagogic mode and political strategy. I shall tend to make reference to primary school pedagogy because that's what I'm most familiar with, but I hope that these remarks will be relevant to all sections of the education system and to our own practice as teachers in higher and further education.

In 1968 I became a primary school teacher. I was swayed by the romantic promise of progressivism in education, and I linked poverty and inner-city decay with the terrible regimentation and the "old-fashioned" repressive and silencing methods. I had read Herbert Kohl's *Thirty-Six Children*[1] and John Holt's *How Children Fail*,[2] and I loved my inner-city children with a fierce passion, for under my nurturance, their illiteracy would be converted into inner-city poetry. There was joy in my classroom. There were also terrible problems: how to control the children, for example. And four o'clock found me frequently sobbing quietly at my desk, behind the shut door where none of the old, strict teachers, who didn't like my ways, could see me.

Clearly, difficult as it all was, the dream of something different was at that moment very important. But since then, the libertarianism upon which the progressivism of the '60s was founded has been re-examined. It is this libertarianism which was crucial in locating the "personal" as a central aspect of the political, and particularly to the development of a whole panoply of therapeutic interventions. However, alongside a concept of liberation as personal freeing was an understanding of power which located it a fixed possession, in this case that of the oppressive, and consequently repressive, teacher. Personal liberty became synonymous with the lifting of that repression.

In response to these ideas, I want to offer two arguments: first, that the concepts of power and liberation are intimately connected to the radical bourgeois project, the formation of the modern state and the modern concept of democratic government. I shall argue that the forms of pedagogy necessary to the maintenance of order, and the regulation of populations, demand a self-regulating individual and a notion of freedom as freedom from overt control. Yet, such a notion of freedom is a sham.

Secondly, the position of women as teachers (particularly in primary schools) is vital to the notion of freeing and liberation implied in such a pedagogy. It is love which will win the day, and it is the benevolent gaze of the teacher which will secure freedom from cruel authority in the family as well as the school. Through the figure of the maternal teacher, the harsh power of the authoritarian father will be converted into the soft benevolence of the bourgeois mother.

Hence, I will argue, aspects of women's sexuality are intimately bound up with the concept of progressivism. Just as women have argued that the sexual liberation of the '60s was a celebration of masculine sexuality, so I shall argue that the liberation of children conceived in these terms did not mean the liberation of women. In some ways, it actually served to keep women firmly entrenched as vital carers. Women teachers became caught, trapped, inside a concept of nurturance which held them responsible for the freeing of each little individual, and therefore for the management of an idealist dream, an impossible fiction.

Critical to my analysis is a questioning of the concept of power employed in previous formulations. I want to suggest that instead of constructing a concept whereby power equals authoritarianism and absence of power equals helpful teacher and democratic relations, such formulations deny power. (I shall return to the concept of denial used in its psychoanalytic sense). Instead, I shall use power in the Foucauldian sense of *power/knowledge*.[3] It is this sense that I want to raise problems for the concept of liberation as freedom from coercion, and to suggest that it is central to the concept of the bourgeois individual.

The transformation of governmental form, and therefore of the notion of power, is located by Foucault as the shift from an overt sovereign power to a "suspicious" and invisible power located within those aspects of the sciences, particularly human sciences, which came to be used as the basis for what he calls technologies and apparatuses of social regulation. Basically, Foucault argues that the form of government depends not on authoritarianism but on normalization; the concept of a calculated, known population. In that sense a variety of governing practices—from medicine and law, to social welfare and schooling—began to be based on a concept of a norm, a normal individual.

In the nineteenth century science was used to calculate and produce a knowledge of the population on an unprecedented scale. The production of "knowledges" became intimately bound with the devising of new techniques of population management. The school was the arena for the development of one set of techniques for "disciplining" the population. The emergence first of popular and then compulsory schooling related specifically to the problems of crime and poverty understood as characteristics of the population: criminality and pauperism.[4] Schooling was seen as one way to ensure the development of "good habits" which would therefore alleviate these twin problems. The original strategy was to engage children in ceaseless activity, with constant surveillance to ensure these habits. Subsequently, this strategy was abandoned in the face of children's ability at rote learning—"to recite the Lord's Prayer for a half-penny"—without actually assuming the right moral habits.

It was at this point that the kind of pedagogy which had been advocated in terms of overt authority began to be challenged. There were many examples of such challenges, from the work of Froebel and Pestalozzi, to Robert Owen and his school in the New Lanark Mills, to Itard and Seguin in France (who Maria Montessori followed).[5] In their differing ways, they began to advocate an education "according to nature".

Here "nature" must be defined in a number of ways; most of those which are important in the inception of psychology involve a sense of "species-being" derived from evolutionary biology. Thus, in these cases, "education according to nature" came to mean "according to a science of human nature." The critical features here were a sense of evolution and heredity, and an environment understood in quasi-biological terms. Their "interaction" varied in different theories, but was rarely stated differently.[6]

This human nature was mapped out in the Child Study Societies which flooded the land. The calculation of the distinct qualities and characteristics of children followed many attempts to link ontogeny to phylogeny—the individual's development to that of the species—the most famous of which is Darwin's study of his infant son.[7] This classification of children proceeded in the same way that the animal/human distinction was being monitored in the Empire. The categorization of children according to the ontogenetic characteristics of their natures was similarly based on certain assumptions about the civilizing process and the place of "a natural environment" in it.[8]

Education according to nature became the way of ensuring a natural path of development, the best kind of civilizing process.[9] Theories of instincts and animality were thus connected to the regulation of the population, many of whom (particularly the urban proletariat) displayed all too obvious signs of animal passions.[10] Degeneracy was seen as an aberration of nature.[11] And the part played by the environment was made clear by the mapping of the city—the spread of typhoid, the city's criminal quarters, and so forth. The environment, too, could be watched, monitored and transformed.

I am glossing over a great deal of political struggle, but my aim is to demonstrate that the advent of naturalism, that is, the ensuring of a correct passage from animal infant to civilized adult, became understood both as "progressive"—according to scientific principles—and effective. It would prevent the threatened rebellion *precisely because* children who were not coerced would not need to rebel—the lessons would be learned and, this time, properly. Docile bodies would become a self-disciplined work force.

What was proposed was a process—a scientific process—whereby the schoolroom could become a laboratory, where development could be watched, monitored and set along the right path. There was therefore no need for lessons, no discipline of the overt kind. Power became that of the possessor of the Word, of rationality, of scientific concepts—reasons's mastery over the emotions. This would ensure a stable populace, and rebellion would therefore be eradicated by natural means. Interference was limited and surveillance was everywhere. The ultimate irony is that the child supposedly freed by this process to develop according to its nature was the most classified, catalogued, watched and monitored in history. Freed from coercion, the child was much more subtly regulated into normality.

These new concepts created "the child" as the object of calculation and pedagogic practice. For example, "language" became that standard presented in reading books created especially for the child. Using concepts derived from Etienne Balibar's examination of the French language,[12] Jacqueline Rose argues[13] that the construction of a unified nation required the production of reading material *for children*. What we now think of as "natural language" was produced specifically as a special text, stripped of the literary style of the educated aristocracy of the time. In that sense, uniformity, natural language, was created out of diversity— a wide variety of dialects, for example—and made the object of those texts used in compulsory schooling. In this way a standard—an educated standard—was produced, with the consequent pathologization of difference as deviance from that standard. (In a similar vein, Keith Hoskin[14] traces the way in which the development of silent reading transformed a system of oral recitation, and particularly facilitated the development of examinations as written work in silence, thus making the mass testing and normalization of the population possible).

At the very moment that nature was introduced into pedagogy, the shift to covert surveillance became enshrined in a word—"love". "Love" was to facilitate the development of the child in a proper supportive environment. This shift is co-terminous with, and related to, another: the entrance of women into elementary school teaching. The emerging human sciences, building upon previous philosophical tenets, had deemed women's bodies unfit for reason, for intellectual activity. The possession of a womb was thought to render a woman unfit for deep thought, which might tax her reproductive powers to make her less amenable to rearing children. Given the state of Empire, the concern with the race as with the species, it was considered potentially injurious to allow bourgeois women to reason.

Nevertheless, women's struggles to enter higher education finally were successful—when elementary teacher training was opened to them. Frances Widdowson argues that the development of teacher training colleges went together with the concern to educate women.[15] Such a concern was not a reversal of the brain/womb polarity, but precisely its opposite. Women were to be educated, in the words of the 1933 Hadow Report,[16] "to amplify their capacities for maternal nurturance". These capacities, while given naturally, could be enhanced so that women teachers could provide a quasi-maternal nurturance to compensate for the

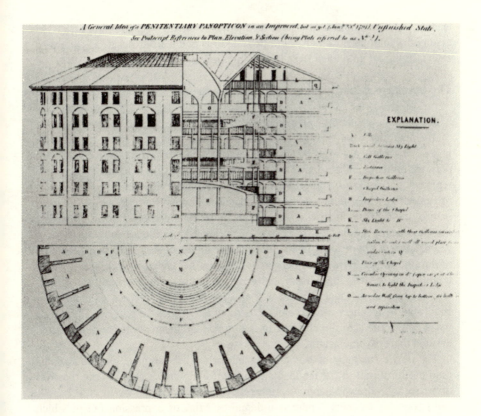

depraved environments of the poor. In addition, women could watch, monitor and map the child's development. Clipboard in hand, these scientific educators could survey each of their small charges, whose development was entrusted to their love.

It was always an impossible fiction. The dream of ensuring each child's pathway to reason turned the schoolroom, where pupils recited their lessons and moved up the form, into the classroom,[17] a place in which each child was considered separately. Discipline became not overt disciplining but covert watching. Regurgitated facts became acquired concepts. Knowledge became naturalized as structure or process. Teachers began to talk about "learning *how* to learn", the surest guarantor of correct rationality. The old ways had to be outlawed to make room for natural reason. Children, therefore, were not taught facts, but were left alone to interact with their environment. The horror of child labor was to be no more. Classroom work was replaced by play—the *proper* medium of expression for children, the most basic and animal-like medium of unconscious fantasies and the recapitulated development of the species.[18] The classroom became the facilitating space for each individual, under the watchful and total gaze of the teacher, who was held responsible for the development of each individual. This assumed a total gaze, which could be stated, as one teacher put it, as "knowing each child as an individual." An impossible fiction.

The psychic economy of the progressive classroom

Let us imagine such a classroom. All has been transformed to make way for "active learning", not "passive regurgitating". This pedagogic space is filled with groups of tables, not rows of desks. There may be no playtime, since work and play are indistinguishable, and work cards and individual assignments may have replaced textbooks. Children may choose their own time tables. Freedom is imagined. A whole fictional space is created, a fantasy-space in which the ideal nature, the most facilitating environment, rather like a greenhouse, is created in the classroom. Away from the decay of the inner city, the air in the classroom smells sweet. The teacher is no authoritarian father figure, but a bourgeois and nurturant mother. Here all can grow properly. In this greenhouse there will be no totalitarianism. It is the nursery and it nurtures, preventing the pent-up aggression leading to delinquency and war and fascism. The freedom of children is suggested by teachers who are not the oedipal father, but the pre-oedipal mother, whose attachment to the children in her care, together with her total presence, ensures their psychic health.

The desire for happiness is a sentiment echoed throughout such classrooms (and deftly caught in Pat Holland's film *What are Schools For?,* where the children are only allowed happy sentiments and happy words: "Wonderful, beautiful", coos the teacher). There is a denial of pain, of oppression (all of which seems to have been left outside the classroom door). There is also a denial of power, as though the helpful teacher didn't wield any (and indeed we progressivists of the '60s believed we could be friends with children, be partners in learning—no power, no hierarchy, called by our first names).

The teacher is there to help, to enable, to facilitate. Only those children with a poor grasp of reality, those poor pathological children, see her power. Because of their own authoritarian families, they react in a paranoid fashion to this nurturance—they are aggressive, they do not speak. They feel they are being watched, and nurtured.[19] Who, one might ask, has not adapted to reality? A bourgeois reality, where it is impossible to see the power invested in your charitable deeds, where the poor and oppressed are transformed into the pathological and inadequate.

But more than this, the happy classroom is a place where passion is transformed into the safety of reason. Here, independence and autonomy are fostered through the presence of the quasi-mother. There is no severance of this mother-child dyad except to autonomy.[20] This leaves the child in a fantasy of omnipotent control over the Other—the teacher. "His" path to rationality, displayed best in mathematics, is a path to omnipotent mastery over a calculable universe (outside time and space—a rationally ordered and controlled world).[21] Passion is superseded by an "attraction to ideas", the "love of order and purity of mathematics." Such power is immensely pleasurable. But whose universe is real?

Is it the universe outside time and space where there will be no war, no pain, no desire, no oppression?

At what cost the fantasy of liberation? I suggest that the cost is borne by the teacher, as it is borne by the mother. She is passive to the child's active, she works to his play. She is the servant of the omnipotent child, whose needs she must meet at all times. Carolyn Steedman[22] suggests that such a role mirrors not the aristocratic mother, but the paid servant of the aristocracy, who is always there to service the children. His majesty the baby becomes his highness the child. The price of intellectual labor (the symbolic play of the Logos) is its Other and opposite, work. The servicing labor of women makes the child, the natural child, possible.

The education of working-class and black children is something of a problem, since they conform rarely to the ideal child. So too, the girl: is she to be a knower or a potential nurturer of knowers? What price her freedom? Although there is much to say about the education of girls and women, let me simply state that regulation of women's sexuality, rendering them fit only for maternal nurturance, is something which, as scholars like Lucy Bland have demonstrated,[23] pathologizes activity and passion. Needs replace desire; affect replaces libido. Indeed, in progressivism, girls are often held up as lacking: they seem to demonstrate either deviant activity, or a passivity which means that they must be found lacking in reason and compensated for this lack. As I tried to show, in "Sex, Power and Pedagogy",[24] it is masculine sexuality, to the point of violence, which is validated by this pedagogy. It is the female teacher who is to *contain* this irrationality and to transform it into reason, where it can do no harm—a transformation of physical violence into the symbolic violence of mastery, the law. And in each case, the woman as container soaks up and contains the irrationality which she best understands.

The extent of validation of violence among boys is shocking in classrooms today. And the downplaying of this aggression in reasoned argument is itself an interesting transformation of power. Here, it is the knower who can win and apparently topple the power of the teacher, through argument. Disciplining becomes knowing.

Although some have suggested that progressivism frees working-class children from harsh authoritarianism, I would suggest precisely the opposite. Progressivism makes powerlessness, the product of oppression, invisible. Within the naturalized discourse it is rendered "unnatural", "abnormal", "pathological"—a state to be corrected, because it threatens the psychic health of the social body. It is therefore very important to reassert the centrality of oppression and its transformation into a pathology in terms of a political analysis of the present social order. For example, what working-class mothers say to their children is either counted as nothing (it doesn't count as natural language in the deprivation literature) or is romanticized and fetishized as the working-class culture of *Nippers* reading books, bingo and chips, the colorful banter of cockney market-traders. Even in the "equal but different" model of working-class language displayed (differently) in the work of William Labov and Harold Rosen, for example,[25] the historical *production* of the "natural" is completely elided. As Jacqueline Rose argues in *The Case of Peter Pan*, "there is no natural language, especially for children." Yet within the progressivists' nurturant welfare state, with its inadequate families aided by our latter-day charity, bourgeois culture is taken as nature.

Meanwhile, meanings are struggled over in the classroom. "The Child" is created as a sign, to be read and calibrated within the pedagogic discourses regulating the classroom. The child is defined and mapped in its relations of similarity and difference with other signs: activity, experience, play rather than passivity, recitation, work and so forth. Through the regulation of this pedagogy children become subjected in the classroom.[26] The classroom, then, is a site of struggle, not of an unproblematic fitting of these categories onto children, but of a constantly erupting pathology, like the unconscious, breaking the smooth surface of the pedagogic discourse.

Many studies, of which the most famous is ORACLE,[27] have claimed that progressivism has never been tried in Britain, that most British classrooms are not child-centered, despite the orthodoxy. We are faced with children working, following the rules, trying to find out what to do. This is despite the fact that there are taken to be no rules, only the pure joy of discovery. It often seems that the teachers produce the very categories that children are taken to be discovering. Children are bewildered because they don't know the rules, and use strategies which aren't supposed to exist. Teachers turn out to be more traditional than expected and feel guilty because the future and "freedom of our children forever" is laid at their door. They are the guardians of an impossible dream, reason's dream of democratic harmony.

Notes

1. Herbert Kohl, *Thirty-Six Children*, Harmondsworth, Penguin, 1971.

2. John Holt, *How Children Fail*, Harmondsworth, Pelican, 1969.

3. Michel Foucault uses the couple *power/knowledge* to examine the positive effectivity of knowledge of populations in the possibility of government. For a general treatment, see Colin Gordon (ed.), *Power/Knowledge*, Brighton, Harvester, 1984. For a specific treatment in relation to primary school pedagogy see Valerie Walkerdine: "Developmental Psychology and the Child-Centred Pedagogy" in Henriques et al. (eds.), *Changing the Subject: Psychology, Social Regulation and Subjectivity*, London, Methuen, 1984. See also Valerie Walkerdine, *Schoolgirl Fictions*, London, Verso, 1991.

4. See Karen Jones and Kevin Williamson, "The Birth of the Schoolroom", *Ideology and Consciousness*, no. 6, 1979.

5. See Valerie Walkerdine, op. cit., and Carolyn Steedman, "Prisonhouses", *Feminist Review, 18,* 1985 for more detail. While the former were attempts in the eighteenth and nineteenth centuries, Montessori followed up by applying the techniques used to train and test the humanity of the "wild boy of Aveyron" to the education of "idiots" and then to the poor of the Italian city slums in 1910–1920.

6. A rare difference was the work of the Soviet psychologist, Lev Vygotsky, working in the 1920s and '30s. Although he did not deviate from a "developmental" model, he made a concerted effort to situate that development within history and not just phylogeny. See for example, F. Newman & L. Holzman, *Lev Vygotzky: Revolutionary Scientist,* London, Routledge, 1992.

7. Charles Darwin, "A Biographical Sketch of an Infant" (1840), reprinted in *Mind 7.*

8. The take-up of "Social Darwinism" had widespread effects, and the emerging anthropology sought to map the animal/human distinction onto nature in different environments in the "discovered" lands of the Empire. Here was a ready test of the "civilizing process."

9. Because it worked *with* nature and not against it, it became a pedagogy of development. Thus the regulation of the population could become self-regulation of a natural system, operating according to universal laws of development. See, for example, Nikolas Rose, *Social Regulation and the Psychology of the Individual,* London, Routledge and Kegan Paul, 1985 and Denise Riley, *War in the Nursery,* London, Virago, 1983. See also N. Rose, *Governing the Soul,* London, Routledge, 1989.

10. The feared uprising of the urban proletariat was associated with the violence of "animal" or "pre-human" emotions.

11. See the work of Nikolas Rose, op. cit. (note 9).

12. Renee Balibar and D. Laporte, *Le francais national,* Paris, Hachette, 1975.

13. Jacqueline Rose, *The Case of Peter Pan or the Impossibility of Children's Fiction,* London, Macmillan, 1985.

14. Keith Hoskin, *Cobwebs to Catch Flies: Writing (and) the Child* (unpublished manuscript), University of Warwick, Department of Education, 1985.

15. Frances Widdowson, *Going up to the Next Class: Women in Elementary Teacher Training,* London, WRRC/Hutchinson, 1983.

16. Consultative Committee of the Board of Education, *Infant and Nursery Schools* (Hadow Report) 1933, London, HMSO.

17. David Hamilton, *On Simultaneous Instruction and the Early Evolution of Class Teaching,* University of Glasgow, Department of Education, 1981.

18. Ideas about play spanned work from child psychologists (Klein) to work on animal ethology demonstrating that young animals played, making it therefore natural. For more discussion, see V. Walkerdine & H. Lucey, *Democracy in the Kitchen,* London, Virago, 1989, as well as E. Singer, *Child Care and the Psychology of Development,* London, Routledge, 1992.

19. For further elaboration, see "On the Regulation of Speaking and Silence", in Valerie Walkerdine, *Schoolgirl Fictions,* op. cit. (note 3).

20. In this discourse, separation from the Mother/Other is not to anywhere or to a relation to the father/phallic/paternal space, but to an autonomy conceived as "individuation."

21. This is further developed in Valerie Walkerdine, *The Mastery of Reason,* London, Routledge, 1988 & 1990.

22. Carolyn Steedman, "The Mother Made Conscious", *History Workshop Journal,* 1985.

23. Lucy Bland, "Guardians of the Race or Vampires upon the Nation's Health? Female Sexuality and its Regulation in Early Twentieth Century Britain", in E. Whitelegg et al. (eds.), *The Changing Experience of Women,* Oxford, Martin Robertson, 1986.

24. Valerie Walkerdine, "Sex, Power and Pedagogy", *Screen Education,* no. 38, 1981, 14–25.

25. William Labov, "The Logic of Non-Standard English", in Ashar Cashdan (ed.), *Language in Education,* Open University and Routledge and Kegan Paul, 1972. For Harold Rosen's critique of Bernstein, see his *Language and Class,* Bristol, Falling Wall Press, 1972, and *The Language and Class Workshop* series.

26. For further elaboration see Valerie Walkerdine, *The Mastery of Reason,* London, Routledge, 1988/90.

27. ORACLE (Observational Research and Classroom Learning Evaluation) was written up as a series of books; for example, Maurice Galton, Brian Simon and Paul Croll, *Inside the Primary Classroom,* London, Routledge and Kegan Paul, 1983.

3

Feminist Politics in Radical Pedagogy

Carmen Luke

Repositioning women from the periphery to the center of social analysis is a central task for feminist theorists, regardless of diverse disciplinary perspectives and theoretical standpoints. Many feminist philosophers, literary, social, cultural and political theorists have tended towards what broadly can be characterized as poststructuralist research: the deconstruction of "master" narratives. Feminist educational theorists, by contrast, have tended largely to focus on critiques of patriarchal assumptions and practices in efforts to document the politics and institutionalization of gendered differences in educational settings and discourses. Explicitly deconstructive work on educational theoretical metanarratives has not been a visible project. This chapter is such an attempt. The narrative under scrutiny here is that of "critical pedagogy", also often referred to as "radical pedagogy."

Following an introductory outline of critical pedagogy's theoretical perspective and historical location, the paper then proceeds in three stages. First, radical pedagogy's construction of the subject will be analysed in terms of its theoretical location in private/public spheres, a dual theoretical and actual space which underlies both liberal theory and historical materialism. The focus is on assumptions central to the critical pedagogy agenda: the public sphere, citizenship, democracy, emancipation. Second, an analysis follows of the individualist ethic presupposed in notions of critical selfhood, personal voice, self-reflexive hermeneutics and critical agency. Third, I briefly examine some principal assumptions of the Frankfurt School's concept of subjectivity as constituted in depth psychology, a concept critical pedagogy adopts as part of its formulation of subject identity and formation.

It will be argued throughout these three sections that, from a feminist position, the discourse of critical pedagogy constructs a masculinist subject which renders its emancipatory agenda for "gender" theoretically and practically problematic. I will further argue that the absence of a coherent and systematic engagement with theorization of "gender" leads to an acritical reinstatement and revalorization of history's "great" patriarchal metanarratives. I conclude with a discussion of how some insights of feminist cultural theory, poststructuralism and postmodernism might provide useful conceptual tools with which to formulate educational questions of the cultural production and reproduction of gendered subjectivities.

Mindful of the substantial and significant recent scholarship by and about women of color such as Amos & Parmar (1987), Carby (1987), Dill (1987), Hill Collins (1990), hooks (1987, 1990), Minh-ha (1989), Mohanty, Russo and Torres (1991), and Spivak (1988a), this paper makes no claims about how their positions would deconstruct and critique the texts I examine here. At every turn in working through this paper, the gender/race intersection of feminine subjectivity revealed itself in need of separate yet related analysis and commentary. Yet the undertheorized concept of "gender" and subjectivity in the critical pedagogy literature identified here has profound ramifications for all women, mapped as we are across the grids of race, class, ethnic, age, and sexuality discourses.

Critical theory in education: radical pedagogy

Beginning in the early 1970s, new sociology developed a phenomenological perspective on school knowledge and relations (e.g., Young, 1971). The emphasis was on agency, reality, interaction, and lived experience as co-constitutive of the production of meaning. It was assumed that once educators took into account children's differential subjectivities and background knowledge, schooling could be transformed and students' class-based failure remediated. The disregard by first-wave new sociologists for those structural ideological, socioeconomic, cultural, and institutional constraints that delimit possibilities for meaning and for lived experience left the field wide open for structural reproduction theory (e.g., Althusser, 1971; Bowles & Gintis, 1976; Bourdieu & Passeron, 1977).

"Second-wave" new sociology emphasized the structural determinants in the reproduction of class and thus of the labor force, subjectivities, and culture. Even student resistance was found to be hegemonized and seemingly served only the reproductive ideology of class and gender oppression (Willis, 1977; McRobbie, 1978; McRobbie & Garber, 1976). Exscribing the voluntarist phenomenological subject, reproduction theorists moved towards the removal of agency from history, the investment of ideological institutions with autonomous, monolithic power, and hence the deletion of all (theoretical) hope for positive intervention at the intersubjective level of the school and classroom.

Historically, critical pedagogy in the 1980s could be seen to constitute a "third wave" new sociology of education (e.g., Giroux, 1981, 1983, 1988; Aronowitz & Giroux, 1985; Giroux & McLaren, 1986; McLaren, 1986, 1987; 1988a,b,c; Giroux & Simon, 1988; Simon, 1987). To counteract the pessimism of reproduction theories, the critical pedagogy project centered on hope, liberation, and equality. Agency and (raised) consciousness were reinstated on center stage, albeit this time with structural constraints acknowledged. Lived experience and intersubjective construction of meaning and identity formation were reauthenticated, and new goals for self-empowerment and critical agency in a critical democracy were set. As with first wave new sociology, critical pedagogy's positive thesis is based on the assumption that if the "text" and experience of schooling are changed (i.e., elimination of racism, sexism, classism), then students' lives and, hence, civil society will be changed for the better. That is, if students are given (equal) opportunity to articulate their cultural experiences, and if teachers help students discover how they self-construct cultural meanings and identities within and against the ideological frameworks of mass culture, institutional settings and discourses—then students will have the critical tools with which to act in morally responsible, socially just and politically conscientious ways against individual and collective oppression. In this view, critical self-determination will lead to a democratic transformation of schooling and society.

Critical pedagogy theoretically is founded on first generation Frankfurt School critical theory, on Gramsci's concept of hegemony and associated concepts of the (organic intellectual) subject and (counter-hegemonic) practice, and on Freire's educational theory and practice of "conscientization". From Marcuse and Gramsci, among others, radical pedagogy derives an amalgamated concept of the subject. Marcuse held that reified social relations, invested with a repressive ideology of control and false needs, permeate the everyday and thus insert themselves in the unconscious and in personality dispositions (Giroux, 1983: 27–34; 147–148). Marcuse's indebtedness and reworking of certain Freudian tenets I leave aside for now; a more detailed discussion follows in the latter part of the paper. For Frankfurt School theorists the practice of de-reification, of personal and political emancipation, was through negative critique: that is, the negation of false consciousness through ideology critique. In Marcuse, emancipatory practice was possible on the basis of Freud's formulation of the pleasure principle. For Freud, the fundamental human drive was towards pleasure; for Marcuse this translated into the drive for the resolution of tension and thus for an escape from domination into freedom (cf. Giroux, 1983: 34). Gramsci provides radical pedagogy theory with another dimension of subjectivity. The Gramscian notion of critical subjectivity is less psychoanalytically based and grants subjects common sense, dialectical thinking, and intellectual possibilities. Hegemonized subjects have the potential to contest their ideological positioning and historical condition since "all men are intellectuals" (Gramsci, 1971: 9). In principle, all have the potential to assume a counter-hegemonic position from which to articulate the values and interests of subordinate groups. In the Gramscian schema, the intellectual who assumes such a position speaks from and for the working class: her or his experience and interests are organic to "real" class interests. For Gramsci, while hegemonic control was powerful, diffuse and complex, it was not seamless. For critical pedagogy, this means that it is within the many small but potentially powerful spaces within institutions of social and ideological control that counter-hegemonic discourses and practices can be organized. The school is one site where organic intellectuals should elaborate a critical language to enable creative and critical consciousness among students.

Freire's (1973, 1978) critical pedagogy of conscientization provides radical pedagogy with the notion of teaching for critical consciousness, the teaching of critical literacy. Freire's pedagogy begins from, rather than precludes, students' problematicization of knowledge, language and lived experience. Its aim, then, is the development among the "Oppressed" of language and concepts, wordings and readings with which to understand the ideological sources of disempowerment and voicelessness. This agenda pivots on the reinstatement via critical pedagogy of what modern schooling militates against: the power to speak, to critique, and to act in ways commensurate with their interests and emancipatory goals.

Taken together, Frankfurt School negative critique, Gramscian counterhegemonic practice, and Freireian conscientization thus provide a powerful agenda for emancipatory education. The target of emancipation for Gramsci and Freire are the oppressed working-class poor and peasantry. For Frankfurtians, all Western culture was oppressed by a repressive technicist and instrumental rationality—a rationality inscribed in reified relations and subjectivities, and these rationalized and naturalized by culture industries and cultural institutions like the mass media, school and family. Power and the sources of domination in all three theoretical frameworks reside with ruling class interests expressed in both economic and cultural structures. The subjugated are the proletarian masses (Gramsci), the disenfranchized peasantry (Freire) and the incorporated working and middle classes (Frankfurt School).

The liberationist social and intellectual movement that began in the late 1960s and variously influenced 1970s new sociology owes a great deal to marxian and neo–marxian theory. Across the West, student movements were accompanied by a surge of interest in the works of Marcuse, Freire and, later, Gramsci and Habermas. In efforts to contest epistemological and theoretical positivism and the conservative politics that historically have characterized the modernist educational enterprise, new sociologists have mapped, in a range of radical to progressivist variants, a neo-marxian materialist and culturalist critique onto the educational discourse. The political importance of the institutionalization of new sociology (and sociologists) in university education departments—that is, the institutional positioning of a discourse of resistance to and critique of theoretical conservativism and the populist discourse of the right—cannot and should not be underestimated. Nonetheless, as Wexler (1987: 42) observes, our collective self-index has been marked by an obsessive leftist critique of liberalism, a critique which some argue has been unable to provide the empirical goods in support of its claims (Liston, 1988). Ideology critique, historical materialism, and (postpositivist) qualitative methodology, then, were historical counter practices to both entrenched sociological positivist and then emergent New Right populist opposition. Yet despite two decades of new sociology's self-production through the discourse of critique—of the other and of each other's work—an apparent current stagnation has emerged where "the rhetoric of resistance ha[s] been preempted by the New Right's public language of reaction and restoration"

(Wexler, 1987: 42). The early 1990s, then, is not the time for those educationists committed to critical social theory and the remaking of practice to fragment over theoretical minutae. There is a need, as Apple (1986), Giroux (1988) and others have rightly noted, to organize our theoretical strategy and practical tactics in a counter-offensive front. However, that front can no longer exclude women, either by failure to critique masculinist theoretical narratives or by an "add-on" approach to matters of practice—both academic and pedagogical. What follows is an attempt to address that exclusion.

The public sphere: citizenship, rationality, critique and action

The "great" Western theoretical secular and non-secular metanarratives have been expressions of and the search for solutions to problems rooted in male experience. Critical inquiry—public speech and writing—although it has an identifiable relation to class privilege is fixed most profoundly to gendered privilege. The language of theory, as Rowbotham (1973: 32) noted almost two decades ago, "only expresses a reality experienced by the oppressors." Male authorship of theory, then, articulated from the standpoint of male experience, and conceptions of critique and action with which to realize visions for a better future, have historically situated the male individual at the center of theoretical, public discourse. Although the term "gender" is increasingly visible in mainstream social and cultural criticism, the theoretical standpoint from which pro-feminist male theorists speak all too often remains unproblematicized and entrenched in masculinist ideology (Morris, 1988).

In the discourse of critical pedagogy, the educational politics of emancipatory self- and social empowerment, and of emancipatory rationality and citizenship education, have been articulated in epistemic relation to liberal conceptions of equality and participatory democracy. These, in turn, are located squarely in (male) individualism constitutive of the public sphere. Despite the critique of liberalism's competitive individualism and technocratic rationality (Giroux, 1983, 1988), the agenda for radical pedagogy remains the restoration of a "creative democracy", a "resurrec[tion]" of "the tradition of liberal democracy" (Giroux, 1988: 202). This pedagogy of self- and social empowerment developed through a language of critique, possibility, and action takes democratic education beyond that envisioned by Dewey. It retains the conceptual centrality of individualism and the pragmatics of experience (and voice) but aims to extend these through a collective affirmation of an ethics of care, solidarity, and liberation (cf. Giroux, 1983, 1988). The emancipatory rationality that underpins a liberatory pedagogy "is based on the principles of critique and action" (Giroux, 1983: 190). In the liberal democratic state, as in liberal theory, critique and action historically have been the prerogatives of men empowered to inscribe and exchange critique and action in the formal public discourse of policy and law, in academic text, cultural (film, TV) text, the editorial page, or the corporate memo. Critique and action in the form of women's protest against inadequate child care, welfare and medical provisions, marital and non-marital rape, abuse, and pornography laws, and against an asymmetrical gendered wage-system remain politically subordinate issues on the public agenda. When women's critique and action is public(ized), it is largely organized and articulated in discourses and texts defined and regulated by men: in sites as diverse as the courts, unions, senate sub committee hearings, the media, policed protest marches, publishing houses and journal editorial boards. Critique and action are not generally available to unwaged housewives or, for that matter, to half the labor force of women working double jobs in predominantly part-time clerical and service employment, and in full-time child care, sexual and domestic service work.

In marxian theory, too, critique and action—resisting and transcending false consciousness and organizing for revolutionary action—resides with the male laborer. Barrett (1987a,b) and other socialist-feminists (e.g., Alexander, 1987; Beechey, 1987; Eisenstein, 1987; Hartsock, 1987a; Nicholson, 1987; O'Brien, 1984; Rowbotham, 1973; Smith, 1987) have pointed out that Marx's unreflectively sexist presuppositions have theoretically and practically entrenched sexual divisions: within the "working class and the organized labour movement" (Barrett, 1987a: 57), as well as in male and feminist marxist theorizing. The marxian legacy in critical pedagogy goes unchallenged on questions of gender. The paternal signifiers of labor, alienation, and the monogendered class dynamic of historical materialism remain taken-for-granted universals. The Marxist theoretical totalization of history in forms of male domination reducible to waged labor in historical modes of production evades the problematic of domination in gender relations. This focus seriously delimits the possibility for theorizing emancipatory interests that it claims to promote. The failure to recognize the gender blindness in marxist theory, as well as its historical genesis in industrial capitalism, leads contemporary neo-marxist social theorists to reflect on "gender" in the post-industrial present with a masculinist theoretical template of another age. Lather (1984: 52) observes that "given the gender blindness of Marxism . . . , it is not surprising that women's struggle should receive only tactical attention." It is that kind of tactical attention that "commatizes" (O'Brien, 1984) gender in the texts of critical pedagogy and which strategically refuses to engage and challenge those master texts which privilege male subjectivity as historical and universal agency. Lather continues: "While male neo-marxists are seen as becoming "rather ominously polite to the women's movement" . . . they have not revised their theories to acknowledge the role of gender relations in historical causation" (52). Marx's androcentric humanism is based on the centrality of labor, and as Barrett (1987a: 48) points out, "although in principle human labour is . . . neither male or female, there is a tendency in Marx's more specific analyses to imply that labour power is generally male." Moreover, "Marx persists . . . in the assumption that the individual of whom he speaks is male and that occasionally cognizance will need to be taken of his wife and family" (57).

It is through (public) wage labor that the subject becomes alienated from "his" essence, his labor, the product of that labor, and finally from his species being. Alienation thus is posited as a male condition and a cultural (public) condition. Domestic labor, by contrast, which does not generate direct market surplus value is implicitly rendered as natural labor. Domestic work, childbearing and rearing thus conceptually are not inherently alienating, and the products of that labor (meals, clean clothes, socialized children) do not confront and alienate the domestic worker. The theoretical implication here is that women in their natural state as mothers and housewives are neither alienated from their essence nor their species being. In other words, the natural, unwaged (private) labor of species production, family and child care, by virtue of being outside visible exploitation and appropriation by the capitalist wage system, constitutes a non-alienating condition in which (female) subject and essence are in a natural and harmonious state. In marxism as in liberalism, women, biology, domestic life and labor symbolize nature: natural and unmediated, non-alienated and non-exploited female essence.

Historical materialism is the history of domination and exploitation among men in the public sphere. The historical struggles inherent in laboring for the other—classes of men for men, not women for men—is the "motor" of history, the history of class struggle. Alexander (1987: 163), for instance, points out that "the political traditions of Marxism have had little to say about feminism or the needs and aspirations of women; while historical materialism, by identifying class struggle as the motor of history pushes the questions of sexual divisions and difference to the periphery of the historical process."

Calls for the reflexive teacher to promote civic and cultural literacy and participatory learning in the democratic classroom (e.g., Apple, 1986; Aronowitz & Giroux, 1985; Giroux, 1983; Giroux & McLaren, 1986; McLaren, 1987, 1988a,b,c) reinstate the private/public liberal dichotomy and the underlying nature/culture split which have been central targets of feminist critiques of liberalism. In liberal theory the principle of equality is founded on the conceptual and actual division between the public and the private. Indeed, the possibility of the public sphere in which "equal" men articulate culture and the law (of the father) which protects androcentric "human" interests, is founded on the subordination and exclusion of the private from the public/political. The conceptual relocation into the public of the feminine, which is theoretically tied in liberal theory to the private/nuclear family/mothering nexus, leaves the dichotomous gendered political structure intact. This move frees persons in the private to assume locations in the public in addition to retaining their "natural" caretaker positions in the private. It does not theoretically rewrite the masculinist public position, which is where the politics of universal, common, and androcentric "human" interests are inscribed. Pateman (1988: 11) writes that women in the liberal state are contracted in to a sphere "that both is and is not in civil society." In other words,

the private, womanly sphere (natural) and the public, masculine sphere (civil) are opposed but gain their meaning from each other, and the meaning of the civil freedom of public life is thrown into relief when counterposed to the natural subjection that characterizes the private realm. . . . What it means to be an "individual", a maker of contracts and civilly free, is revealed by the subjection of women within the private sphere" (p. 11).

Granting voice to girls in the public sphere of the democratic classroom is an add-on tactic of incorporation. Such conceptual tactics do not begin to address the more fundamental problems of the gendered requirements of citizenship (cf. Dietz, 1989; Fraser, 1987), or of "democratic" participation within the social relations of school settings. For, without a rewriting of the masculine public subject, women end up doubly inscribed in marginal public positions and in "natural" caretaking positions in the private. Public man, liberated from routinized domestic drudgery and the particularized, trivial needs and interests of children and household, thus remains free to defend public, universally human interests as a full-time (pre)occupation.

The failure to take into theoretical consideration this fundamental argument within feminisms reveals a patriarchalism among those who today make the most vocal claims to be pro-feminist, to be struggling on behalf of the socially, economically, and educationally disadvantaged. For we might ask who is theorizing on what epistemological grounds about, as Apple (1986: 200) correctly notes, mostly women's labor (i.e., teaching). Liberalism grants women citizenship and a place in the public by replicating the public/private power structure: women's teaching, health care and service labor is seen as a "natural" extension of their domestic abilities.

Once the gender-neutral concept of citizenship in the democratic liberal state is recast as gender specific, then "female citizenship" reads as a double positioning: a guaranteed right to a location in the public, and yet the responsibility to sustain the private. Hence equal pay legislation, equal educational and employment clauses, or language and curricular reform, are classic liberal strategies that grant ostensible equality of public participation to women (and minorities) but that leave embedded epistemic structures intact. It is those epistemic gendered dualisms and oppositions that can guarantee equality at the level of anti-sexist legislative tactics while guaranteeing the continuation of unequal positioning and power, even when women are admitted to the public. Female citizenship is not equivalent to the concept of citizenship in liberal discourse—it is not subsumable, theoretically or practically, under the patriarchal ideal of equality and "human" citizenship. Conceptual "add-on" tactics serve strategically to retain a theoretical structure in which the other can effectively be incorporated and made visible into an epistemology which privileges public man and his speech. A truly radical pedagogy cannot afford to leave its theoretical assumptions beyond self-critique, particularly if that pedagogy claims to be centrally based on self-reflexive practice.

A self-reflexive politics of action would require of critical pedagogy theorists the application of the kind of reflexive and self-critical awareness demanded of teachers, to deconstruct the ideology and rational theorizing embodied in their own texts. It would require that critical educational theorists ask those same questions of their own pedagogical (textual) practice that they demand teachers ask themselves. As McLaren (1988a: 9) quite accurately observed, teachers need to ask: "What can we learn about making our own pedagogies more critical by understanding how groups of students are differentially oppressed according to race, class, and gender? . . . What diversity do we silence in the name of liberatory pedagogy?" The same question should be asked of critical pedagogy theorists: what diversity is being silenced in critical pedagogy that appeals to the patriarchal model of classical Greek citizenship education (Giroux, 1983: 168), and to the fathers of American progressivism as lost foundations upon which to build a liberatory pedagogy sensitive to the *general* categories of race, class, and gender? The point is that the critical pedagogy project ignores gender by a failure systematically to engage with specific feminist theoretical and practical concerns, and by a de facto erasure of women altogether, through appeals to patriarchy's exclusionary grand narratives as the cornerstones for a new educational rationality.

Let us consider the latter. Appeals to education's "greats," such as John Dewey and George Counts, revalorize an early 20th-century vision of a "democratic tradition" from which American education is currently judged to be in retreat (Giroux & McLaren, 1986: 216). Dewey was quite clear on who his object of study was, on the separation of the private and public: "When men act, they act in a common and public world" (1944 [1916]: 297). Without an acknowledgment of the deeply embedded masculinist standpoint in Dewey's democratic vision or, for that matter, of Frankfurt School's theoretical worldview, their incorporation into the critical pedagogy text of the 1980s is no more than a dangerous extension—a dangerous memory—of conceptions of male individualism, power, and public speech disguised in the rhetoric of universalized self- and social empowerment. Consider this version of the ideal of citizenship education:

> In the classical Greek definition of citizenship education, a model of rationality can be recognized that is explicitly political, normative, and visionary. Within this model, education was seen as intrinsically political, designed to educate the [male] citizen for intelligent and active participation the civic community . . . intelligence was viewed as an extension of ethics, a manifestation and demonstration of the doctrine of the good and just life. . . . the relationship between the individual and the society was based on a continuing struggle for a more just and decent political community. Giroux (1983: 168).

Giroux admits that liberal democratic theory has supported "noble ideals for its citizens" (women's struggle for the vote?) but laments "that such ideals have not found their way, in general, into the day-to-day practices of schools, either historically or in more recent times" (168). What were these "ideals" and for whom were they ideal? This is not the place to review Greek political theory, nor does Giroux detail which foundational Greek theory he means to involve. But I do wish to point out that the Greek political ideal for citizenship education is not a sufficient scaffold to support a feminist pedagogy. Citizenship, the good and just life—according to a presumably Aristotelean, "classical Greek definition" (Giroux, 1983: 168)—was public life, the life of male community and citizenship which celebrated public speech in the pursuit of knowledge and truth. Aristotle (and Plato) silenced and privatized women and slaves in the *idion* (the private) of the *oikos* or household. Plato's ostensibly egalitarian educational and social theory and Aristotle's political theory and metaphysics wrote woman as inferior, as *idion*/idiot, as servant, as ruled rather than ruler. For both, the masculine standard was the first principle against which women's capacities and social position were judged. The gendered private/public, *polis*/*oikos* divisions laid down by the "fathers" of democracy have been foundational to western political thought. Elshtain (1981: 53) in her rereading of Greek political theory from a feminist perspective suggests: "That Aristotle himself excluded certain categories of persons from politics places no continuing claims on us if we determine that slave production and Aristotle's version of the production and reproduction of the 'oikos' need not serve as structural supports for political activity."

Yet to what extent one can ignore, and attribute to naive historical omission, the position of women in the domestic private sphere as a natural and necessary counterpart to the political public activities of men who (freed from the *oikos*) enable and sustain the democratic *polis*, is itself theoretically problematic, if the logic and integrity of the explanatory frame depends on that very separation. Elshtain points out that "the key is to assay what one can drop without so eroding the overall structure of the theory that one's favored alternatives are dropped as particular dimensions of explanation are rejected" (53). Marxist and liberal political theory and the logic of capitalism have depended upon, and taken as naturally given, this gendered division between the male public and female private, between culture and nature, reason and emotion, ruler and ruled. I submit that Western patriarchal rule and its economic expressions in (global) capitalism and epistemological expressions in, *inter alia*, Western religions and science are one and the same discourse (cf. Spivak, 1988a). That discourse was first formalized through its fixing in print for infinite recirculation and valorization in those "great" Greek metanarratives of "a just and decent political community" (Giroux, 1983: 168). It is there that we find the conceptual groundwork for a "democratic" politics of the sexual division of mental and manual labor and asymmetrical participation in public life.

I do not here posit "founding texts" or causal points of origin for the historical structural separations of gendered spheres in Western political, economic, social and epistemological organization. From an archaeological perspective, such texts and the discursive branchings they engendered are part of a "discursive constellation" (Foucault, 1972) which, historically, can be traced to the construction of particular political, socio cultural, epistemological, and subject formations. Hence, to what extent we can epistemologically or theoretically overlook not just "innocent" historical omission but explicitly misogynist articulations of exclusion and dehumanization, and then accept these master narratives as unproblematic "ideals", and as epistemological and theoretical cornerstones of a liberatory, democratic pedagogy that purports to be grounded in a politics of gender, race, and class is a serious problem indeed. It is a serious political problem of practice through theorizing, of writing text that promises transformation while it silently rallies around a re-formation of untenable and invalid 'founding' principles. Such a discourse points to an idealist and gender-blind valorization of master discourses which promote and legitimate the very social relations and subject positions for which critical pedagogy claims to provide a language of critique, of critical reflection and understanding. McLaren (1988a: 9) comments that "a critical pedagogy must assist students in developing a language of critique . . . from the standpoint of understanding what is necessary for the capitalist social structure to sustain its most oppressive social relations: e.g. . . . an inurement to discourses which encourage subject positions uncritical of racism, sexism, and class exploitation." The standpoint from which critical pedagogy speaks reveals an inurement to those discourses which laid the foundation for innumerous discursive constructions of public "man" in political society, all of which militated against women, racial differences, and underclasses. Radical teachers and teacher educators of "dangerous memory"—those who teach "the histories of women, blacks, working-class groups, and others whose histories challenge the moral legitimacy of the structures of society" (Giroux & McLaren, 1986: 227) should be cautious of reiterating the dangerous memory of a liberal idealism which centers on the primacy of male consciousness.

The hermeneutic experience: individualism and the public confessional

A liberal individualist ethic is written into the pedagogical agenda for the self-reflexive teacher. S/he is encouraged to empower students to become politically active and critical citizens by valuing their experience and voice; in short, to develop in students a sense of "critical agency" (McLaren, 1988a: 6) with which to work towards a critical democracy. The transformative task is for teachers to enable students to name and give voice to their experience (their subject positions) and then transform and give meaning to those experiences by critically examining the discourses that give meaning to those experiences. Teachers must be taught, and in turn provide students with, a language of critique with which to demystify and politicize the discursive production of meaning students (and teachers) use to articulate their own experience and, as well, to analyze those institutional discourses applied to and against them. One way to open up a forum in the classroom for expressing subjectivity and experience is to give voice to those commonly silenced: working-class girls and boys ("class"), girls in general ("gender"), and girls and boys of racial and ethnic backgrounds ("race"). This is seen as a political counter-hegemonic and emancipatory move against the systemic and systematic class culture reproduction found among marginalized girls' (McRobbie, 1978) and boys' (Willis, 1977) decidedly non-emancipatory resistance to schooling.

Viewed historically and epistemologically, what does the critical pedagogy agenda propose for concrete action, other than signify an optimistic epistemological turn, a reinstatement of liberalism's idealized individual and democratic ideals, a new celebration of democratic (critical) education as the hard work of freedom? In terms of that oppressed triad—race, class, gender—how will critical and dialectical thinking, expressions of subjectivity and cultural experience, and a language of critique transform the real material conditions of, for instance, inner-city girls and women of color, mapped as they are on blind spots in a "democratic" political economy that has given them token equal access in principle to education and the workplace? Eisenstein (1987), for instance, rightly notes that under liberalism women are given access to the public. The problem in Eisenstein's view is that the liberal state can grant legal and equal opportunities of access to the public sphere without providing for women the conditions for equal participation. This move, in turn, denies them equal access to the power (and rewards) with which to articulate and legislate change in their diverse interests.

Women vote, work for wages, serve on city councils, teach school, type the nation's memos and wipe its restaurant tables; they make beds and scrub toilets across the country in hospitals, hotels, theaters, and government offices. Women's asymmetrical yet numerically equal participation in the public remains confined to the extension of their domestic labor. Primary and preschool teaching, health care, clerical, food, cleaning and sexual service work are not sites from which to participate authoritatively or equally about "substantive political problems". For many women, substantive political problems often are private and not the same as those deemed as public, common interest. Men support and will inscribe on the public agenda those private (property) issues that challenge the male vision of "family", "child", or "wife." Hence, the profamily, anti-abortion movement addresses a contentious public matter over which men (and hegemonized women) wield considerable power. We have yet to see men organize to lobby for their right to housework, to childrearing, or to bring their wages in line with women. It is unquestionably important to give students the analytic tools with which to understand the forces that shape their experience, the first step of which is encouraging students to articulate their experiences and sense of self. Acts of naming and speaking one's identity and location give access to the many discourses and interdiscursive combinations students (indeed all of us) use to make sense of ourselves and our experiences. Yet encouraging critical classroom dialogue and legitimating personal voice *within* the extant structure of schooling and contemporary society and culture, assumes that institutionalized interpretive "praxis" will or should somehow enable the dismantling of the contradictions of patriarchal structures and supporting discourses. To expect that women students in the university, for instance, will readily reveal their personal cultural histories to a male academic, even when given equal opportunity and encouragement to "speak", grossly underestimates the sexual politics that structure classroom encounters (cf. Lewis & Simon, 1986; Orner, this volume). A related problem, of course, is the realism and authenticity assumed to underly subjective disclosures. Confessions of the self, particularly when naturalized as unmediated expressions of real experience, can be valorized as "authentic" (and beyond critique) regardless of the cultural meanings (e.g., racism, sexism, or classism in minority subcultures) that structure those expressions and experiences. Presumably in such cases the reflexive, psychoanalyst-teacher interprets student speech along more politically critical and correct lines, thus demystifying students' imaginary (ideological) relations to the real (culture). Privileging experience as foundational to knowledge, or as a transparent window to the "real", denies its situatedness in discourses that constitute subjectivities in the first place, and that enable articulation of experience from discursively constructed subject positions (cf. Fuss, 1989; Henriques et al., 1984; Walkerdine, 1990). Both teacher and student subject are equally implicated in discursive networks. Students' articulation of "real" experience and teachers' interpretive, emancipatory task *within* the institutional discourse of schooling do not reside outside of interlocking discourses and networks of institutionalized gender and power relations. This does not mean that emancipatory action in the classroom is precluded by the ideological weight of interpellated subjects. It does mean, however, that critique and action, deployed at the classroom level *without* critique of the metanarratives that theoretically and practically sustain the structures and discourses of schooling in the liberal state, may miss the point altogether. Equal opportunity to speak in the classroom, like equal representation in imagery and language in curricular text, will do little to challenge the outer limits of the epistomological horizon where the masculinist logic of the universal subject and its naming of the other is firmly inscribed.

The point is this: to grant equal classroom time to female students, to democratize the classroom speech situation, and to encourage marginal groups to make public what is personal and private does not alter theoretically or practically those gendered structural divisions upon which liberal capitalism and its knowledge industries are based. Those very divisions have generated countless discourses of, strategies and pleas for "equalities" in the first place. The emancipatory strategy of the public confessional may both be an illusory reading of classroom gender politics and of students' "critical" responses. Consider, for instance, that few critically oriented teacher educators would disagree that many students (female or male) are quick to admit to the need for teaching against oppression, for developing and in fact using in classroom dialogue and writing a "language of critique." Many female and male student teachers produce critical self-knowledge and "demonstrate" critical dialectical thinking, a language of critique, and even a pro-feminist stance in the seminar essay and debate. Yet it is women who look after children while studying, miss classes to tend to sick children, and will encounter obstacles to "academic success" by male academics that male students by and large do not confront. They will still tend overwhelmingly to opt for primary school teaching and join teachers' unions (the collective project for better pay and working conditions) while maintaining their domestic careers. They will have to keep their feminist politics in check in order to qualify for tenure and promotion, and to retain their jobs in a patriarchal system that writes their positions and possibilities for them.

Armed with the intellectual tools of critical thinking, a language of critique and possibility, female students who continue with university studies will be initiated into the male discourse of sponsorship mobility, the sexual (and racial) politics of which have yet to be systematically documented. A language of critique does help women students to understand the processes of masculine and feminine subject positioning in those hallowed sites of knowledge production. But the very gendered divisions of power and authority that enable and deny female academic mobility still tend to render a feminist language of critique politically counterproductive for women, who still continue overwhelmingly to depend upon men for sanctioning of research topics, allocation of research funds, decreeing what knowledge counts as relevant and citeable, for thesis examination, degree granting, promotion, and tenure.

My point is that disclosure of the self, sharing and problematizing cultural experience and subjectivity, critique, dialectics, theory, are unquestionably a more politically responsible pedagogy than conservative skills transmission models—whether behaviorist or neo-classical. How personal voice, dialectical thinking and critical agency are supposed to translate into a "critical democracy", however, is not at all clear. In other words, without a theoretical analysis of how emancipatory resistance through a critical education for citizenship can transform liberal capitalism's fundamental structural separations and politics of sexual division and subjugation, critical pedagogy's agenda reads as a humanist discourse of progressivism rewritten in the language of critical theory. How problematicizing race, class and gender in the classroom, and providing the conceptual tools of emancipatory critique will provide, beyond a more socially just and moral classroom, for the possibility of political action to enable those structural transformation required to liberate the "disenfranchised and dispossessed", and to alleviate "human suffering" (McLaren, 1988a: 8) is never spelled out in critical pedagogy's agenda. How exactly is the "remaking of the capitalist character structure" (8) through adherence to a "principle of sociality in our pedagogical project" (8) supposed to alter the hegemony of white patriarchal rule and its historical expression in the liberal post-industrial capitalist state? Wexler (1987) rightly notes New Sociology's deflated critique of liberal conceptions of schooling in the face of the current New Right enemy. But the turn for critical pedagogy is, ironically, a retreat to a discursively radicalized but nonetheless idealist liberalism. The turn that may hold some promise is towards what Donna Harraway calls "cyborg politics": an anti-restorationist project based on an epistemology of provisional and partial knowledges and identities, and on irreducible differences and standpoints linked in coalition through affinity, not identity (Haraway, 1990: 197). I turn to discuss this more at length at the end of this chapter.

The critical individual (teacher and student) is radical pedagogy's centered and neutered object of study. By its failure to address female teachers and female students in terms other than the insistent reference to "gender", which skirts altogether the politics of gender that structure the possibilities (of critique) for women teachers and female students, the (textual) discourse of critical pedagogy constructs and addresses an androgynous and colorless subject. The ethic of individualism—historically envisioned by and a vision of the constitutive male subject—that is inscribed in the egalitarian ideals of participatory democracy, translates in the critical pedagogy agenda into critical selfhood enabled by equal and non-coercive participation in classroom dialogue. Exhortations to provide equal opportunities for the expression of personal voice, to encourage dialectical thinking and to foster critical agency do not provide the conceptual tools with which to rewrite those theoretical narratives and structural conditions that historically have formed the basis of institutionalized gender asymmetries of power. To argue for the "donation" (Lewis & Simon, 1986) of classroom time for equal voice and critical dialogue skirts the structural problematic of who, in schools or universities, has the authority to speak, to critique, and to judge what is worthwhile (student) speech and critique.

The imaginary equality presupposed among subjects in public speech contexts such as the school is premised upon liberal notions of disembodied, dispassionate subjects capable of equal and impartial (perspectiveless) normative reasoning (Young, 1987, 1990; Fraser, 1987, 1989). Young and Fraser, for instance, have argued that the logic of unity and sameness implied by an idealized and egalitarian dialogic situation theoretically excludes those groups of persons whose ontology and cultural identity constructions associate them with the triviality of particularized interests, with the savagery of emotions, desire, the body, and with relational rather than abstract moral reasoning abilities (cf. Gilligan, 1982, 1987; Benhabib, 1987). Pateman (1987: 120), in her discussion of the private/public split in liberal theory, comments that the discourse of democratic, equal and public communication is based on the presupposition that the public is the political within civil society which historically excludes the personal–private–domestic. In this symmetrized division, in which only one side of the equation rules both, only the concerns of the ruling public domain are open for political and rational debate, and are constituted as common concerns of humanity and of the community. Radical pedagogy's textual and theoretical privileging of the "public sphere," "democracy," "citizenship," and the individualism implied in citizenship and reflective hermeneutics, without theoretical qualifications that, at the very least, acknowledge what the public's "other" is, indicates a profound gender-blindness to the fact that such a problem exists theoretically and historically. Such a position ignores women's concrete embodiments and locations in discursive power relations.

The unwillingness to address issues placed on the contemporary critical agenda by feminist theorists precludes an articulation of an educational politics that adequately can explain what is meant by "link[ing] the personal and the political so as to understand how power is reproduced, mediated, and resisted at the level of daily existence" (Giroux, 1983: 238). Theorists who do not engage substantively with feminist theory and research, of course, cannot be expected to contribute to a feminist reworking of theory or politics, or to renounce the patriarchal signifier in the theories and texts that they unequivocally do valorize as applicable to the many cross configurations of gender, class, race, and other socially "disabling" marks of identity. The general refusal by male academics to engage with feminist theory, and to self-reflect on their own work from the perspective of a male reading of feminist critiques, seriously undermines whatever gender(ed) messages they may claim to have for women about women. The discourse of critical pedagogy is one such instance. The need to "deal with feminism" often amounts to no more than a few obligatory citations—marginalia. To cite "key" feminist authors in the burial site of the bibliography is not the same as knowing and using their work. Morris (1988: 15) comments:

> In spite of many rhetorical flourishes from men about their recognition and acceptance of feminism's "contribution" to cultural and political theory, not very many men have really read extensively, or kept on reading, very many women's books and essays—particularly those published off the fast-track of prestige journals, or in strictly feminist contexts. The bottom line of any working bibliography is not, after all, a frame, but a practical prerequisite: you have to know it to use it.

With very few exceptions (e.g., Connell, 1987; Heath, 1987), male theorists do not deal seriously or constructively with feminist theory. This, however, is not to overlook serious and reconstructive (as in self-serving) colonizing moves among some male theorists, who are claiming feminine ways of knowing, seeing, reading and writing as that "other" side of male vision which, in a moment of masculinist fervor (modernity) men temporarily lost sight of (e.g., Scholes, Derrida, Ross, Eagleton). But apart from a handful of theoretical imperialists, few male academics are aware of the diversity of feminist critiques, of the various theoretical strands of feminism, of internal theoretical debates within these strands (cf. deLauretis, 1989; Hirsch & Fox Keller, 1990), or of feminists' current perceptions of theoretical gains, impasses, and "backlash" (cf. Stacey, 1986).

The subject in critical theory

Concepts of culture and subjectivity derived from the Freudian and marxian legacies reworked by Horkheimer and Adorno (1972 [1944]) and Marcuse

(1955, 1964, 1968) form the theoretical basis for radical pedagogy's cultural critique and analysis and concept of the psycho-social subject. The assumptions underlying what Frankfurt School theorists conceptualized as the psychic and social development of the individual within capitalist economic and cultural values and relations testifies to male experience translated into epistemology—into an abstract masculinity, to be read as that which is universally human.

Marcuse (1955) redefines and politicizes Freud's "death instinct" as mediated by the desire (instinct) for pleasure and not, as Freud had claimed, by the desire for self-destruction. This move enables Marcuse to formulate an essentialist and universal unconscious desire for a social order and subjectivity that is not repressive and repressed, reified and falsified. This positive desire for freedom from social and internalized psychic repression and domination (i.e., "surplus repression" institutionalized in, for instance, the family and school), in turn, constitutes the psychic (individualist) dynamic which conceptually enables negative critique for liberation from unfreedom. For Marcuse, as for the psychological subject in radical pedagogy, the death instinct still holds as a primary "autonomous drive." But because it is reconceptualized as mediated by a modified pleasure principle ("the need to resolve tension"), negative critique can thus—theoretically, at least—lead to a de-reification of values and relations. It can lead to "a better future", and thus to a more pleasurable and less repressive consciousness and social experience. The conceptual terminus of the search for pleasure, gratification, and freedom, however, remains the death instinct. While this apparent ontological movement may read theoretically and epistemologically as a "dialectical" moment, it is but one more moment in the historical reproduction of the fundamentally dualist project within Western philosophy. Conceptual dualisms are as ancient as any secular and non-secular epistemologies. Hartsock (1987a: 170) comments that such dualisms are rooted historically and specifically in male consciousness and experience. The classic life/death, self/other, subject/object, nature/culture, thesis/antithesis oppositions "have absorbed a great deal of philosophical energy, . . . have structured social relations for centuries," and served as explanatory frameworks both generated from and used to rationalize that experience. The discourse of radical pedagogy, and specifically its concept of the subject and subjectivity, is theoretically founded on such a framework. To find the "death instinct" textually present and posited as an unproblematic conceptual underpinning of subjectivity in the discourse of radical pedagogy warrants at least minor deconstruction. Giroux (1983: 29) writes: "Freud's studies on psychopathology, particularly his sensitivity to *humanity's* capacity for self-destructiveness and his focus on the *loss of ego stability* and the *decline of the influence of the family* in contemporary society added significantly to the Frankfurt School analyses (my emphases)." Acknowledgement of Marcuse's politicization of "Freud's important notion of the death instinct" (34) attests to a symptomatically masculinist reading. The oppositional life/death doublet has a long-entrenched epistemological history which feminist theorists have critiqued at length. Some of these critiques are worth noting here, since the very logic of liberation from oppression and repression is founded upon a (masculinist/universal) subjectivity conceptualized in a life-death struggle with itself and the other.

Hegel's and Lacan's self-conscious subjects, for instance, emerge out of negation: the loss of an essential self through the recognition of the self as other, and in seeing in the other only its own self. Benhabib (1987: 84–85) comments:

> The story of the autonomous male ego is the saga of this initial sense of *loss* in confrontation with the other, and the gradual recovery from this original narcissistic wound through the sobering experience of war, fear, domination, anxiety and death. The last installment of this drama is the social contract: the establishment of the law to govern all . . . to reestablish the authority of the father in the image of the law."

Hartsock (1987a), arguing for a feminist historical materialism, also comments on Hegel's conceptualization of the relationship between "self and other as a statement of male experience: the relation of the two consciousnesses takes the form of a trial by death. As Hegel describes it, 'each seeks the death of the other' " (169). She goes on to explain:

> Hegel's analysis makes clear the problematic social relations available to the self which maintains itself by opposition: . . . the male experience when replicated as epistemology leads to a world conceived as, and (in fact) inhabited by, a number of fundamentally hostile others whom one comes to know by means of opposition (even death struggle) and yet with whom one must construct a social relation in order to survive" (170).

Those relations for men historically are oppositional and confrontational (e.g., the struggle with nature), instrumental (object-centered production, alienation from and exchange of commodities), and dominating (nature, the other, life). The preoccupation with death and destruction is an historically and philosophically inscribed male valuation of the order of things. In Hartsock's (1984: 1987a) view, "perhaps the most dramatic (though not the only) reversal of the proper order of things characteristic of the male experience is the substitution of death for life" (1987a: 171). This perversion she considers at least partially the result of the sexual division of labor in childrearing and, I would add, in the biological division of labor in childbearing. Arguing from an object relations perspective in psychoanalytic theory, Chodorow (1978) has argued that ego formation in boys is dependent upon successful oedipal resolution (separation from the mother). The essentialist character of Chodorow's construct of mothering notwithstanding, her explanations, along with Gilligan's (1982) work on feminine moral development, provide insightful analyses of the social organization of self/other orientations. According to Chodorow, a boy's construction of self-identity is dependent upon strong boundary formations that separate him from the primary (female) parenting agent. His learning of social rules, roles and self is structured by an absent and idealized concept of masculinity. Because of the primacy of female parenting and the domestic absence of the father, a boy's world and sense of self is disconnected, strongly boundary-defined and thus separate and oppositional, rather than relational as is (theoretically) the case with girls. "The boy's construction of self in opposition to unity with mother, his construction of identity as differentiation from the other, sets a hostile and combative dualism at the heart of both the community men construct and the masculinist world view by means of which they understand themselves" (Hartsock, 1987a: 169). This masculinist worldview is the Lacanian symbolic order—the rule of language and the father—a mirror for men which reflects the masculine self, identity, experience, and history in sharp opposition to all that which stands for difference from itself. The male sense of self, then, is socially produced and bounded by rigid ego-boundaries. He experiences the self as discontinuous with others, and expresses relationality through the production, competition, control and exchange of objects and objectified others (e.g., knowledge, commodities, nature, women). The male mental and manual modus operandi is instrumental. Drawing on Bataille, Hartsock continues:

> As a consequence of this experience of discontinuity and aloneness, penetration of ego-boundaries, or fusion with another is experienced as violent. . . . Insisting that another submit to one's will is simply a milder form of the destruction of discontinuity in the death of the other since in this case one is no longer confronting a discontinuous and opposed will, despite its discontinuous embodiment. This is perhaps one source of the links between sexual activity, domination, and death. (p. 172).

That death, in all its metaphoric and conceptual shades, should figure so prominently in male authored theory and literature, and be so unproblematically taken by men as universally given, may very well lie historically in the collective social experience of specifically male embodiment.

By contrast, as some would argue, women's reproductive consciousness and potential, their connectedness to the production of life, the ontological significance of their physiological and cultural relation to genetic time and species (re)production locates their experience of self and others in an embodied relation to and in continuum with life, not death. One aspect of women's relational consciousness, Hartsock proposes, "is centered on the experience of living in a female rather than male body" (p. 167) (cf. Irigaray, 1985). Concrete physiological differences do not practically or theoretically suggest an essentialism on which to hinge justifications for the sexual division of childrearing, domestic or waged labor, but they do suggest a sexually differentiated set of embodied boundary configurations which may very well have do with different orientations to the other, to life, death, and the self. Man's egocentric, boundary-dependent self, his exclusion from the relational, bodily experience of life, and thus his self-objectification through the domination and devaluation of life (of nature, of the feminine) was quite clear for Freud (1961: 12): "there is nothing of which we are more certain than the feeling of ourself, or our own ego. This ego appears to us as something autonomous and unitary, marked off distinctly from everything else."

Finally, the historical record bears testimony that "humanity's capacity to self-destruction" is not a universally human, but an exclusively male condition. Death and killing in the search for peace, unity, harmony, or life, are inscribed in the phallocentrism of historical and contemporary military apparatuses (cf. Lloyd, 1986), and in the cultural myths, fables, and literary texts that construct ancient and contemporary heroes in search of love for the price of death. Not least, the life/death conflation is brutally inscribed in pornographic texts: male authorship and spectatorship of imageries of hostility, violence and even death, torture and dismemberment superimposed on fetishized variations of the life-creating act of sexual intercourse.

From the above, we can begin to see that Frankfurt School critique of instrumental rationality is, at its epistemological core, an expression of male subjectivity both in its understanding of consciousness and in its critique of its own masculinist ideology, culture, and history. It is a critique of the social structures and relations of patriarchy. It fails, however, to recognize that its object of study *is* patriarchy by universalizing and naturalizing its masculinist understanding as applicable to humanity, to human nature, and to history. While the material, social, and political activities of history can indeed be characterized by collective and individual power plays of domination and subjugation, they are located via any analysis in male rule, authority, authorship. How can feminist educators take serious an agenda for political education that bases its concept of subjectivity on a concept of "man" whose aim for a better future, for a less repressed subjectivity lies in "creating a new environment 'in which the non-aggressive, erotic, receptive faculties of man, in harmony with the consciousness of freedom, strive for the pacification of man and nature' (Marcuse, 1969)" (Giroux, 1983: 40). On a literal reading, the noble striving for the pacification of man and nature represents a deeper and distinctly male reality of the historically hostile oppositions between man and nature, between self and other, between dominant masculinity and subordinate femininity, both actual and symbolic. I am not claiming here an essentialist reading of femininity qua nature, as untainted by the oppositional logic of subordination/domination. I am, however, unconvinced that Frankfurt School depth psychology—derived as it is from the master theorist of phallocentrism—is an adequate psychological and social theory for the explanation of identity formation and development in any subjects other than Western (and Westernized) males. As such, it is appropriately authored by those to whom the theory speaks, and can be read as politically relevant for those upon whom such an epistemological standpoint is both derivative of and centered upon.

Critical theory in the postindustrial age: who and where is the subject?

The sedimented discursive configurations that historically have and continue to structure labor, life and language are being stripped of their "natural" truth veneer and political legitimacy. Feminist criticism is deconstructing the master narratives of patriarchy and thereby moving gender onto the critical agenda even if, in many discourses, it remains institutionally contained at the margins. Post-structuralism has decentered the subject, power, and knowledge. Postmodernism has decentered realism, de-authorized the cultural canons of representation, "auteur" and authority in art and literature. In renegade quarters in philosophy, literary and cultural theory, talk of the "death of the subject", the end of Man, Meaning, Truth, History, and the Real is already no longer novel nor fashionably avant-garde. The old dichotomies and essentialist and foundationalist assumptions that underlie the subject-in-history implicated by the classic epistemological dualisms are being demoted by feminist cultural theorists, poststructuralists and postmodernists to the status of conceptual residue of the age of modernity. If we can accept, as critical pedagogy unhesitantly does, that new socio-historical conditions have emerged in tandem with new cultural spheres and knowledge/ information technologies, then the critique of subjectivity and culture in the age of modernity postulated by first generation critical theorists Adorno, Horkheimer and Marcuse may no longer be theoretically wholly adequate to the tasks of analysis, critique, and conceptualization of contemporary socio-cultural conditions. As I have tried to show, Frankfurtian critical theory translated into a pedagogical agenda argues for androcentric essentialism, for realism, and for a generalized emancipation from generalized social oppression and psychological repression. The emancipatory space within which subjects are to be mobilized into collective action is seen somehow to be located outside of discourse and history, and exterior to power inscriptions. If anything, critical theory is an historical text which can be read on two levels of analysis: first, it serves as a useful history or philosophy lesson on masculinist epistemology of which it is *sine qua non* an exemplary text; secondly, it constitutes the historical positivity of critique of the age of modernity.

A preoccupation with the state of knowledge, culture, and subjectivity in "info-tech" capitalism marks contemporary postmodernist, poststructuralist, and feminist cultural theory, although encounters between feminism and postmodernism have been guarded and tenuous (cf. Alcoff, 1988; Flax, 1987; Fraser & Nicholson, 1988; Hartsock, 1987b; Nicholson, 1990; Probyn, 1987; Yeatman, 1991). Poststructuralism has for some time now focused its critique on the discourses of modernity, whereas postmodernism is more concerned with mapping and theorizing crises (in meaning, representation) in postmodernity. Feminist critical theory in literature and cultural studies, by contrast, is pursuing the feminine subject in the poststructuralist track of deconstructing master narratives, and in the postmodernist track of locating and freeing the feminine subject from the containment of the male gaze in systems of (linguistic) signification and (visual) representation.

Skepticism and incredulity towards the totalizing schemes of metanarratives— whether literary, philosophical, psychoanalytic, or cultural aesthetic—character- ize contemporary "radical" social and cultural critique everywhere except in post–"New" Sociology of Education quarters where, oddly enough, concerns with the social, the cultural, subjectivity, and critique of the master discourses of positivism have long been privileged objects of study. With few exceptions (e.g., Wexler, 1987), male and feminist New Sociology theorists have avoided ques- tioning how a pedagogy might be theorized to fit within newly emergent social relations that are configured in the symbolic networks of technological informa- tional-communicational exchange systems (cf. Luke, 1992). The question of how a feminist pedagogy might be articulated within such a framework has not been raised for extensive theoretical and practical debate. And, aside from cri- tiques of institutionalized patriarchy in the school, systematic deconstruction of educational master narratives also has not been undertaken. The works in this volume are one move in that direction.

Educational theorists' (i.e., those identifying with 1980s post–"New" Sociol- ogy offshoots) reluctance to engage with current anxieties over the crisis in knowledge, the collapse of meaning, and the decimation of the subject has pre- cluded male and feminist New Sociologists from posing questions about the ap- parent contradictions between the death of the subject, the referent, the social, and feminism's birth of the female subject, her referents and social forms and expression. It is widely suggested that language, knowledge, culture, and labor are undergoing significant transformations as part of a more general transforma- tion of industrial capitalism (the modern age) to post-industrial, informational capitalism (the postmodern age). Within these new relations the subject increas- ingly is fragmented and multiplied, decentered and counterposed in the commo- dified sign logic of simulated difference (cf. Baudrillard, 1980, 1983). If this is the case, then what are the pedagogical (and theoretical) implications of feminist efforts to construct a positivity—a privileged referent—of female subjectivity? Is postmodernism's project of erasure, both of the canon and the subject, at all compatible with feminist projects?

These are questions that need to be posed and worked through in the process of theorizing towards a feminist pedagogy: one that would claim to be histori- cally relevant and politically radical in an age where the old patriarchal para- digms apparently have lost legitimacy, and where symbolic, semiotic technolog- ical configurations constitute labor, commodities, culture and thus subjectivities. Further, what is required is a feminist pedagogy that will recognize industrial model schooling—its texts, practices, and (meta)discourses that underwrite the whole educational enterprise—for the phallogocentric monolith that it is, one in desperate need of being written over. Such a pedagogy, therefore, needs to be sensitive to the dilemmas posed by advocating a feminist pedagogy that, for the time being, will need to fit in with the institutional structures of modernist school apparatuses. Some feminists (e.g., Bannerji, Carty, Dehli, Heald & McKenna, 1991; Gaskell & McLaren, 1987; Lather, 1991; Weiler, 1988; the authors in this volume) have begun to outline the practical and theoretical problems encountered by educators with distinctly feminist emancipatory interests. Yet how and whether a feminist pedagogy of emancipation unproblematically fits in with the liberation models of critical pedagogy tends to remain largely unquestioned. The first step towards such a project I have provisionally attempted here. To close, I will now outline what I think holds potential for a re-vision of feminist pedagogy, one that I think needs to form the basis of an epistemological standpoint from which a politics of knowledge and a political pedagogy can be mobilized.

To begin, I would not question, as Spivak does (1988b), whether the subaltern can speak. The postmodernist move to local sites and knowledges, to the naming of identities and location, and the belated feminist move from woman to women, is indicative that the subaltern can indeed speak. It is what we want to speak about and to whom that is at issue, not whether we can speak. And while the risk of essentialism should be seen as a genuine theoretical and actual danger, I suggest that the postmodernist intellectual and cultural moment allows for a strategic essentialism that characterizes "all others", and that provides the space for what Donna Haraway names cyborg politics. In other words, this is the time to stand firm on those certainties that we can provisionally claim are essential to our shades of otherness: our skepticism of the kinds of certainties promised by modernist discourses, the irreducible fluidity and complexity of our identities and locations, our insider/outsider locations, knowledges, and visions. The multiplicity of our differences, as Fraser and Nicholson (1988), Hartsock (1990), and Probyn (1990) warn us, need not degenerate into a view form everywhere and thus from nowhere. They key for theorists and feminist teachers is to avoid slipping into a relativism of endless difference by standing firm on contextual and theoretical limits. These limits to difference, uncertainty, partiality, the local and location, are commitments to locating perspective, experience, and knowledge in historical, political, and cultural contexts.

Elizabeth Grosz (1988) explains that a situational, perpsectival theory of knowledge is by definition a relational theory of knowledge which is not the same as relativism. Social subjects, social theories and research are always located in specific historical, cultural and political trajectories which are always in historical relation to other trajectories, other relations of domination. As such, persons, practices, knowledges are "neither neutral nor indifferent to individual particularities (as the objectivist or absolutist maintains), nor purely free-floating, a position any subject can occupy at will (as the subjectivist or relativist maintains)" (p. 100). There is nothing incompatible about speaking from and of particular historical locations of difference and joining those in collective subversions and affirmations along axes that connect others through points of affinity. And one of those points of affinity that women of all colors share is that while we know some things about ourselves in relations of domination, we don't know and can't claim to know everything about each other. This is our undecidability, our situatedness in the politics of difference and location, our commitment to a historical standpoint in what Mani (1989) calls "different temporalities of struggle". This applies to students and teachers in classrooms, and to feminist theorists in the 1990s struggling through and with language, with the postmodernist death of the subject and the birth of other subjects, with the vexing problem of essentialism, with rewriting self/other boundaries, and with a politics of difference for subjects in western postmodernist sites and subjects in decidedly pre-modernist third world and eastern European sites.

Feminist privileging of undecidability and partiality and feminist visions of cyborg irreverence, of "transgressed boundaries, potent fusions, and dangerous possibilities" suggest what Haraway (1990: 198) envisions as a political struggle, a social and bodily reality "in which people are not afraid of permanently partial identities and contradictory standpoints". Contradictory standpoints are not the same as positions that float uncommitted on a sea of postmodernist theoretical indeterminacy. A feminist pedagogy does not disclaim foundation; instead, it grounds its epistemology on a foundation of difference. Undecidability, partiality and uncertainty *within* a theoretical commitment to the specificity and irreducibility of difference, to historical trajectories and moments, generate a pedagogical ethics which Mary Lydon (1988:141) calls "pedagogy as an ars erotica". Such a pedagogy "resist[s] the confessional impulse" and instead, as Dianne Fuss (1989: 118) proposes, takes as its starting and end points "the responsibility to historicize, to examine each deployment of essence, each appeal to experience, each claim to identity in the complicated contextual frame in which it is made."

Such a political and ethical standpoint means that we cannot claim one method, one approach, or one pedagogical strategy for student empowerment or for making students name their identity and location. It means that we are not politically and ethically justified to assume positions of authority on 'negative identities': to assume that we have the power to empower or the "language of critique" with which to translate student speech and give it back to them in politically correct terms. Nor can we claim to know what the politically correct end points for liberation are for others. Take, for instance, the bedrock feminist critique of the family or abortion rights. The emancipatory endpoints of these critiques are anathema to Australian Aboriginal women whose political task is to reclaim their decimated culture from the brink of genocide. For women whose families were fragmented through forced separation by the reserve system, whose mothers and grandmothers underwent forced sterilizations, whose children suffer the highest disease and infant mortality rate in Australia, abortion rights do not carry the same political weight and urgency as they do for Anglo-European women.

Deferrals to the local and to specificity do not mean that anything goes, that we do not take a position in classroom encounters, in positions available to us in the discourses of various kinds of schooling. And that position, in my estimation, can only be emancipatory if our attention to the politics of the local (of struggles, identities) are tied to dedicated engagement with and teachings of the politics of global structures and justifying narratives of oppression. In other words, the feminist (and postmodernist) risk of slippage into endless difference and local narratives can easily obscure attention from historical structures of domination and exploitation. We should regard with caution the consequences of the postmodernist denouncement of totalizing grand narratives, because such a move potentially subverts feminist efforts to critique those grand historical and contemporary systems of oppression of which local narratives are diverse variations on familiar themes (patriarchy, capitalism, imperialism, etc.). And this returns us to Haraway's "affinity": genealogical discontinuities and differences may be irreducible, but there are nodal points of affinity that do link those differences along different historical axes of power and subjugation. We cannot afford to privilege experience at the expense of theory, the local at the expense of the global. Nor can we afford to be seduced by vanguard revolutionary or postmodernist theory. Our attention to history must not sidetrack our attention to contemporary theory which, if left unexamined, has potential disastrous ethical and political effects. The feminist political and theoretical tasks of writing ourselves from the ground up, of dismantling the long history of misogynist epistemology, and of fending off the current double moves of theoretical appropriations of the feminine on one hand and the elimination of the subject on the other, are tasks unprecedented in history. The fathers had it much easier: writing and speaking "truth" from the singular location of insider, an insider with unifocal and monochromatic vision, are no great accomplishments.

Critical social theories which today fail to recognize the theoretical inadequacy of universalized, androcentric subjectivities dug out from the master narratives of old and which, moreover, fail to acknowledge the theoretical efforts made by feminists to destabilize the one-dimensional "grand recits" of the West, cannot serve real women (or men) as a template for social (or pedagogical) action and possibility. What I have suggested here is the urgent need for a serious skepticism of and critical attention to those contemporary educational narratives that claim to be emancipatory, ideologically critical, self-reflexive, and politically conscientious, and yet remain theoretically entrenched in gender- and color-blind patriarchal liberalism.

References

Alcoff, L. (1988) Cultural feminism versus post-structuralism: The identity crises in feminist theory. *Sings, 13*(3), 405–36.

Alexander, S. (1987) Women, class and sexual difference. In A. Phillips (Ed.), *Feminism and equality* (pp. 160–175). Oxford: Blackwell.

Althusser, L. (1971) Ideology and ideological state apparatuses. In *Lenin and philosophy, and other essays* (B. Brewster, trans.). New York: Monthly Review Press.

Amos, V. & Parmar, P. (1987) Resistances and responses: The experiences of black girls in Britain. In M. Arnot & G. Weiner (Eds.), *Gender and the politics of schooling* (pp. 211–22). London: Open University Press.

Apple, M. (1982) *Cultural and economic reproduction in education.* London: Routledge & Kegan Paul.

Apple, M. (1986) *Teachers and texts.* London: Routledge & Kegan Paul.

Aronowitz, S. & Giroux, H. (1985) *Education under siege.* South Hadley, MA: Bergin & Garvey.

Bannerji, H., Carty, L., Dehli, K., Heald, S. & McKenna, K. (1991) *Unsettling relations: The university as a site of feminist struggles.* Toronto: Women's Press.

Barrett, M. (1987a) Marxist-feminism and the work of Karl Marx. In A. Phillips (Ed.), *Feminism and equality* (pp. 44–61). Oxford: Blackwell.

Barrett, M. (1987b) Gender and class: Marxist feminist perspectives on education. In M. Arnot & G. Weiner (Eds.), *Gender and the politics of schooling* (pp. 50–64). London: Open University Press.

Baudrillard, J. (1980) The implosion of meaning in the media and the implosion of the social in the masses. In K. Woodward (Ed.), *The myths of information: Technology and postindustrial culture* (pp. 137–150). Madison, WI: Coda Press.

Baudrillard, J. (1983) *Simulacra and simulations.* New York: Semiotext(e).

Beechey, V. (1987) *Unequal work.* London: Verso.

Benhabib, S. (1987) The generalized and the concrete other. In S. Behabib & D. Cornell (Eds.), *Feminism as critique* (pp. 77–95). London: Polity.

Bourdieu, P. & Passeron, J. (1977) *Reproduction: In education, society and culture.* London: Sage.

Bowles, S. & Gintis, H. (1976) *Schooling in capitalist America.* New York: Basic Books.

Carby, H. (1987) Black feminism and the boundaries of sisterhood. In M. Arnot & G. Weiner (Eds.), *Gender and the politics of schooling* (pp. 64–75). London: Open University Press.

Chodorow, N. (1978) *The reproduction of mothering.* Berkeley, CA: University of California Press.

Connell, R. W. (1987) *Gender and power.* Sydney: Allen & Unwin.

deLauretis, T. (1989) The essence of the triangle or, taking the risk of essentialism seriously: Feminist theory in Italy, the U.S., and Britain. *differences, 1*(2), 3–37.

Dewey, J. (1944 [1916]) *Democracy and education.* New York: The Free Press.

Dietz, M. G. (1989) Context is all: Feminism and theories of citizenship. In J. K. Conway, S. C. Bourque & J. W. Scott (Eds.), *Learning about women: Gender, politics & power* (pp. 1–24). Ann Arbor, MI: University of Michigan Press.

Dill, B. (1987) The dialectics of black womanhood. In S. Harding (Ed.), *Feminism and methodology* (pp. 97–108). Bloomington, IN: Indiana University Press.

Eisenstein, H. (1987) Patriarchy and the universal oppression of women: Feminist debates. In M. Arnot & G. Weiner (Eds.), *Gender and the politics of schooling* (pp. 35–49). London: Open University Press.

Elshtain, J. (1981) *Public man, private woman.* Oxford: Martin Robertson.

Flax, J. (1987) Postmodernism and gender relations in feminist theory. *Signs, 12*(4), 621–643.

Foucault, M. (1972) *The archaeology of knowledge* (A. Sheridan, trans.). New York: Harper.

Fraser, N. (1987) What's critical about critical theory? In S. Benhabib & D. Cornell (Eds.), *Feminism as critique* (pp. 31–55). London: Polity.

Fraser, N. & Nicholson, L. (1988) Social criticism without philosophy: An encounter between feminism and postmodernism. *Theory, Culture and Society, 5*, 373–94.

Freire, P. (1973) *Pedagogy of the oppressed*. New York: Seabury Press.

Freire, P. (1978) *Education for critical consciousness*. New York: Seabury Press.

Freud, S. (1961) *Civilization and its discontents*. New York: Norton.

Fuss, D. (1989) *Essentially speaking*. New York: Routledge, Chapman and Hall.

Gaskell, J. & McLaren, A. (Eds.) (1987) *Women and education: A Canadian perspective*. Calgary: Detselig.

Gilligan, C. (1982) *In a different voice: Psychological theory and women's development*. Cambridge, MA: Harvard University Press.

Gilligan, C. (1987) Woman's place in man's life cycle. In S. Harding (Ed.), *Feminism and methodology* (pp. 57–73). Bloomington, IN: University of Indiana Press.

Giroux, H. (1981) *Ideology, culture and the process of schooling*. Philadelphia, PA: Temple University Press.

Giroux, H. (1983) *Theory and resistance in education*. London: Heineman.

Giroux, H. (1988) *Schooling and the struggle for public life*. Minneapolis, MN: University of Minnesota Press.

Giroux, H. & McLaren, P. (1986) Teacher education and the politics of engagement: The case for democratic schooling. *Harvard Educational Review, 56*(3), 213–27.

Giroux, H. & Simon, R. (1988) Critical pedagogy and the politics of popular culture. *Cultural Studies, 2*(3), 294–320.

Gramsci, A. (1971) *Selections from prison notebooks* (Q. Hoare, ed. & trans.). New York: International Publishers.

Grosz, E. (1988) The in(ter)vention of feminist knowledges. In B. Caine, E. Grosz & M. de-Lapervanche (Eds.), *Crossing boundaries* (pp. 92–104). Sydney: Allen & Unwin.

Haraway, D. (1990) A manifesto for cyborgs: Science, technology, and socialist feminism in the 1980s. In L. Nicholson (Ed.), *Feminism/postmodernism* (pp. 190–233). New York: Routledge, Chapman and Hall.

Hartsock, N. (1984) Gender and sexuality: Masculinity, violence, and domination. *Humanities in Society, 7*(1 & 2), 19–46.

Hartsock, N. (1987a) The feminist standpoint: Developing the ground for a specifically feminist historical materialism. In S. Harding (Ed.), *Feminism and methodology* (pp. 157–80). Bloomington, IN: University of Indiana Press.

Hartsock, N. (1987b) Rethinking modernism: Minority vs. majority theories. *Cultural Critique, 7*, 187–206.

Hartsock, N. (1990) Foucault on power: A theory for women? In L. Nicholson (Ed.), *Feminism/postmodernism* (pp. 157–175). New York: Routledge.

Heath, S. (1987) Men in Feminism: Men in feminist theory. In A. Jardine & P. Smith (Eds.), *Men in feminism* (41–46). New York: Methuen.

Henriques, J., Hollway, W., Urwin, C., Venn, C. & Walkerdine, V. (1984) *Changing the subject*. New York: Methuen.

Hill Collins, P. (1990) *Black feminist thought*. London: Unwin Hyman.

Hirsch, M. & Fox Keller, E. (Eds.) (1990) *Conflicts in feminism*. New York: Routledge.

hooks, b. (1987) Feminism: A movement to end sexist oppression. In A. Phillips (Ed.), *Feminism and equality* (pp. 62–76). Oxford: Blackwell.

hooks, b. (1990) *Yearning: Race, gender, and cultural politics*. Boston, MA: South End Press.

Horkheimer, M. & Adorno, T. (1972 [1944]) *The dialectic of enlightenment*. New York: Herder.

Irigaray, L. (1985) *Speculum of the other woman* (G. C. Gill, trans.). Ithaca, NY: Cornell University Press.

Lather, P. (1984) Critical theory, curricular transformation and feminist mainstreaming. *Journal of Education, 166*(1), 49–62.

Lather, P. (1991) *Getting smart: Feminist research and pedagogy with/in the postmodern.* New York: Routledge.

Lewis, M. & Simon, R. (1986) A discourse not intended for her: Learning and teaching within patriarchy. *Harvard Educational Review, 56*(4), 457–472.

Liston, D. (1988) Faith and evidence: Examining marxist explanations of schools. *American Journal of Education, 96*(3), 323–350.

Lloyd, G. (1986) Selfhood, war and masculinity. In C. Pateman & E. Gross (Eds.), *Feminist challenges* (pp. 63–76). Sydney: Allen & Unwin.

Luke, C. (1992) Television curriculum and popular literacy: Feminine identity politics in family discourse. In B. Green (Ed.), *The insistence of the letter.* Basingstoke, UK: Falmer.

Lydon, M. (1988). Foucault and feminism: A romance of many dimensions. In I. Diamond & L. Quinby (Eds.), *Feminism and Foucault* (pp. 135–148). Boston, MA: Northeastern University Press.

Mani, L. (1989) Multiple mediations: Feminist scholarship in the age of multinational reception. *Inscriptions, 5,* 1–25.

McLaren, P. (1986) *Schooling as a ritual performance: Towards a political economy of educational symbols and gestures.* London: Routledge.

McLaren, P. (1987) Education as counter-discourse: Towards a critical pedagogy of hope. *The Review of Education, 13*(1), 58–68.

McLaren, P. (1988a) Language, social structure and the production of subjectivity. *Critical Pedagogy Networker, 1*(1 & 2), 1–10.

McLaren, P. (1988b) Culture or canon? Critical pedagogy and the politics of literacy. *Harvard Educational Review, 58*(2), 213–34.

McLaren, P. (1988c) On ideology and education: Critical pedagogy and the politics of education. *Social Text, 19/20,* 153–185.

McRobbie, A. (1978) Working class girls and the culture of femininity. In Women's Study Group, Centre for Contemporary Cultural Studies, *Women take issue* (pp. 96–108). London: Hutchinson.

McRobbie, A. & Garber, J. (1976) Girls and subcultures: An exploration. In S. Hall & T. Jefferson (Eds.), *Resistance through rituals* (pp. 209–29). London: Hutchinson.

Marcuse, H. (1955) *Eros and civilization.* Boston: Beacon Press.

Marcuse, H. (1964) *One dimensional man.* Boston: Beacon Press.

Marcuse, H. (1968) *An essay on liberation.* Boston: Beacon Press.

Marcuse, H. (1969) Repressive tolerance. In R. Wolff, B. Moor Jr., & H. Marcuse (Eds.), *A critique of pure tolerance.* Boston, MA: Beacon Press.

Minh-ha, T. T. (1989) *Woman, native, other.* Bloomington, IA: University of Indiana Press.

Mohanty, C. T., Russo, A. & Torres, L. (Eds.) (1991) *Third world women and the politics of feminism.* Bloomington, IA: Indiana University Press.

Morris, M. (1988) *The pirate's fiancee: Feminism, reading, postmodernism.* London: Verso.

Nicholson, L. (1986) *Gender and history: The limits of social theory in the age of the family.* New York: Columbia University Press.

Nicholson, L. (1987) Feminism and Marx. In S. Benhabib & D. Cornell (Eds.), *Feminism as critique* (pp. 16–30). London: Polity.

Nicholson, L. (Ed.) (1990) *Feminism/postmodernism*. New York: Routledge.

O'Brien, M. (1984) The commatization of women: Patriarchal fetishism in the sociology of education. *Interchange, 15*(2), 43–60.

Pateman, C. (1987) Feminist critiques of the public/private dichotomy. In A. Phillips (Ed.), *Feminism and equality* (pp. 103–126). Oxford: Blackwell.

Pateman, C. (1988) *The sexual contract*. London: Blackwell.

Probyn, E. (1987) Bodies and anti-bodies: Feminism and postmodernism. *Cultural Studies, 1*(3), 349–360.

Probyn, E. (1990) Travels in the postmodern: Making sense of the local. In L. Nicholson (Ed.), *Feminism/postmodernism* (pp. 176–189). New York: Routledge.

Rowbotham, S. (1973) *Woman's consciousness, man's world*. Middlesex: Pelican.

Simon, R. (1987) Empowerment as a pedagogy of possibility. *Language Arts, 2,* 370–82.

Smith, D. (1987) Women's perspective as a radical critique of sociology. In S. Harding (Ed.), *Feminism and methodology* (pp. 84–96). Bloomington, IN: University of Indiana Press.

Spivak, G. (1988a) *In other worlds: Essays in cultural politics*. New York: Routledge.

Spivak, G. (1988b) Can the subaltern speak? In C. Nelson & L. Grossberg (Eds.) *Marxism and the interpretation of culture* (pp. 271–313). Urbana, IL: University of Illinois Press.

Stacey, J. (1986) Are feminists afraid to leave home? The challenge of conservative pro-family feminism. In J. Mitchell & A. Oakley (Eds.), *What is feminism?* (pp. 219–248). Oxford: Blackwell.

Weiler, K. (1988) *Women teaching for change: Gender, class and power*. Bergin & Garvey.

Walkerdine, V. (1990) *Schoolgirl fictions*. London: Verso.

Wexler, P. (1987) *Social analysis of education*. London: Routledge & Kegan Paul.

Willis, P. (1977) *Learning to labour*. Lexington, MA: D. C. Heath.

Yeatman, A. (1991) The epistemological politics of postmodern feminist theorising. *Social Semiotics, 1*(1), 30–48.

Young, I. (1987) Impartiality and the civic public: Some implications of feminist critiques of moral and political theory. In S. Benhabib & D. Cornell (Eds.), *Feminism as critique* (pp. 56–76). Oxford: Blackwell.

Young, I. (1990) *Justice and the politics of difference*. Princeton, NJ: Princeton University Press.

Young, M. (Ed.) (1971) *Knowledge and control*. London: Open University Press.

4

What We Can Do for You! What *Can* "We" Do For "You"?: Struggling over Empowerment in Critical and Feminist Pedagogy

Jennifer Gore

"Empowerment" is a term used in a range of current educational discourses. For example, there are conservative discourses (e.g. Maeroff, 1988) which equate empowerment with professionalization and seem to employ the term for rhetorical purposes which result in little shift in relations of power; liberal humanist discourses (e.g. Yonemura, 1986) which aim at the "empowerment" of *individual* teachers, student teachers and students and the alteration of power relations *within* the classroom; and critical and feminist discourses (e.g. Culley, 1985; Giroux, 1988; McLaren, 1988; Miller, 1990; Shor & Freire, 1987; Shrewsbury, 1987; Simon, 1987) which are concerned with societal relations of power and hold more collective and avowedly political notions of empowerment. Because of their roots in specific liberatory and emancipatory political projects, we might be least likely to question the claims to empowerment of the critical and feminist discourses. Precisely for this reason, and because my own practice as a teacher educator is grounded in critical and feminist traditions, I limit this paper to an analysis of discourses within those traditions.[1]

My major aim is to point to some weaknesses or shortcomings in the construction of "empowerment" by critical and feminist educational discourses which create problems internal to those discourses. Rather than seek to legitimate or celebrate critical and feminist discourses, I want to look for their dangers, their normalizing tendencies, for how they might serve as instruments of domination despite the intentions of their creators (Sawicki, 1988). Michel Foucault says "Thought is freedom in relation to what one does, the motion by which one detaches oneself from it, establishes it as an object and reflects on it as a problem" (Rabinow, 1984, p. 388). As is consistent with many poststructural analyses (e.g. Ellsworth, 1989; Popkewitz, 1991; Sawicki, 1988), my aim is to be "thoughtful" about constructions of truth, power, knowledge, the self, and language in these discourses. Specifically, I draw on Foucault's notion of "regime of truth" to reflect on problems of power relations and knowledge internal to the critical and feminist discourses which are my focus here. To do so, I have selected examples which illustrate clearly the potential dangers of those discourses.

At the same time, however, I wish to acknowledge that some work within the critical and feminist traditions at least begins to address the kinds of weaknesses I outline here (e.g. Britzman, 1991; Cherryholmes, 1988; Ellsworth, 1989; Lather, 1991; Lewis, 1988, 1989; Marshall, 1989). Of particular relevance to my argument is the feminist poststructuralist work of scholar/teacher Elizabeth Ellsworth (1989). Following her initiative, this paper cautions those of us who profess and practice empowerment within critical and feminist discourses against didactic claims of "what we can do for you". My aim is not to immobilize or paralyze us from continuing that work. Rather, I hope to strengthen my own, and others', understanding and practice within critical and feminist traditions.

My focus is on those critical and feminist educational discourses that emphasize empowerment. Interestingly, the same discourses seem to also claim for themselves the label "pedagogy"; that is, discourses of "critical pedagogy" and "feminist pedagogy". While other critical educational discourses and other feminist discourses address pedagogy and have relevance to pedagogy, they do not claim to be centrally about pedagogy. Nor, curiously, is "empowerment" central to these "non-pedagogy" discourses. This observation leads me to ponder, as a secondary aim of the paper, the connection of empowerment and pedagogy in discourses of critical and feminist pedagogy. I shall explicitly address this issue near the end of the paper.

The fields of critical pedagogy and feminist pedagogy are complex and fragmented. Through an analysis of contemporary academic literature that claims for itself the label "critical pedagogy" or "feminist pedagogy", I have begun to explore not only the separation of these two fields, but distinctions within each field (Gore, 1989b, in press). Within the field of critical pedagogy two main discursive strands can be identified. The central distinction between the two strands centers on different approaches to the question of pedagogy, whereby one strand emphasizes the articulation of a broad (and shifting) social and educational vision while the other shows greater concern for instructional practices in specific contexts. In making this distinction between "systems of thought" in critical pedagogy, the prominence of its "authors", the proponents of the two strands, is striking, with Henry Giroux and Peter McLaren the key advocates and representatives of the first strand and Paulo Freire and Ira Shor the key advocates and representatives of the second. In the field of feminist pedagogy, two discursive strands can also be identified. The central distinction between these strands lies in the emphasis of one strand on instructional aspects of pedagogy and the emphasis of the other strand on feminism(s). While "authors" can be named (e.g. Margo Culley, Carolyn Shrewsbury, and Nancy Schniedewind as representative of the first strand; Madeleine Grumet and Frances Maher as representative of the second), these "systems of thought" are most closely linked to the institutional location of their proponents, with the first strand of feminist pedagogy emerging from Women's Studies departments and the second from schools of education. Another distinction within feminist pedagogy can be drawn around the variety of stances within feminism that are reflected but often not acknowledged in the discourses of feminist pedagogy. Simply stated, much of the feminist pedagogy literature to date has emerged out of liberal and radical feminist traditions.[2] It is not within the scope of this paper to map out these distinctions in detail. However, acknowledging the complexity of the "objects" of my analysis is important in countering any "unity" implied in the following discussion of points of coincidence in constructions of empowerment.

It is from the outlined discursive strands of critical and feminist pedagogy that I will be drawing examples as I return to my primary aim of identifying weaknesses in constructions of empowerment. It is not my purpose to criticize specific discourses as having specific weaknesses so much as I hope to illustrate, through examples, general tendencies among the critical and feminist pedagogy discourses. The normalizing tendencies, or dangers, of these discourses can be located in: (1) presuppositions inherent in the term empowerment which are taken on by the discourses and, closely related, (2) their unreflexive use of empowerment rhetoric. I elaborate each of these in turn.

Problematic presuppositions

The term "empowerment" has no particular meaning prior to its construction within specific discourses; that is, it is important to acknowledge that the meanings of words are always "up for grabs", that there are no essential meanings— only ascribed meanings (Weedon, 1987). Social definitions of terms are products of the contexts surrounding their use and the discourses in which they are embedded.

Nevertheless, while its specific meanings must be identified within discourses, the term "empowerment" often does, more generally, presuppose (1) an agent of empowerment, (2) a notion of power as property, and (3) some kind of vision or desirable end state. It is my contention that discourses of critical and feminist pedagogy construct empowerment in ways consistent with these underlying presuppositions. I elaborate these arguments by addressing each of the three presuppositions in turn: first, clarifying how the presupposition seems inherent to the term "empowerment"; next, illustrating its manifestation in some discourses of critical and feminist pedagogy; and finally, pointing to theoretical weaknesses and oversights within these discourses that are created by taking on the presupposition in the construction of empowerment.

The agent of empowerment

To em-power denotes to give authority, to enable, to license. As such, it is a process which requires an agent—someone, or something, to em-power. Even the notion of "self-empowerment" presumes an agent—the self.

When discourses of critical and feminist pedagogy espouse "self-empowerment" the distinction made is not around the agent of empowerment but around the subject of empowerment—that is, who is (to be) empowered. Giroux (1988) and McLaren (1989), for instance, speak frequently of "self and social empowerment", distinguishing between, and connecting, the empowerment of individuals and social positions. The following statement by McLaren (1989) provides an example: "Teachers must engage unyieldingly in their attempt to empower students both as individuals and as potential agents of social change by establishing a critical pedagogy that students can use in the classroom and in the streets" (221). The agent of empowerment in this example, and generally in critical pedagogy, is the teacher while the subject of empowerment is more than the individual student.

Strong senses of human agency and optimism pervade claims about the teacher as empower-er in ways which portray the teacher's role as crucial and sometimes even as omnipotent. Culley (1985) provides an extreme example of this approach to empowerment: "The feminist teacher can be a potent agent of change who, through combinations of course content and process, has the power to replace self-hatred with self-love, incapacity with capacity, unfreedom with freedom, blindness with knowledge" (21). Likewise in critical pedagogy, we find statements which place the teacher as the agent of empowerment. For example, McLaren (1989) in addressing the "kinds of theories educators should work with" and the "knowledge they can provide in order to empower students", says "empowerment means not only helping students to understand and engage the world around them, but also enabling them to exercise the kind of courage necessary to change the social order where necessary" (182). The teacher, as the agent of empowerment, is accorded great importance in these discourses.

My major concerns are that these claims to empowerment attribute extraordinary abilities to the teacher, and hold a view of agency which risks ignoring the context(s) of teachers' work. Teachers are constrained by, for example, their location in patriarchal institutions (Grumet, 1988) and by the historical construction of pedagogy as, and within, discourses of social regulation (Gore, in press; Hamilton, 1989; Luke, 1989). Overly optimistic views of the agent of empowerment also set up serious shortcomings in the use of empowerment rhetoric which shall be elaborated later.

Power as property

Another major shortcoming of constructions of empowerment in critical and feminist pedagogy discourses is that they conceive of power as property, something the teacher has and can give to students. To *em*-power suggests that power can be given, provided, controlled, held, conferred, taken away. For example, Shrewsbury (1987) describes the vision of feminist pedagogy as including "a participatory, democratic process in which at least some power is shared" (7) and "the goal is to increase the power of all actors, not to limit the power of some" (8). While Giroux (1988) and McLaren (1989) have recently begun to refer to power as embodied in concrete practices, they still talk of "sharing power" in ways which remained locked within a view of power as property. "Giroux assumes that schools must be seen . . . as complexes of dominant and subordinate cultures, each ideologically linked to *the power they possess* to define and legitimate a particular construction of reality" (McLaren, 1989, 200) (emphasis added).

Power as property is often, but not necessarily, connected with a "zero-sum" understanding of power which suggests that there is only so much power and that if teachers "give" some of it to students, they must "give up" some of their own power. Such an understanding of power is implied in Kathryn Pauly Morgan's (1987) characterization of the paradox of democratic pedagogy:

> If the feminist teacher actively assumes any of the forms of power available to her—expert, reward, legitimate, maternal/referent—she eliminates the possibility of educational democracy in the feminist classroom; if she dispenses with these in the name of preserving democracy, she suffers personal alienation, fails to function as a role model, and abandons the politically significant role of woman authority. In short, she stops functioning as a feminist teacher. (51)

Some of the early "resistance" work in education points to the inadequacy of conceptions of power as property or zero-sum. For example, in Paul Willis' (1977) study, *Learning to Labour,* the teachers were not alone in being able to exercise power. The "lads" exercised their own power also. And the effects of the exercise of power were contradictory and partial.

While Willis' study only pointed to the operation of power as contradictory, Foucault (among others) has elaborated a view of power which reveals weaknesses of the property and zero-sum conceptions. Rather than conceiving of power as a possession or a commodity, a thing to be held or exchanged, Foucault (1980) argued instead that power is "exercised, and . . . only exists in action" (89):

> Power must be analysed as something which circulates, or rather as something which only functions in the form of a chain. It is never localised here or there, never in anybody's hands, never appropriated as a commodity or piece of wealth. Power is employed and exercised through a net-like organisation. And not only do individuals circulate between its threads; they are always in the position of simultaneously undergoing and exercising this power. They are not only its inert or consenting target. They are always also the elements of its articulation. In other words, individuals are the vehicles of power, not its points of application. (98)

Theoretically, Foucault's analysis of power raises questions about the possibility of empowering. First, it refutes the idea that one can give power to (can *empower*) another. Thus, to accept a view of one's work as giving power (as property) to others/Others (I will return to this in my discussion of the use of empowerment) is to overly simplify the operation of power in our society. Given

Foucault's conception of power as "circulating", "exercised" and existing "only in action", empowerment cannot mean the giving of power. It could, however, mean the exercise of power in an attempt (that might not be successful) to help others to exercise power. That is, Foucault's analysis of power doesn't preclude purposeful or politically motivated action; it does point out the rather strong possibility that our purposes might not be attained.

Second, conceiving of power *as exercised* points immediately to the need for empowerment to be context-specific and related to practices. As I have already indicated, discourses of critical and feminist pedagogy have tended to "decontextualize" empowerment. Their concern for context at the broad level of societal relations and institutions and ideologies (be they capitalist and/or patriarchal) leads to totalizing or universalizing tendencies which imply their concern is for "all teachers" or "all students" or "all women". Understanding power as exercised, rather than as possessed, requires more attention to the microdynamics of the operation of power as it is exercised in particular sites, that is conducting an "*ascending* analysis of power, starting . . . from its infinitesimal mechanisms" (Foucault, 1980, 99).

What is the vision of empowerment anyway?

Critical and feminist pedagogy discourses frequently perpetuate a simplistic dichotomy between empowerment and oppression through a level of abstraction which mystifies the meanings ascribed to either term (empowerment or oppression). Ellsworth (1989) has illustrated this point by citing some of the ways in which critical discourses answer the question "Empowerment for what?" The vision is of empowerment

> for "human betterment", for expanding "the range of possible social identities people may become" and "making one's self present as part of a moral and political project that links production of meaning to the possibility for human agency, democratic community, and transformative social action" (307).

But what does all this mean at the level of the school or classroom? And how are teachers to turn this "macro" vision into the "micro" of their daily practices in classrooms? Such questions have historically plagued radical educational work, as it struggles with the contradictory demands of traditional radical political ideals and institutional work in the academy (Ladwig, 1992; Liston & Zeichner, 1991; Wexler, 1987).

The perpetuation of a dichotomy between empowerment and oppression also stems from a shift in conceptions of power as repression to power as productive, such that empowerment is linked with a productive conception of power and oppression is linked with a repressive conception. For example, Shrewsbury (1987) states that "by focusing on empowerment, feminist pedagogy embodies a concept of power as energy, capacity, and potential rather than as domination"

(8). In this view, power is *either* productive *or* repressive. I will argue shortly that attempts to empower can (and probably will) have inconsistent effects.

What I find most troubling is the theoretical *pronouncement* of these discourses as empowering or liberatory. For example, McLaren (1989) claims that:

> We can consider *dominant* discourses (those produced by the dominant culture) as "regimes of truth", as general economies of power/knowledge, or as multiple forms of constraint. . . . A critical discourse is . . . self-critical and deconstructs dominant discourses the moment they are ready to achieve hegemony (181).

In this statement, critical discourses are presented as liberatory because they challenge dominant discourses, not because they have been liberatory for particular people or groups. Meanwhile, the "self critical" nature claimed for critical discourses seems more rhetorical than actual. While Giroux and McLaren occasionally reframe or clarify aspects of their argument as their project continues to shift with time, the possibility that their own academic construction of critical pedagogy might not be the emancipatory discourse it is intended to be is rarely articulated by these theorists. Rather, teachers are exhorted to "take as their first concern the issue of empowerment"; empowerment which "depends on the ability of teachers in the future to struggle collectively in order to create those ideological and material conditions of work that enable them to share power, to shape policy, and to play an active role in structuring school/community relations" (Giroux, 1988, 214). In short, empowerment depends on teachers using and actualizing this discourse of critical pedagogy.

Contrary to this view, Sawicki (1988) argues that "no discourse is inherently liberating or oppressive. . . . The liberatory status of any discourse is a matter of historical inquiry, not theoretical pronouncement" (166). Does this suggest that by focussing only on "dominant" discourses McLaren has missed an opportunity afforded by the concept "regime of truth"? Bové (1988) argues that many leading humanistic intellectuals misread Foucault "to blunt the political consequences of his critique of their disciplines', their discourses', and their own positions within the knowledge/power apparatus" (xi). The political consequences of Foucault's critique include questioning of the ideological, discursive, and political positions of "oppositional" discourses. To capitalize on this interpretation of Foucault's work would require more contextualization of empowerment rhetoric. That is, in addition to the theoretical pronouncement about emancipatory potential currently found, there would need to be more historical or empirical inquiry of empowerment in particular sites and discourses.

This general problem of decontextualization is perhaps more apparent in the critical discourses than it is in the feminist pedagogy discourses where there can be found many more attempts to address specific contexts. With the 1960s radical feminist premise that "the personal is political" (Jaggar, 1983), an insight which still has currency in contemporary feminisms, the feminist pedagogy literature reveals a much greater emphasis on actual classrooms and classroom practices (e.g., consider the collections edited by Bunch & Pollack, 1983; Culley & Portuges, 1985; Schniedewind & Maher, 1987) and seems less inclined toward grand theorizing. However, many of these accounts are rather descriptive and individualistic in their presentation of context and pay little attention to the location of their practices in educational institutions. Despite any differences related to "feminist process" or "feminist pedagogy", or to a student population consisting primarily of women, teaching feminism in a Women's Studies classroom remains an act of pedagogy in an educational institution.

When much of the empowerment rhetoric pertains to practices which could or should take place within universities and schools, we must ask how much freedom can there be within the institutional and pedagogical exigencies of teaching? More attention to contexts would help shift the problem of empowerment from dualisms of power/powerlessness, and dominant/subordinate, that is, from purely oppositional stances, to a problem of multiplicity and contradiction. It may be helpful to think of social actors negotiating actions within particular contexts. I hasten to add here that I am not advocating a notion of context as simply a pseudonym/synonym for the present or the immediate. Rather, I would argue that context must be conceived as filled with social actors whose personal *and* group histories position them as subjects immersed in social patterns. Thus, contexts for the work of empowerment need to be defined historically and politically with acknowledgment of the unique struggles that characterize the exercise of power at the micro levels.

Unreflexive use

My major concern about the politics of empowerment within discourses of critical and feminist pedagogy stems from conceptions of the agent of empowerment. Having established that the agent of empowerment is usually the teacher, and that the subject (or object) of empowerment is Others, a distinction is immediately set up between "us" and "them". Even if some teachers attempted to empower other teachers, the distinction remains between those who aim to empower and those who are to be empowered. As a given in any relation which aims at empowerment, the agent becomes problematic when the us/them relationship is conceived as requiring a focus only on "them". When the agent of empowerment assumes to be already empowered, and so apart from those who are to be empowered, arrogance can underlie claims of "what we can do for you". This danger is apparent both in the work of the teacher who is to empower students, and in the work of the academic whose discourse is purportedly empowering for the teachers (and others).

In the focus on Others there is a danger of forgetting to examine one's own (or one's group's) implication in the conditions one seeks to affect. Consider, for example, the following statement by Giroux (1988):

Teachers' work has to be analyzed in terms of its social and political function within particular "regimes of truth". That is, teachers can no longer deceive themselves into believing they are serving on behalf of truth when, in fact, they are deeply involved in battles "about the status of truth and the political role it plays". (212)

In his insistence that teachers are intellectuals who need to be conscious of the contradictory effects of their work, it seems Giroux has ignored the possibility that his own position as an intellectual is also vulnerable as a "regime of truth". Although Giroux (1991) argues that "educators need to be skeptical regarding any notion of reason [that] purports to reveal the truth by denying its own historical construction and ideological principles" (51), he does not articulate, with any specificity, his own complicity. It is possible that he has misread Foucault in a way which costs him his critical openness (Bové, 1988). His insight on teachers seems to be his oversight when it comes to his own work. In the (well-intentioned) focus on empowering others there is a danger of overlooking the reflexivity which, rhetorically,[3] is considered integral to critical practice.

Moreover, setting oneself apart as teacher/intellectual/leader can easily foster an arrogance which assumes to know what empowerment means for teachers or students. And it assumes that "we *can* do for you". Bové (1986) puts it like this:

Leading intellectuals tend to assume responsibility for imagining alternatives and do so *within* a set of discourses and institutions burdened genealogically by multifaceted complicities with power that make them dangerous to people. As agencies of these discourses that greatly affect the lives of people one might say leading intellectuals are a tool of oppression and most so precisely when they arrogate the right and power to judge and imagine efficacious alternatives—a process that we might suspect, sustains leading intellectuals at the expense of others (277).

Rather than making pronouncements about what we can do, we need to ask "what *can* we do for you?".

If empowerment is constructed as the exercise of power in an attempt to help others to exercise power (rather than as the giving of power), we confront the unforeseeable and contradictory effects of the exercise of power and must be more humble and reflexive in our claims. It is not at all clear we can do anything. For example, in my own practice as a teacher educator, I have encouraged student teachers to question practices of the education systems in which they will work and have exposed them to ideas of collective political action as having potential for social change. These efforts were aimed at "empowering" student teachers as they enter the salaried workforce. But my teaching will not/has not always had the effects I hoped it would (Gore, 1990; Gore & Zeichner, 1991). Some students decided that they couldn't bear to teach in such an oppressive system and never entered teaching. Some taught for only a brief time and then pursued alternative careers. Some have struggled to find peers with whom to engage in "collective political action" and, in "going it alone", have been ostracized within their schools and have risked job security. Others have accepted "the way things are".

In attempts to empower others we need to acknowledge that our agency has limits, that we might "get it wrong" in assuming we know what would be empowering for others, and that no matter what our aims or how we go about "empowering", our efforts will be partial and inconsistent.

Regimes of truth

Each of the concerns about empowerment I have articulated above—an overly optimistic view of agency, a tendency to overlook context, an overly simplistic conception of power as property, the theoretical pronouncement of discourses as liberatory, a lack of reflexivity—can be illuminated through Foucault's notion of "regimes of truth".

In pointing to the nexus of power and knowledge, regime of truth highlights the potential dangers and normalizing tendencies of all discourses, including those which aim to liberate. Foucault (1983) said "My point is not that everything is bad, but that everything is dangerous" (231). Foucault (1980) explains "regime of truth" as follows: " 'Truth' is linked in circular relation with systems of power which produce and sustain it, and to effects of power which it induces and which extend it" (133), and

> Each society has its regime of truth, its general politics of truth: that is, the types of discourse which it accepts and makes function as true; the mechanisms and instances which enable one to distinguish true and false statements, the means by which each is sanctioned; the techniques and procedures accorded value in the acquisition of truth; the status of those who are charged with saying what counts as true (131).

McLaren and Giroux, from whose work I have drawn many of my examples thus far, both employ the concept "regime of truth" to talk about the nexus of power and knowledge. My interpretation of the concept differs however, in my application of it to more than one "society" (the "dominant" society) with a single regime. My use allows us to posit that, for example, feminisms may have their own power-knowledge nexuses which, in particular contexts or at particular historical moments, will operate in ways which are oppressive and repressive to people within and/or outside of that "society". As evidence, consider the anger many women of color have expressed at the alienation and marginalization they felt from what developed as a primarily white, middle-class form of feminism in the academy (e.g. hooks, 1984; Lorde, 1984; Omolade, 1985; Spelman, 1988). Similarly, I argue, contemporary discourses of critical and feminist pedagogy have their own politics of truth—systems of power which produce and sustain truth and effects of power which the discourses induce and by which the discourses are extended—at the same time as they are positioned within the larger regimes of our present.

Michel Foucault (1983) and Michel Feher (1987) have articulated points of focus that can be used as a methodological guide for the study of regimes of truth.[4] The framework articulates two sets of questions or concerns central to Foucault's work; the first identifies the *political* aspects of the regime, focussing on the relations of power, what goes on between people; the second identifies the *ethical* aspects of the regime, the relation to one's self and the way that relation shifts. The political aspects of the regime can be identified through a study of the system of differentiations made, the functions and objectives of those differentiations (or relations of power), the specific techniques and practices which actualize the relations of power, the institutions which integrate these practices, and the formation of knowledge which describes the regime. The ethical component of the regime can be identified by studying the aspects of the self or body that are considered problematic or in need of disciplining in any given regime, in the name of what the self is disciplined or styled, the specific techniques that are developed to achieve a particular self-styling, toward what goal. The ethical "is at once intertwined with and autonomous to the political. . . . The two . . . work together. . . . The ethical affects the mechanisms of power as much as the political, and there is as much resistance in the political as there is in the ethical" (Feher, 1987, 165).

It is not within the scope of this paper, nor it is my aim, to attempt a detailed analysis of regimes of truth in critical and feminist pedagogy. Rather, I elaborate central features of regimes of truth in critical and feminist pedagogy which might help in understanding their constructions of empowerment rhetoric and practices. In particular, I focus on some of the differentiations made, the institutions involved, and the relations to "self" articulated within the discourses. I emphasize that these aspects of the regime are connected to each other and separated here for purposes of analysis and clarity.

In the Neo-Marxist discourses of critical pedagogy there has been a self-proclaimed shift from "a language of critique" to "a language of possibility" (e.g., Aronowitz & Giroux, 1985; Simon, 1987). This differentiation is connected with the shift from conceptions of power as repressive to power as productive, and with a shift from an emphasis on ideology and structure to an emphasis on agency. Resistance theories can be located at the transition between critique and possibility. Willis' (1977) study, for example, pointed to a productive aspect of power but concluded with an elucidation of the oppressive structures which kept "the lads" in their class position. "Empowerment" has been constructed in ways that take the productive moment of power further, and so go "beyond resistance". This movement to a language of possibility is part of a general shift in critical educational discourse toward acknowledging that education has played a role in social movement and not just in social reproduction (Wexler, 1987). There has been movement beyond encouraging teachers to recognize the structural constraints under which they work to having them also acknowledge "the potential inherent in teaching for transformative and political work" (Weiler, 1988, 52). The strong sense of agency found in empowerment rhetoric (particularly in critical pedagogy) can be connected to the language of possibility in which it is embedded. Indeed, it is with this shift to a language of possibility that we saw the emergence of "critical pedagogy" discourse and the linking of empowerment and pedagogy which I shall examine shortly.

Despite this move to power as productive, the Neo-Marxist roots of the discourse perhaps account for the retention of a notion of power as property which still pervades the rhetoric of critical pedagogy. In its "vulgar" form, the Neo-Marxist conception of power is clearly encapsulated in the following passage from Burbules' (1986) "A Theory of Power in Education":

> In order to identify power relations in schools, we have to begin with the questions Where are the conflicts of interest? Where are the zero-sum games? In principle, education need not involve power relations at all; the learning of one student does not necessarily entail the disadvantaging of another. In principle, teachers can function as legitimate authorities, not as authoritarian masters. In principle, schools can *educate* and . . . minimize power relations and promote the basis for informed, consensual, and egalitarian human relations (109).

While Giroux and McLaren might argue with Burbules' theory, traces of power as property can still be found in their work; for example, critical pedagogy retains dualisms of the dominant and subordinate, the oppressed and the privileged, in which power is located in the hands of the dominant and the privileged.

Likewise, in feminist pedagogy conceptions of power as property remain. For example, Clare Bright (1987) says:

> Discussion of the student/teacher relationship must include a frank look at the power of the teacher. Feminists have often avoided the topic of power, preferring structures and situations where power is shared. However, the educational system is not an egalitarian one, and regardless of the extent to which a teacher tries to minimize her power, it can not be completely given away (98).

Inasmuch as feminisms seek to change "patriarchal structures" and "existing power relations between men and women" (Weedon, 1987), notions of power as property and power as productive inhere and are carried into the discourses of feminist pedagogy. For instance, Shrewsbury (1987) claims that

> Empowering pedagogy does not dissolve the authority or power of the instructor. It does move from power as domination to power as creative energy . . . a view of power as creative community energy would suggest that strategies be developed to counteract unequal power arrangements. Such strategies recognize the potentiality for changing traditional unequal relationships. Our classrooms need not always reflect an equality of power, but they must reflect movement in that direction (9,8)

When we consider the specific practices that are to empower we confront what Michael Apple (1988) has discussed as a paradox in the democratic call for social change from "the ground up" and the need to offer possibilities or models from which people can act. This paradox helps account for the tendency toward abstract and decontextualized (at the micro levels) claims for empowerment. In the attempt not to impose an agenda on others, critical (and, to a lesser extent, some feminist) pedagogy discourses have opted instead for rather abstract theories of empowerment. And yet, they have imposed a requirement on teachers to do the work of empowering, to be the agents of empowerment, without providing much in the way of tangible guidance for that work. An exception is the recent feminist poststructuralist attention to pedagogy which situates itself in particular contexts but has also begun to raise questions about the possibility of empowering (e.g. Ellsworth, 1989; Gardner, Dean & McKaig, 1989; Lather, 1991; Lewis, 1989; Mahony, 1988)—questions that point to multiplicity, contradiction and partialness.

The institutional location of much critical and feminist pedagogy discourse, in an academy which rewards the development of theory over struggles to teach, can account for some of the theoretical pronouncement and inattention to context which I have been discussing. As part of *academic* discourses, the constructions of empowerment discussed in this paper often reveal a "will to knowledge", characteristic of much intellectual work, that is so strong that the need, desire or willingness to question one's own work is lost in the desire to believe that one has found "truth", that one is "right". This aspect of the regime of truth is manifested (and problematic) in critical and feminist pedagogy discourses of empowerment by a tendency to present the discourses in a fixed, final, "founded" form which "protects *them* from rethinking and change. It turns what was once 'critical' in their work into a kind of norm or law—a final truth, a final emancipation. For Foucault that is just what critical 'truth' cannot be" (Rajchman, 1985, 93).

Taubman (1986) makes this point in his review of *Gendered Subjects: The Dynamics of Feminist Teaching* claiming it is

> informed by essentialist and separatist arguments and assumptions. . . . Therein . . . lies the danger of a feminist pedagogy. The old dualities are preserved. The origin of truth is found in anatomy. . . . Feminist pedagogy loses its usefulness to the extent that it sees itself as synonymous with good teaching, having an exclusive claim on good teaching. . . . It loses its force to the extent that it locates the origin and horizon of pedagogy in and on the bodies of women (93).

These essentializing tendencies might be accounted for by the emergence of much feminist pedagogy from liberal and radical feminist traditions, both of which have tended to "attempt to define women's nature once and for all" (Weedon, 1987, p. 135). Similarly, the connection of critical pedagogy to Neo-Marxism might account for its totalizing tendencies, whereby dominant dis-

courses are bad and must be overturned and oppositional discourses are liberatory.

The will to knowledge of much academic work also helps us understand the
lack of reflexivity which is a danger in the use of empowerment rhetoric in some
of these discourses. A more detailed attempt to map out the regimes of truth of
critical and feminist pedagogy[5] (Gore, 1989b) reveals a tendency to neglect the
ethical[6]—one's relation to oneself. That is, these discourses rarely address ways
in which teachers, students, or the theorists themselves need to style or discipline
their gestures, postures or attitudes. The rhetoric is of freedom, not of control.
And yet, the discourses have the effect of disciplining teachers to practice critical
and feminist pedagogies. This neglect of the ethical brings us full circle to the
institutions which integrate critical and feminist discourses, primarily universities, and to the differentiations made in the academy and within the discourses
themselves. The focus is generally on the broader political questions of interests
and institutions with, especially in some discourses of critical pedagogy, little
attention to self. How then, does the rhetoric of empowerment connect with the
practice of pedagogy?

Pedagogy and empowerment

To understand the relation of pedagogy to empowerment in these discourses of
critical and feminist pedagogy, I want to highlight two aspects of the preceding
analysis. First, my analysis of presuppositions points to a general congruence
between the two enterprises of pedagogy and empowerment. In very general
terms, pedagogy seems to involve a teacher (an agent) who "gives" knowledge,
responsibility, and more (as property) to students, and aims to produce a particular conception of the educated student (a vision, a desired end state); that is,
pedagogy seems to hold the same presuppositions as empowerment. It is not
surprising, then, that it is the critical and feminist discourses which claim a focus
on pedagogy that also emphasize empowerment.

Moreover, constructions of critical and feminist pedagogies and of empowerment have both occurred within discourses that have gone beyond a conception
of power as primarily repressive: empowerment suggests the productive capacity
of power (while frequently posing it in opposition to power as domination and so
maintaining the dichotomy); critical and feminist pedagogy come out of a history
of "progressive" schooling in which instead of controlling/disciplining/con-
straining learners, the teacher was to use her or his authority to facilitate/to empower.

While the congruence of empowerment and critical and feminist pedagogies
can be understood, it remains to be seen whether they can be actualized as conceived. That is, while the desire may be to move from a conception of power as
repression to em-power-ment (in a dichotomous fashion with great optimism and
human agency), the institutional location (context, again) of much pedagogical

practice may militate against it. The pedagogical relation of teacher to students is, at some fundamental level, one in which the teacher is able to exercise power in ways unavailable to students. Teaching remains embedded within a history of moral and cultural regulation. Moreover, as Foucault (1977) and others (e.g. Walkerdine, 1985, 1986; Walkerdine & Lucey, 1989) have argued about disciplinary power, practices which decrease overt regulation can increase surveillance and regulation through covert and more dangerous means. These conditions suggest that attempts to "give up power" and "share power" in the name of empowerment might be misdirected. Rather, the energies of those of us who advocate critical and feminist pedagogies might be better directed at seeking ways to exercise power toward the fulfilment of our espoused aims, ways that include humility, skepticism and self-criticism.

Second, my reconstruction (following Foucault) of empowerment as the exercise of power in an attempt to help others to exercise power, suggests that empowerment must occur in sites of practice. Indeed if pedagogy is conceived as the process of knowledge production (Lusted, 1986), a meaning consistent with much critical and feminist work that tends to deny constructions of pedagogy as "instruction", then we can argue that empowerment must be pedagogical—a process of knowledge production. Of course, the work of theorizing can certainly be pedagogical to the degree that we can identify processes of knowledge production. But when we consider the rhetoric of much of this work to be for the empowerment of teachers and students *as* teachers and students and as "critical citizens" (critical pedagogy) or women (feminist pedagogy), while the primary site of knowledge production is the university, we can better understand why these discourses have seemed to some critics to be rather ineffectual. For example, Giroux's work has certainly been pedagogical and empowering for many of us *in the academic field*. Critiques of his work for the inaccessibility of its language (e.g. Bowers, 1991; Schrag, 1988; Miedema, 1987) point out that his work may not have been as pedagogical or empowering at the ostensibly targeted sites of school and classroom. Of course, we need to take these criticisms cautiously, given that they are other academic articulations, just as my own critique must be positioned within the academic context of its construction.

Nevertheless, the argument that empowerment must be linked to pedagogical practice reiterates and strengthens two threads of this paper: first, discourses of critical and feminist pedagogy need to pay much closer attention to the contexts in which they aim to empower; second, they need to provide better guidance for the actions of the teachers they hope to empower or they hope will empower students. This is not to suggest that detailed prescriptions for practice should, or even could, be given. But if teachers are to exercise power in an attempt to help their students exercise power both in and outside of the classroom or, as McLaren (1989) put it, "in the classroom and in the streets", then teachers need some contextualized guidance as to ways in which they might proceed. I am fully aware that this paper does not directly assist with the task of providing such contextualized guidance. My purpose here was limited to an elaboration of concerns with constructions of empowerment as a precursor to such a task for my own work in teacher education and, hopefully, for the work of others within the critical and feminist traditions.

Conclusion

None of this discussion of shortcomings or power or regimes of truth is to say that the impulse to empower groups who have historically been oppressed is bad or wrong, or that academics should divorce themselves from struggles that are not perceived to be immediately their own. On the contrary, I believe academics must continue the kinds of political struggles which are the concern of critical and feminist pedagogies but should do so while constantly questioning the "truth" of their/our own thought and selves. Of course, my own thoughts presented here must also be questioned. They represent a moment in my ongoing struggle to understand and practice pedagogies informed by the feminist and critical traditions.

In this paper I have tried to demonstrate ways in which (my interpretations of) Foucault's analyses of power and intellectual work are useful for this endeavor. Foucault's rejection of conceptions of power as property points to a rethinking of empowerment as the exercise of power in an attempt to help others to exercise power. And, in the emphasis on power as action, Foucault's work demands greater attention to the contexts in which empowerment is advocated and/or attempted. Furthermore, Foucault's analysis of power and knowledge as connected through regimes of truth, calls for greater reflexivity and acknowledgment of the limitations of what "we" can do for "you".

Acknowledgment

My thanks to James Ladwig for his insightful comments and criticisms on numerous versions of this paper. I am also grateful to Elizabeth Ellsworth, Tom Popkewitz, Michael Apple, Ken Zeichner and Alison Dewar, each of whom has had significant influences on my thinking about "empowerment".

Notes

1. See Gore (1989a) for an elaboration of the construction of empowerment within conservative and liberal humanist discourses.

2. See Jaggar (1983) and Weedon (1987) for characterizations of the variety of stances within feminism. Also see Acker (1987) for a consideration of the educational applications of the various theoretical frameworks. The recent poststructuralist feminist attention to pedagogy differs from this earlier work in feminist pedagogy in several ways, not the least of which, given my delimitations in this paper, is its reluctance to call itself "feminist pedagogy".

3. Consider, for example, McLaren's (1989) statement cited earlier in this paper that critical dis-

courses are "self-critical" or the statement "Nor must we ever give up becoming more theoretically vigilant on the basis that we are morally innocent. To claim immunity from our exercising domination over others on the basis that we have good intentions is to euphemistically dodge Michel Foucault's injunction that we judge truth by its effects and to deny our complicity in economies of oppression on the grounds of our theoretical ignorance" (McLaren, 1988, p. 70). There is a confessional nod of complicity here, but no explication, elaboration, or articulation of the *specific* form that complicity takes.

4. I thank Elizabeth Ellsworth for introducing me to Feher's (1987) work and for suggesting its relevance as a methodology for my work on critical and feminist pedagogies.

5. See Gore (1989b) for an attempt to map out the regimes of truth in critical and feminist pedagogy around issues of authority.

6. This sense in which Foucault uses "ethical" is not to be confused with the commonsense use of the term, which often conflates ethics with morality.

References

Acker, S. (1987). Feminist theory and the study of gender and education. *International Review of Education, 33*(4), 419–435.

Apple, M. W. (1988). Curriculum, capitalism, and democracy: A response to Whitty's critics. *British Journal of Sociology of Education, 7*(3), 319–327.

Aronowitz, S. & Giroux, H. A. (1985). *Education under siege.* Massachusetts: Bergin & Garvey.

Bové, P. A. (1986). *Intellectuals in power: A genealogy of critical humanism.* New York: Columbia University Press.

Bové, P. A. (1988). Foreword: The Foucault phenomenon: The problematics of style. In G. Deleuze *Foucault* (trans. S. Hand), (pp. vii–xl). Minneapolis: University of Minnesota Press.

Bowers, C. A. (1991). Some questions about the anachronistic elements in the Giroux-McLaren theory of a critical pedagogy. *Curriculum Inquiry, 21*(2), 239–252.

Bunch, C. & Pollack, S. (Eds). (1983). *Learning our way: Essays in feminist education.* Trumansburg, New York: The Crossing Press.

Bright, C. (1987). Teaching feminist pedagogy: An undergraduate course. *Women's Studies Quarterly, 15*(3&4), 96–100.

Britzman, D. (1991). *Practice makes practice: A critical study of learning to teach.* Albany: State University of New York Press.

Burbules, N. C. (1986). A theory of power in education. *Educational Theory, 36*(2), 95–114.

Cherryholmes, C. (1988). *Power and criticism: Poststructural investigations in education.* New York: Teachers College Press.

Culley, M. (1985). Anger and authority in the introductory Women's Studies classroom. In M. Culley & C. Portuges (Eds). *Gendered subjects: The dynamics of feminist teaching,* (pp. 209–218). Boston & London: Routledge & Kegan Paul.

Culley M. & Portuges, C. (Eds). (1985). *Gendered subjects: The dynamics of feminist teaching.* Boston & London: Routledge & Kegan Paul.

Ellsworth, E. (1989). Why doesn't this feel empowering? Working through the repressive myths of critical pedagogy. *Harvard Educational Review, 59*(3), 297–324.

Feher, M. (1987). On bodies and technologies. In H. Foster (Ed). *Discussions in contemporary culture,* (pp. 159–172). Seattle: Bay Press.

Foucault, M. (1977). *Discipline and punish: The birth of the prison.* New York: Pantheon.

Foucault, M. (1980). Truth and power. In C. Gordon (Ed). *Power/knowledge: Selected interviews and other writings 1972–1977*, (pp. 109–133). New York: Pantheon Books.

Foucault, M. (1983). The subject and power. In H. L. Dreyfus & P. Rabinow (Eds). *Michel Foucault: Beyond structuralism and hermeneutics*, 2nd edition, (pp. 208–228). Chicago: University of Chicago Press.

Gardner, S., Dean, C. & McKaig, D. (1989). Responding to difference in the classroom: The politics of knowledge, class, and sexuality. *Sociology of Education, 62* (Jan.), 64–74.

Giroux, H. A. (1988). *Schooling and the struggle for public life: Critical pedagogy in the modern age*. Minneapolis: University of Minnesota Press.

Giroux, H. A. (Ed). (1991). *Postmodernism, feminism, and cultural politics: Redrawing educational boundaries*. Albany: State University of New York Press.

Gore, J. M. (1989a). Agency, structure and the rhetoric of teacher empowerment. Paper presented at the American Educational Research Association Annual Conference, San Francisco, California, March 27–31.

Gore, J. M. (1989b). The struggle for pedagogies: Critical and feminist discourses as "regimes of truth". Paper presented at the Eleventh Conference on Curriculum Theory and Classroom Practice, Bergamo Conference Center, Dayton, Ohio, October 18–22.

Gore, J. M. (1990). Pedagogy as text in physical education teacher education. In D. Kirk & R. Tinning (Eds). *Physical education, curriculum and culture: Critical issues in the contemporary crisis*, (pp. 101–138). London, New York & Philadelphia: The Falmer Press.

Gore, J. M. (in press). *The struggle for pedagogies: Critical and feminist discourses as "regimes of truth"*. New York: Routledge.

Gore, J. M. & Zeichner, K. M. (1991). Action research and reflective teaching in preservice teacher education: A case study from the United States. *Teaching and Teacher Education, 7*(2), 119–136.

Grumet, M. (1988). *Bitter milk*. Amherst: The University of Massachusetts Press.

Hamilton, D. (1989). *Towards a theory of schooling*. London, New York & Philadelphia: The Falmer Press.

hooks, b. (1984). *Feminist theory: From margin to center*. Boston: South End Press.

Jaggar, A. M. (1983). *Feminist politics and human nature*. Sussex: The Harvester Press.

Ladwig, J. G. (1992). A theory of methodology for the sociology of school knowledge. Ph.D. thesis, University of Wisconsin-Madison.

Lather, P. (1991). *Getting smart: Feminist research and pedagogy with/in the postmodern*. New York: Routledge.

Lewis, M. (1988). *Without a word: Sources and themes for a feminist pedagogy*. Ph.D. thesis, University of Toronto.

Lewis, M. (1989). Problems of practice in radical teaching. A feminist perspective on the psycho/social/sexual dynamics in the mixed gender classroom. Paper presented at the American Educational Research Association Annual Conference, San Francisco, California, March 27–31.

Liston, D. & Zeichner, K. (1991). *Teacher education and the conditions of schooling*. New York: Routledge.

Lorde, A. (1984). *Sister outsider*. Trumansburg, NY: Crossing Press.

Luke, C. (1989). *Pedagogy, printing and protestantism: The discourse on childhood*. Albany: State University of New York Press.

Lusted, D. (1986). Why pedagogy? *Screen, 27*(5), 2–14.

Maeroff, G. I. (1988). *The empowerment of teachers: Overcoming the crisis of confidence*. New York & London: Teachers College Press.

Mahony, P. (1988). Oppressive pedagogy: The importance of process in Women's Studies. *Women's Studies International Forum, 11*(2), 103–108.

Marshall, J. D. (1989). Foucault and education. *Australian Journal of Education, 33*(2), 99–113.

McLaren, P. (1988). Schooling the postmodern body: Critical pedagogy and the politics of enfleshment. *Journal of Education, 170*(3), 53–83.

McLaren, P. (1989). *Life in schools: An introduction to critical pedagogy in the foundations of education.* New York & London: Longman.

Miedema, S. (1987). The theory-practice relation in critical pedagogy. *Phenomenology + Pedagogy, 5*(3), 221–229.

Miller, J. L. (1990). *Creating spaces and finding voices: Teachers collaborating for empowerment.* Albany: State University of New York Press.

Morgan, K. P. (1987). The perils and paradoxes of feminist pedagogy. *Resources for Feminist Research, 16*(3), 49–52.

Omolade, B. (1985). Black women and feminism. In H. Eisenstein & A. Jardine (Eds). *The future of difference.* New Brunswick: Rutgers University Press.

Popkewitz, T. S. (1991). *A political sociology of educational reform: Power/knowledge in teaching, teacher education, and research.* New York: Teachers College Press.

Rabinow, P. (1984). Polemics, politics, and problemizations: An interview with Michel Foucault. In P. Rabinow (Ed). *The Foucault reader,* (pp. 381–390). New York: Pantheon Books.

Rajchman, J. (1985). *Michel Foucault: The freedom of philosophy.* New York: Columbia University Press.

Sawicki, J. (1988). Feminism and the power of Foucauldian discourse. In J. Arac (Ed). *After Foucault: Humanistic knowledge, postmodern challenges,* (pp. 161–178). New Brunswick and London: Rutgers University Press.

Schniedewind, N. & Maher, F. (Eds). (1987). Special feature: Feminist pedagogy. *Women's Studies Quarterly, 15*(3&4).

Schrag, F. (1988). Response to Giroux. *Educational Theory, 38*(1), 143–144.

Shor, I. & Freire, P. (1987). *A pedagogy for liberation: Dialogues on transforming education.* Massachusetts: Bergin & Garvey.

Shrewsbury, C. M. (1987). What is feminist pedagogy? *Women's Studies Quarterly, 15*(3&4), 6–14.

Simon, R. I. (1987). Empowerment as a pedagogy of possibility. *Language Arts, 64*(4), 370–382.

Spelman, E. V. (1988). *Inessential woman: Problems of exclusion in feminist thought.* Boston: Beacon Press.

Taubman, P. (1986). Review article "Gendered subjects: The dynamics of feminist teaching", Margaret Culley & Catherine Portuges (Eds.) *Phenomenology + Pedagogy, 4*(2), 89–94.

Walkerdine, V. (1985). On the regulation of speaking and silence: Subjectivity, class and gender in contemporary schooling. In C. Steedman, C. Unwin, & V. Walkerdine (Eds). *Language, gender and childhood* (pp. 203–241). London, Boston & Henley: Routledge & Kegan Paul.

Walkerdine, V. (1986). Progressive pedagogy and political struggle. *Screen, 27*(5), 54–60.

Walkerdine, V. & Lucey, H. (1989). *Democracy in the kitchen: Regulating mothers and socialising daughters.* London: Virago Press.

Weedon, C. (1987). *Feminist practice and poststructuralist theory.* Oxford: Basil Blackwell.

Weiler, K. (1988). *Women teaching for change: Gender, class and power.* South Hadley, Massachusetts: Bergin & Garvey.

Wexler, P. (1987). *Social analysis of education: After the new sociology.* London & New York: Routledge & Kegan Paul.

Willis, P. (1977). *Learning to labour.* Westmead: Saxon House.

Yonemura, M. (1986). Reflections on teacher empowerment and teacher education. *Harvard Educational Review, 56*(4), 473–480.

5

Interrupting the Calls for Student Voice in "Liberatory" Education: A Feminist Poststructuralist Perspective

Mimi Orner

Issues concerning the power and authority of teachers are crucial for those of us committed to education against a variety of such oppressive formations as those based on race, class, gender, sexuality, ethnicity, and ability. Critical and feminist theories and epistemologies of education offer a wide range of strategies for intervention in the "business as usual" of teaching. But some of these discursive and material practices are constructed around problematic assumptions regarding what it means to be a student and/or youth. I will show that students/youth are positioned as Other by Anglo-American feminist and critical pedagogy. I will argue for a reexamination of some of the fundamental conceptions regarding students/youth which inform emancipatory projects in education.

Defining the problem

Feminist poststructuralist discourse views the struggle over identity within the subject as inseparable from the struggle over the meanings of identities and subject positions within the culture at large. The meanings of terms used to represent social groups which have historically been targets of oppression are continuously undergoing transformation in ways that render as violent and exclusionary any attempt to focus on a singular definition. The meanings of "woman", "person of color", "person with disabilities", "impoverished", "old", "working-class", "lesbian", "gay", "bisexual", "Jew", "ethnic", "minority", are constantly being renegotiated by groups acting strategically in specific social and historical contexts. As a "Jewish", "fat", "heterosexual", "white", "young", "middle class", "woman", I see the terms I have used here to describe myself as highly unstable, since the culturally generated meanings and understandings articulated to these terms continually undergo personal and social transformation. Instead of framing the slipperiness of identity as a problem to be solved or an obstacle to be avoided, feminist poststructuralists regard the inability to fix our identities and to be known through them in any definitive way as a powerful means through which we can "denaturalize" ourselves and embrace change. As a "feminist" "educator", the social construction and contestation of identity leads me to ask certain questions.

What does it mean for those of us who are teachers to struggle against oppression inside the classroom? How can we understand "resistance" by students to education which is designed to "empower" them? How do we speak as teachers *and* as members of various social groups? How do we understand our own embodiment of privilege and oppression, both historical and current? How do we teach as allies to oppressed groups of which we are not a part? What does it mean to teach as an ally? What are the implications of these concerns and commitments for pedagogy?

Until recently, the only discourses available which allowed me to address these questions were Anglo-American feminist and critical theories of education. But growing concern with unexamined aspects of these discourses and practices has fostered a significant body of work by educational theorists who utilize poststructuralist analyses to question Anglo-American feminist and critical approaches to pedagogy and educational theory. Frameworks and concepts derived from feminist appropriations of poststructuralist discourse have fueled powerful critiques of the pedagogical and political limitations of what have been called the "emancipatory" and "liberatory" educational traditions. One of the goals of this study is to demonstrate the significance of feminist poststructuralist theories for those identifying and working against oppressive relations in schools.

Demands for student voice in the educational writings of critical and Anglo-American feminist theorists presuppose subject positions for teachers and students which are highly problematic when seen through the lenses of feminist poststructuralist theories. Student voice, as it has been conceptualized in work which claims to empower students, is an oppressive construct—one that I argue perpetuates relations of domination in the name of liberation. All of us in this volume, working in different institutions and socio-historical contexts, and indeed in different countries, have begun to interrogate the calls for student voice as they operate within specific historical contexts. In this exploration, I will build on my colleagues' work as I deconstruct some of the metaphors, concepts and frameworks which are taken for granted in the "emancipatory" educational traditions generally and in the myriad calls for student voice in particular. I will show that demands for student voice in the Anglo-American feminist and critical traditions are highly suspect, given the reformulations of key concepts offered by feminist poststructuralist perspectives.

What I argue here is that calls for "authentic student voice" contain realist and essentialist epistemological positions regarding subjectivity which are neither acknowledged specifically nor developed theoretically. I will show that concepts such as subjectivity, identity, language, context, and power which are central to deconstructivist work in other areas, such as literary theory, philosophy and religion, have much to offer the field of education. More specifically, I will argue that these terms necessitate and help initiate a re-thinking of emancipatory discourses and practices involved with schooling.

Student voice in theory and practice

Historically, the demand by academics and other powerful groups for an "authentic" people's voice or culture to be heard has been received by disenfranchised groups with a great deal of suspicion. Why must the "oppressed" speak? For whose benefit do we/do they speak? How is the speaking received, interpreted, controlled, limited, disciplined and stylized by the speakers, the listeners, the historical moment, the context? What use is made of the "people's voice" after it is heard?

Theorists of feminist pedagogy in Britain and North America have had as a focus for student voice "the valuing of women's experiences inside the classroom, and the disruption of power hierarchies which have kept women silent" (Culley, 1985, p. 213). Critical theorists of pedagogy

> argue that the language of schooling and everyday life has to provide teachers and students with the skills they will need to locate themselves in history, find their own voices, and establish the convictions and compassion necessary for exercising civic courage, taking risks, and furthering the habits, customs and social relations essential to democratic public forms. (Freire and Giroux, 1989, p. viii)

But the concept of voice has other meanings and uses in education as well. As Britzman explains:

> . . . the concept of voice spans literal, metaphorical and political terrains: In its literal sense voice represents the speech and perspectives of the speaker; metaphorically, voice spans inflection, tone, accent, style and the qualities and feelings conveyed by the speaker's words; and politically, a commitment to voice "attests to the *right* of speaking and being represented." (Britzman, 1989, p. 146)

The literal sense of student voice is exemplified by the oracy project in Britain, where the focus on student voice is part of a concern with questions of student competence in talking and listening. Similarly, instructional designers of discussion generating films for use in classrooms see student voice as the "affective response" to a provocative film or televisual stimulus. It is important to note the currency that the concept of student voice has across the so-called "paradigms" of educational research. Different rationales have been offered to justify the solicitation of student voice. It is clear that why students are being asked to talk, and what they are being asked to talk about, varies along with the social, political, economic and cultural commitments of an array of research and teaching agendas. But what is more deeply entrenched, and less examined across the various calls for student voice, are patterns of relating to students and youth as Other. These patterns are virtually unassailable, given currently dominant conceptualizations in both mainstream and oppositional education theory of the unified, rational subject.

Discourses of feminist poststructuralism

Feminist poststructuralist frameworks provide a way of looking at the long-term silences of all the received intellectual traditions of the West, including Marxist and Anglo-American feminist approaches to understanding and working against oppression. Feminist poststructuralist perspectives challenge the discourses of emancipation and the assumptions of fixed identity and unified, rational subjectivity found in some feminist and much critical literature and in work on student voice in particular.

In her book, *Gynesis: Configurations of Woman in Modernity* (1985), Alice Jardine locates poststructuralist work as arising out of a rejection by French intellectuals of 19th-century European political and philosophical conceptual frameworks. According to Jardine, this rejection necessarily includes humanist modes of thought that are based in movements of human liberation.

> Why this rejection? The major reason has been cautiously and painstakingly laid out in texts written over the past twenty-five years: our ways of understanding in the West have been and continue to be complicitious with our ways of oppressing. . . . The clearest way, perhaps, to contain in one word the gesture theorists in France have performed on the texts and contexts of humanist ideology is to focus on the word *denaturalization:* they have denaturalized the world that humanism naturalized, a world whose anthro-pology and anthro-centrism no longer make sense. (Jardine, 1985, p. 24)

It is the "anthro-pology and anthro-centrism" of educational discourses which claim "liberatory" status for themselves that I hope to denaturalize by focusing on the concept of student voice. Calls for students to speak in the name of their own liberation and empowerment must be scrutinized. Educators concerned with changing unjust power relations must continually examine our assumptions about our own positions, those of our students, the meanings and uses of student voice, our power to call for students to speak, and our often unexamined power to legitimate and perpetuate unjust relations in the name of student empowerment. To paraphrase Patti Lather, What are the sins of imposition we commit in the name of liberation? "Whether the goal of one's work is prediction, understanding or emancipation, all are ways of disciplining the body, normalizing behavior, administering the life of populations" (Rajchman in Lather, 1987b, p. 19).

By interrogating what have been called the master (ie., white, European, male) narratives which have legitimized and naturalized Western thought, and which have excluded, repressed, spoken for and about women and men of color, white women, Jews, lesbians and gays, those with physical and mental disabilities and others, poststructuralists have helped denaturalize what has historically been constructed as "natural", "normal", "seamless", "real", and "true" by the master narratives. This has not been an easy task. As Jardine explains:

> Going back to analyze [the master narratives] . . . has meant going back to the Greek philosophies in which they are grounded and, most particularly, to the originary relationships posited between . . . all the dualistic oppositions that determine our ways of thinking . . . [Ways] which are inadequate for under-standing a world of multiple causes and effects which interact in complex and nonlinear ways, and which are rooted in a limitless array of historical and cul-tural specificities. (Jardine, 1985, p. 24)

Dualisms which we contend with daily and which ignore the complexity and interrelatedness of the terms exemplify a mode of thought which has serious consequences for us all. Binary oppositions such as: Day/Night, Man/Woman, Father/Mother, Sun/Moon, Activity/Passivity, Culture/Nature, Sense/Non-Sense, Reason/Madness, Central/Marginal, Surface/Depth, Matter/Spirit, Mind/Body, Veil/Truth, Text/Meaning, Interior/Exterior, Representation/Presence, Appearance/Essence, and particularly prevalent for radical pedagogues, Theory/Practice, Structure/Agency, Production/Reproduction, Subject/Object, Teacher/Student, Oppressor/Oppressed, and Voice/Silence are inadequate and dangerous, as they have historically been accompanied by the essentializing of both terms and the privileging of the first term over the second. For example, mind and body are split off from each other, essentialized and then prioritized to read "mind over body." The same goes for day over night, man over woman, theory over practice, and teacher over student. It is crucial that we see how the terms interrelate, how they have been historically constructed as opposites, and how they have been used to justify and naturalize power relations.

Scrutinizing binary oppositions in order to get at what has been the master narratives' own "non-knowledge," the "second term," has been an important as-pect of poststructuralist work. Concepts such as Man, the Subject, Truth, His-tory, and Meaning have been denaturalized and deconstructed in attempts to re-cover each of their second terms, to find out what has been erased, silenced, and rejected in their names.

The subject and subjectivity

Central to work of this nature are the terms subject and subjectivity. These terms signify a crucial break with humanist, binary conceptions of the individual which have been central to Western philosophy, politics and social organizing. The term "subject" refers to something quite different from the more familiar term "individual".

> The latter term dates from the Renaissance and presupposes that "man" is a free, intellectual agent and that thinking processes are not coerced by historical

or cultural circumstances. This view of Reason is expressed in Descartes' philosophical work. Consider this phrase: "I think, therefore I am." Descartes' "I" assumes itself to be fully conscious, and hence self-knowable. It is not only autonomous but coherent; the notion of another psychic territory, in contradiction to consciousness, is unimaginable. (Sarup, 1989, p. 1)

Unlike the term "individual," the term "subject" encourages us to think of ourselves and our realities as constructions: the products of signifying or meaning-making activities which are both culturally specific and generally unconscious. The term "subject" calls into question the notion of a totally conscious self. The "subject" is always both conscious and unconscious. As Chris Weedon observes,

"Subjectivity" is used to refer to the conscious and unconscious thoughts and emotions of the individual, her sense of herself and her ways of understanding her relation to the world. Humanist discourses presuppose an essence at the heart of the individual which is unique, fixed and coherent and which makes her what she is. . . . poststructuralism proposes a subjectivity which is precarious, contradictory and in process, constantly being reconstituted in discourse each time we think or speak. (Weedon, 1987, p. 32)

Discourses on student voice are premised on the assumption of a fully conscious, fully speaking, "unique, fixed and coherent" self. These discourses, enmeshed in humanist presuppositions, ignore the shifting identities, unconscious processes, pleasures and desires not only of students, but of teachers, administrators and researchers as well. Discourses on student voice do not adequately recognize that one's social position, one's voice, can "at best be tentative and temporary given the changing, often contradictory relations of power at multiple levels of social life—the personal, the institutional, the governmental, the commercial" (Ellsworth and Selvin, 1986, p. 77).

"Liberatory" educational discourses call for the transformation of "reality" through a consciousness of one's social position through the articulation of one's voice. Little or no attention is given to the multiple social positions, multiple voices, conscious and unconscious pleasures, tensions, desires, and contradictions which are present in all subjects, in all historical contexts. Teachers and students must be thought of as "unfixed, unsatisfied, . . . not a unity, not autonomous, but a process, perpetually in construction, perpetually contradictory, perpetually open to change" (Belsey, 1980, p. 132).

Language

For feminist poststructuralist theorists, language is a crucial concept. Whereas Anglo-American feminist and critical pedagogies call for authentic student voice, poststructuralist theories of language see authentic student voice as an impossibility. Unlike discourses of humanism, poststructuralist theories of language do not see language simply as a tool we use. Rather, poststructuralists see language as a site of struggle where subjectivity and consciousness are produced.

> Language is not transparent as in humanist discourse, it is not expressive and does not label a 'real' world. Meanings do not exist prior to their articulation in language and language is not an abstract system, but is always socially and historically located in discourses. Discourses represent political interests and in consequence are constantly vying for status and power. (Weedon, 1987, p. 41)

Jacques Lacan's theoretical and psychoanalytical work has been integral to poststructuralist understandings of the importance of language. In a departure from the structuralism of Ferdinand de Saussure (a structuralism that sees truth as being "behind" or "within" a text), poststructuralism stresses the interaction of the reader and text as a productivity. For poststructuralists, reading is not the passive consumption of a pre-made product, as it is for structuralism. Reading is a negotiation between the reader and the text which takes place in, and is profoundly influenced by, particular contexts and historical conjunctures. For poststructuralists, nothing and no one is ever fully present in language. It is an illusion to believe that we can ever be fully present in speaking or writing, because using language entails using signs that are "half ours and half someone else's" (Bakhtin, 1981, p. 345).

> Knowledge of the world, of others and of self is determined by language. Language is the precondition for the act of becoming aware of oneself as a distinct entity. . . . But language is also the vehicle of a social given, a culture, prohibitions and laws. The young child is fashioned and will be indelibly marked by it without being aware of it (Sarup, 1989, p. 9)

Poststructuralist discourse throws into question the transparency, authenticity and self-referentiality of language embedded in calls for student voice. "Liberatory" educational strategies, which "allow students to find their own voices, to discover the power of authenticity" (Shrewsbury, 1987, p. 9), are inadequate in a poststructuralist framework because they ignore the mediating aspects of language and the unconscious. Furthermore, calls for student voice in education presume students, voices, and identities to be singular, unchanging and unaffected by the context in which the speaking occurs. I will examine the significance of contextual constraints for "authentic student voice" in the next section, as I continue to denaturalize the calls for student voice in "pedagogies of emancipation".

The importance of context

When we focus on the multiple voices and contradictions present in specific sites at specific historical moments, it becomes impossible to support universal calls for student voice. Feminist poststructuralist analysis, in order to avoid the "master's position" of formulating a totalizing discourse, is contextually based: "Its details cannot be specified in advance since the precise configuration of power relations in any situation will determine how best we can act" (Weedon, 1987, p. 139). There are times when it is not safe for students to speak: when one student's socially constructed body language threatens another; when the teacher is not perceived as an ally. It is not adequate to write off student silence in these instances as simply a case of internalized oppression. Nor can we simply label these silences resistance or false consciousness. There may be compelling conscious and unconscious reasons for not speaking—or for speaking, perhaps more loudly, with silence. As Patti Lather argues: "We must be willing to learn from those who don't speak up in words. What are their silences telling us?" (Lather, 1987a, p. 12).

How power relations in the classroom are manifest is crucial. How do the subject positions inhabited by one student connect with the subject positions of everyone else in the room? How do these multiple identities and positions inform who speaks and who listens? Who is comfortable in the room and who is not? Who was insulted and who did the insulting in the hall just before class? It seems impossibly naive to think that there can be anything like a genuine sharing of voices in the classroom. What does seem possible, on the other hand, is an attempt to recognize the power differentials present and to understand how they impinge upon what is sayable and doable in that specific context.

In a course on gender and education that I recently taught at the University of Wisconsin-Madison, I had a number of opportunities to hear students talk about silence. During the last few minutes of a class session in which the readings and discussion had centered on homophobia in schools, several students began expressing their fears, anxieties, and processes of self-censorship regarding the issues raised that day. Several class members found it difficult to discuss homophobia in a classroom with so many people they did not know. One woman strongly disagreed and offered that it was precisely because she did have friends in class that she felt unable to participate in the discussion. Some lesbians who were out in the class felt uncomfortable talking to "straights" about heterosexual privilege. Others wanted to answer questions or respond to the comments and/or misconceptions of their classmates. After class, I was approached by one woman who said she had never heard the word "lesbian" spoken out loud before and just needed time and space to take it all in.

There were many silences and voices in operation in the classroom on that day, including my own. The speakings and silences of those who were there occurred in an extremely complex environment where shifting relations of power between and among the members of the class combined with a multitude of subjectivities, lived identities, political and philosophical positions, and institutional constraints. Additionally, the class was located historically in a context which included the recent murder of a gay man at a location very close to where we were meeting, and a time when huge numbers of U.S. troops were being sent to the Persian Gulf as the university debated its affiliation with the Reserve Officers Training Corp (R.O.T.C.), which openly denies access to lesbians and gay men. The complexity of the classroom and of the utterances and silences of those present that day must also be seen in relation to earlier class meetings, other class discussions, personal experiences, controversies and issues that students were engaged in.

The contexts in which all these silences and speakings occurred were complex conjunctures of histories, identities, ideologies, local, national and international events and relations. Those who would distill only singular, stable meanings from student silence ignore the profoundly contextual nature of all classroom interaction. Those who would "read" student silence simply as resistance or ideological-impairment replicate forms of vanguardism which construct students as knowable, malleable objects rather than as complex, contradictory subjects.

The local struggles of students and teachers in classrooms and the social and historical contexts in which classrooms are located form the basis for feminist poststructuralist approaches to teaching. Feminist poststructuralist discourse offers educators powerful tools for analyzing the mechanisms of power locally and the possibilities for change. In the next section, I will examine theories which provide insight into the local relations of power, operating inside as well as outside of the classroom, informing all interactions between and among teachers and students.

Power-in-context

Traditionally, power has been thought of negatively, as that which limits, prohibits, refuses, and censors. The work of Michel Foucault calls into question negative, judicial formulations of power and replaces them with technical and strategic ones. For Foucault, power is a relation not a possession or a capacity. Power is not subordinate to or in the service of the economy. It is not the property of an individual or class, nor is it a commodity which can be acquired or seized (see Gore, this volume). Modern power operates through the construction of "new" discourses and modes of activity rather than by setting limits on pre-existing ones. Foucault saw the threads of power everywhere, as woven in networks. He shifted the focus away from questions such as "Who is powerful?" or "What are the intentions of those with power?", to questions regarding the processes by which subjects are constituted as effects of power.

Foucault's articulation of power contrasts abruptly with the monarchical conception of power subsumed by much "liberatory" work in education. In "What is Feminist Pedagogy" Carolyn Shrewsbury redefines power in "positive" terms but she does not question the notion of power as possession. Shrewsbury writes,

> By focusing on empowerment, feminist pedagogy embodies a concept of power as energy, capacity, and potential rather than as domination . . . This

conception of power recognizes that people need power, both as a way to maintain a sense of self and as a way to accomplish ends. (Shrewsbury, 1987, p. 8)

Those who call for student voice often do so as a corrective to the silencing of students and youth in the culture at large. It is the *lack of power* students and youth are claimed to have that necessitates intervention. Critical and Anglo-American feminist pedagogues want to *empower* students to find and articulate their silenced and/or delegitimated voices. They want students and youth of various social, political and economic groups to see how they have been dominated by those *with power.*

In contrast to monarchical power, Foucault posited that we, as subjects, internalize systems of surveillance to the point that we become our own overseer. This concept is known as disciplinary power.

> The transformation of Western societies from monarchical (or sovereign) power to disciplinary power is epitomized in Foucault's description of the Panopticon, an architectural device advocated by Jeremy Bentham towards the end of the eighteenth century. In this circular building of cells no prisoner can be certain of not being observed from the central watch-tower, and so the prisoners gradually begin to police their own behaviour. This new mode of power, which we can call panopticism, was first of all in schools, barracks and hospitals. People learned how to establish dossiers, systems of marking and classifying. Then there was the permanent surveillance of a group of pupils or patients; and at a certain moment in time these methods began to be generalized . . . In [Foucault's book] *Discipline and Punish* the likeness between the Panopticon (the "all-seeing") and the Christian God's infinite knowledge . . . is also similar to Freud's concept of the super-ego as the internal monitor of unconscious wishes. (Sarup, 1989, p. 75)

Discourses of "liberatory" pedagogy which claim to empower students do not overtly support relations in which students are monitored by others as they discipline themselves. Yet, it is important to explore anew those aspects of our teaching that we take for granted. Foucault's description of the panopticon raises questions regarding the hidden curriculum of the "talking circle"—the long-cherished form of the democratic classroom. In a Foucauldian framework, the talking circle represents an expression of disciplinary power—the regulation of the self through the internalization of the regulation by others. Similarly, Foucault's analyses of the all-knowing confessor and the regulatory and punitive meanings and uses of the confessional bring to mind curricular and pedagogical practices which call for students to publicly reveal, even confess, information about their lives and cultures in the presence of authority figures such as teachers.

It is indeed necessary for educators and educational theorists to discard monarchical conceptions of power and shift focus to notions of power as productive and present in all contexts, regulating all discourses and social interactions. I am in accordance with Foucault's position that

> . . . one should not assume a massive and primal condition of domination, a binary structure with "dominators" on one side and "dominated" on the other, but rather a multiform production of relations of domination. (Foucault, 1980, p. 142)

A disciplinary notion of power renders untenable the metaphysics underlying critical and feminist conceptions of the "liberatory" classroom as a safe and democratic space where students find and articulate their voices. A disciplinary notion of power renders untenable the metaphysics of any educators claim to a "liberator" identity. By and large, Anglo-American feminist and critical classrooms are envisioned as egalitarian places where power is dispersed and shared by all. The culture, the school, and even other teachers are named as oppressive. But the "liberatory" teacher is not. By positing only rational, unified beings, fully conscious intentions, and the binarism and mutual exclusivity of the terms "empowerer" and "oppressor", "liberatory" pedagogues are not prepared to deal with the oppressive moments in their own teaching. For feminist poststructuralists, it is the gaps and ruptures in practice—the breaks, confusion and contradiction that are always a part of the interplay in teaching—that offer the greatest insight and possibilities for change. Pedagogies informed by feminist poststructuralist perspectives can grapple with the "return of the repressed"—the uncanny and truly oppressive moments in teaching—in ways that "liberatory" education cannot.

In the next section, I will show how the construct of a "liberatory" identity relies on presumptions of unified subjectivity, rationality and universality. I will demonstrate how ahistorical and decontextualized conceptualizations of the "liberatory" teacher and "transformative intellectual" leave no room for those who claim these identities to see themselves as in process, making mistakes, and failing to be perceived as an ally by those marginalized others the educator is attempting to "liberate" or "transform". In contrast, I will show how feminist poststructuralist discourse embraces the multiplicity and partiality of all knowledge and the ongoing processes of identity formation and renegotiation.

Identity

Those of us who live in capitalist economies are continually beckoned by the consumerism and individualism of our cultural institutions to assert ourselves and stake out our identity—an identity that is singular, fixed and true for all time. We are constantly called upon to locate those aspects of ourselves that are unique, different (but not too different) that make us who we are. But as conscious and unconscious subjects, we can never really know ourselves or others in any definitive way. There is always the possibility (and actuality) of a gap, of misinterpretation, of misrecognition when we try to make sense of our relation to others. We can never be certain of the meaning of others' responses. We can never be certain of the meaning of our own responses.

For feminist poststructuralists, identities come from a wide variety of factors and often involve attempts to understand the contradictions between those factors. Class, gender, sexuality, history, language, culture, "individual experience" and so on, all contribute to what we understand to be our identities—to what we recognize as our voices. Working with the multiple, overlapping and contradictory aspects of identity is a complicated matter. Martin and Mohanty point to some of the issues raised by identity and identity politics. They examine the

> . . . irreconcilable tension between the search for a secure place from which to speak, within which to act, and the awareness of the price at which secure places are bought, the awareness of the exclusions, the denials, the blindnesses on which they are predicated. (Martin & Mohanty in de Lauretis, 1986, p. 206)

How can we present and explore identity and difference not as instruments of division, but as unifying forces, without creating a repressive fiction of unity? Mary Gentile (1985) argues that instead of grounding an analysis solely on an examination of an oppressed group's status as Other, we ground it in an analysis of the practice of constructing the Other in all of us.

> It seems that [we] have little choice but to open [our] analysis up in this manner. As soon as we begin to recognize the ways in which theory and practice— be it political, psychological, cultural, social—function to construct our image and our sense of ourselves, we also begin to recognize the ways in which this theory and practice create limitations and conflict for any group or individual that feels slightly out of sync with the "image in the mirror," the "ego ideal" reflected back to this group or this individual by society. Any "marginal" group experiences this dissonance, be they [white] women or men and women of color or the working class or the disabled or children or the elderly or gays and lesbians. I suggest, however, that individual members of the dominant class, race, sex and so on, also experience such a dissonance. Everyone is someone else's "Other." The dissonance may be less intense, easier to ignore, and it may not threaten their basic survival in the ways it does for marginal groups. It does, however, trigger a defensive reaction. Those who "just miss" the ideal will be more invested in presenting and defending it, in disguising all signs of nonconformity and in "passing." (Gentile, 1985, p. 7)

It is important to clarify Gentile's position with regard to difference. She does not suggest a denial of difference that draws attention away from the oppression of one group, by claiming that everyone is victimized. Instead, Gentile wants,

> . . . to assert difference . . . in all its forms and manifestations, to find a commonality in the experience of difference without compromising its distinctive realities and effects. [Gentile posits] a "multiple perspective" that can comprehend alternate viewpoints, not so as to excuse oppression but rather to clarify it, to expose the pain of one individual group without denying that of another. (Gentile, 185, p. 7)

Gentile's approach to acknowledging difference "in all its forms and manifestations" offers crucial insight for educators working against Eurocentrism, masculinism, heterosexism and so on in schools. If our subject positions, versions of history, and interpretations of experiences are seen as temporary and contingent understandings within an on going process in which any absolute meaning or truth is impossible, then our voicing of our differences ought not be received as if we are speaking some solemn Truth about our lives. We must refuse the tendency to attribute "authenticity" to people's voices when they speak from their own experience of difference, as if their speech were transparent and their understanding of their experience unchanging.

At the same time, we need to accept responsibility for our implication in actual historical social relations. "A denial that positionalities exist or that they matter, the denial of one's own personal history and the claim to a total separation from it," results in naturalizing and essentializing who we think we are (Martin & Mohanty in de Lauretis, 1986, p. 208). As an example, Martin and Mohanty question "the exclusions and repressions which support the seeming homogeneity, stability, and self-evidence of 'a white identity,' which is derived from and dependent on the marginalization of differences within as well as 'without'" (Martin & Mohanty in de Lauretis, 1986, p. 193). Minnie Bruce Pratt (1986) argues that stable notions of self and identity are based on exclusion and secured by terror.

> Each of us carries around those growing up places, the institutions, a sort of backdrop, a stage set. So often we act out the present against the backdrop of the past, within a frame of perception that is so familiar, so safe that it is terrifying to risk changing it even when we know our perceptions are distorted, limited, constricted by that old view. (Pratt in de Lauretis, 1986, p. 196)

When Anglo-American feminist and critical pedagogues call for students to find and articulate their voice, they presume singular, essential, authentic, and stable notions of identity. The following quote from the literature on critical pedagogy points to the tendency on the part of educators to deny their own subjectivity, their own positionality, the partiality of their own voices. Len Masterman writes: "Only when pupils value their own language, background and personalities and are not demeaned by them, will they recover their eagerness for expression" (Masterman, 1980, p. 141). Masterman takes it for granted that students do not already value their own language, background and personalities prior to being "empowered" by him to do so. It is as if students have no communities outside of school where they are appreciated and validated. Those of us who are members of marginalized groups know how we validate our own languages, backgrounds and personalities. I question the kind of validation, institutional recognition and legitimation offered by feminist and critical educators. Whose interests are furthered by the institutional recognition of students' languages, backgrounds and personalities? Students? Critical and feminist peda-

gogues? Both? How is the institutional validation offered in the classroom different from the validation offered by others within one's marginalized community?

The affirmation of student voice in the critical and Anglo-American feminist
classroom is not automatic. Upon speaking, students' voices may be subject to
the disciplining and stylizing of the teacher as well as other students. Henry
Giroux asks: "How do we affirm student voices while simultaneously encouraging the interrogation of such voices?" (Giroux & Simon, 1989, p. 231). I ask,
who interrogates whom, and why? How does the threat of interrogation keep
students from feeling safe to speak about their understandings and experiences of
the world? Which voices are cast out once they have indeed spoken up?

Feminist and critical educators are clearly the ones who are in a position to
interrogate students' voices. They are the ones who can empower and interrogate
because they are the ones who know. We are to believe that critical and feminist
teachers have already dealt conclusively with their own inscription and involvement in oppressive power dynamics. Given the binarism and unified subjectivity
which underlies much "liberatory" education, educators see themselves as "em-
powerers"—not as "oppressors". Anglo-American feminist and critical pedagogues allegedly understand and never contribute to the racism, ethnocentrism,
classism, sexism, heterosexism and so on that their students experience. In the
final instance, it is the critical or feminist pedagogue who determines if and when
students have succeeded in valuing their own language, background and personalities. These paternalistic tendencies in critical and Anglo-American feminist
education ultimately replicate racist, classist and sexist forms for students. Educators stand above their students, and guide them in their struggle for "personal
empowerment" and "voice." The only call for change is on the part of the students. The only people who get "worked over" are the students. The only call is
for student voice. Critical and feminist teachers, we are to assume, have already
found and articulated theirs.

Drawing to a close

How can we locate the recent calls by Anglo-American feminist and critical
educators for student voice? Is the attempt to empower students to find and articulate their voices a controlling process—one that demands verbal collaboration?
How do unexamined issues regarding the power and authority of "liberatory"
teachers render problematic their calls for student voice? Does the demand for
student voice "welcome selective inhabitants of the margin in order to better
exclude the margin?" (Spivak, 1987, p. 107). How do the micro-politics of the
"emancipatory" classroom differ from the macro-politics of imperialism?

An analysis of whose interests are served when students speak is needed. What
happens to students who refuse the solicitation of student voice? Some of the
most compelling arguments for denaturalizing student voice come out of critiques of mainstream classrooms by critical pedagogues themselves. Shor

(1980), in referring to how silence in the mainstream classroom can be seen both as a form of defense and as a form of resistance, argues that the refusal to talk prevents others from knowing what students think or feel and using it against them. The "culture of silence", as Freire calls it, is common when oppressed groups come face to face with authority, even when that authority espouses radical or emancipatory politics.

Shor refers to the impatience with "talk" in schools, workplaces, courts of law, the media and other important institutional sites of mass culture where many commands are given and little dialogue is allowed. This enforced silence, he claims, "dishabituates people from gaining the experience of group discussion" (Shor, 1980, p. 7). Working people and students, "talk a lot among themselves, but grow quiet in the presence of authorities. To talk a lot in an institution, at work, at school, or in front of superiors," says Shor, "is to be guilty of collaborating with the enemy" (Shor, 1980, p. 72). If one's "talk" in a classroom is too enthusiastic, the student may be thought of as a teacher's pet. If the "talk" is too rebellious, the teacher may consider the student to be a troublemaker. Shor writes,

> In a culture where superiors regularly humiliate subordinates, it becomes understandable for students to stay self-protectively silent in class. . . . Because a power struggle surrounds the use of words in every institution of life, there are tense rules and high prices to pay for talking. At the very least, supervisors discourage people talking to each other because it interferes with productivity; in school, teachers dissuade students from talking to each other, or out of turn, not only to maintain order but also to maintain the teacher as the sole regulator of the talking. (Shor, 1980, p. 72)

Feminist post-structuralist theories offer powerful tools for analyzing the mechanisms of power locally and the possibilities for change. In education, the call for voice has most often been directed at students. Where are the multiple, contradictory voices of teachers, writers, researchers and administrators? The time has come to listen to those who have been asking others to speak.

References

Bakhtin, M. M. (1981) *The Dialogic Imagination: Four Essays by M. M. Bakhtin.* Austin: University of Texas Press.

Belsey, C. (190). *Critical Practice,* London: Methuen.

Britzman, D. (1989) "Who Has the Floor? Curriculum, Teaching, and the English Student Teacher's Struggle for Voice" *Curriculum Inquiry,* 19:2, pp. 143–162.

Culley, M. (1985) "Anger and authority in the introductory Women's Studies classroom." In M. Culley & C. Portuges (Eds.), *Gendered subjects: The dynamics of feminist teaching* (pp. 209–218). Boston & London: Routledge & Kegan Paul.

Culley, M. and Portuges, C. (Eds.) (1985) *Gendered Subjects: The Dynamics of Feminist Teaching,* Boston: Routledge and Kegan Paul.

de Lauretis, T. (1986) *Feminist Studies/Critical Studies*, Bloomington: Indiana University Press.

Ellsworth, E. and Selvin, A. (1986) "Using Transformative Media Events for Social Education," *New Education*, 8 (2), 70–77.

Foucault, M. (1980) *Power/Knowledge: Selected Interviews and Other Writing, 1972–1977*. Edited by Colin Gordon. New York: Pantheon Books.

Freire, P. and Giroux, H. (1989) "Pedagogy, popular culture and public life: An introduction." In Giroux, H. and Simon, R. (Eds.) *Popular Culture Schooling & Everyday Life* (pp. vii–xii). MA: Bergin & Garvey Publishers, Inc.

Giroux, H. and Simon, R. (1989) "Schooling, popular culture, and a pedagogy of possibility." In H. Giroux & R. Simon (Eds.), *Popular culture: Schooling and everyday life* (pp. 219–235). Massachusetts: Bergin & Garvey Publishers Inc.

Jardine, A. (1985) *Gynesis: Configurations of Woman and Modernity*. Ithaca, New York: Cornell University Press.

Lather, P. (1987a) "Feminist Perspectives on Empowering Research Methodologies," Paper presented at the National Women's Studies Association (NWSA), Atlanta, Georgia.

Lather, P. (1987b) "Educational Research and Practice in a Postmodern Era," Paper presented at Ninth Conference on Curriculum Theory and Classroom Practice, Dayton, Ohio.

Masterman, L. (1980) *Teaching About Television*, London: Macmillan Press Ltd.

Sarup, M. (1989) *An Introductory Guide to Post-Structuralism and Postmodernism*, Athens, Georgia: The University of Georgia Press.

Shor, I. (1980) *Critical Teaching and Everyday Life*, Boston: South End Press.

Shrewsbury, C. (1987) "What is Feminist Pedagogy?" *Women's Studies Quarterly*. Volume XV, (3 & 4) Fall/Winter, 6–14.

Spivak, G. (1987) *In Other Worlds: Essays in Cultural Politics*, New York: Routledge.

Weedon, C. (1987) *Feminist Practice & Poststructuralist Theory*. Oxford: Basil Blackwell Ltd.

6

Why Doesn't this Feel Empowering? Working Through the Repressive Myths of Critical Pedagogy

Elizabeth Ellsworth

In the spring of 1988, the University of Wisconsin-Madison was the focal point of a community-wide crisis provoked by the increased visibility of racist acts and structures on campus and within the Madison community. During the preceding year, the FIJI fraternity had been suspended for portraying racially demeaning stereotypes at a "Fiji Island party," including a 15–foot high cutout of a "Fiji native," a dark-skinned caricature with a bone through its nose. On December 1, 1987, the Minority Affairs Steering Committee released a report, initiated and researched by students, documenting the university's failure to address institutional racism and the experiences of marginalization of students of color on campus. The report called for the appointment of a person of color to the position of vice-chancellor of ethnic minority affairs/affirmative action; effective strategies to recruit and retain students of color, faculty, and staff; establishment of a multicultural center; implementation of a mandatory six-credit ethnic studies requirement; revamping racial and sexual harassment grievance procedures; and initiation of a cultural and racial orientation program for all students. The release of the report, and the university's response to it and to additional incidents such as the FIJI fraternity party, have become the focus of ongoing campus and community-wide debates, demonstrations, and organizing efforts.

In January, 1988, partly in response to this situation, I facilitated a special topics course at UW-Madison called "Media and Anti-Racist Pedagogies," Curriculum and Instruction 607, known as C&I 607. In this chapter, I will offer an interpretation of C&I 607's interventions against campus racism and traditional educational forms at the university. I will then use that interpretation to support a critique of current discourses on critical pedagogy.[1] The literature on critical pedagogy represents attempts by educational researchers to theorize and operationalize pedagogical challenges to oppressive social formations. While the attempts I am concerned with here share fundamental assumptions and goals, their different emphases are reflected in the variety of labels given to them, such as "critical pedagogy," "pedagogy of critique and possibility," "pedagogy of student voice," "pedagogy of empowerment," "radical pedagogy," "pedagogy for radical democracy," and "pedagogy of possibility."[2]

I want to argue, on the basis of my interpretation of C&I 607, that key assumptions, goals, and pedagogical practices fundamental to the literature on critical pedagogy—namely, "empowerment," "student voice," "dialogue," and even the term "critical"—are repressive myths that perpetuate relations of domination. By this I mean that when participants in our class attempted to put into practice prescriptions offered in the literature concerning empowerment, student voice, and dialogue, we produced results that were not only unhelpful, but actually exacerbated the very conditions we were trying to work against, including Eurocentrism, racism, sexism, classism, and "banking education." To the extent that our efforts to put discourses of critical pedagogy into practice led us to reproduce relations of domination in our classroom, these discourses were "working through" us in repressive ways, and had themselves become vehicles of repression. To the extent that we disengaged ourselves from those aspects and moved in another direction, we "worked through" and out of the literature's highly abstract language ("myths") of who we "should" be and what "should" be happening in our classroom; we moved into classroom practices that were context-specific and seemed to be much more responsive to our own understandings of our social identities and situations.

This chapter concludes by addressing the implications of the classroom practices we constructed in response to racism in the university's curriculum, pedagogy, and everyday life. Specifically, it challenges educational scholars who situate themselves within the field of critical pedagogy to come to grips with the fundamental issues this work has raised—especially the question, "What diversity do we silence in the name of "liberatory" pedagogy?"

Pedagogy and political interventions on campus

The nation wide eruption in 1987–1988 of racist violence in communities and on campuses, including the University of Wisconsin-Madison, pervaded the context in which Curriculum and Instruction 607, "Media and Anti-Racist Pedagogies" was planned and facilitated. The increased visibility of racism in Madison was also partly due to the UW Minority Student Coalition's successful documentation of the UW system's resistance to and its failure to address monoculturalism in the curriculum, to recruit and retain students and professors of color, and to alleviate the campus culture's insensitivity or hostility to cultural and racial diversity.

At the time that I began to construct a description of C&I 607, students of color had documented the extent of their racial harassment and alienation on campus. Donna Shalala, the newly appointed, feminist chancellor of UW-Madison, had invited faculty and campus groups to take their initiatives against racism on campus. I had just served on a university committee investigating an incident of racial harassment against one of my students. I wanted to design a course in media and pedagogy that would not only work to clarify the structures of institutional racism underlying university practices and its culture in spring

1988, but that would also use that understanding to plan and carry out a political intervention within that formation. This class would not debate whether or not racist structures and practices were operating at the university; rather, it would investigate *how* they operated, with what effects and contradictions—and where they were vulnerable to political opposition. The course concluded with public interventions on campus, which I will describe later. For my purposes here, the most important interruption of existing power relations within the university consisted of transforming business-as-usual—that is, prevailing social relations—in a university classroom.

Before the spring of 1988, I had used the language of critical pedagogy in course descriptions and with students. For example, syllabi in the video production for education courses stated that goals of the courses included the production of "socially responsible" videotapes, the fostering of "critical production" practices and "critical reception and analysis" of educational videotapes. Syllabi in the media criticism courses stated that we would focus on "critical media use and analysis in the classroom" and the potential of media in "critical education." Students often asked what was meant by "critical"—critical of what, from what position, to what end?—and I referred them to answers provided in the literature. For example, "critical pedagogy" supported classroom analysis and rejection of oppression, injustice, inequality, silencing of marginalized voices, and authoritarian social structures.[3] Its critique was launched from the position of the "radical" educator who recognizes and helps students to recognize and name injustice, who empowers students to act against their own and others' oppressions (including oppressive school structures), and who criticizes and transforms her or his own understanding in response to the understandings of students.[4] The goal of critical pedagogy was a critical democracy, individual freedom, social justice, and social change—a revitalized public sphere characterized by citizens capable of confronting public issues critically through ongoing forms of public debate and social action.[5] Students would be empowered by social identities that affirmed their race, class, and gender positions, and provided the basis for moral deliberation and social action.[6]

The classroom practices of critical educators may in fact engage with actual, historically specific struggles, such as those between students of color and university administrators. But the overwhelming majority of academic articles appearing in major educational journals, although apparently based on actual practices, rarely locate theoretical constructs within them. In my review of the literature I found, instead, that educational researchers who invoke concepts of critical pedagogy consistently strip discussions of classroom practices of historical context and political position. What remains are the definitions cited above, which operate at a high level of abstraction. I found this language more appropriate (yet hardly more helpful) for philosophical debates about the highly problematic concepts of freedom, justice, democracy and "universal" values than for thinking through and planning classroom practices to support the political agenda of C&I 607.

Given the explicit antiracist agenda of the course, I realized that even naming C&I 607 raised complex issues. To describe the course as "Media and Critical Pedagogy," or "Media, Racism, and Critical Pedagogy," for example, would be to hide the politics of the course, making them invisible to the very students I was trying to attract and work with—namely, students committed or open to working against racism. I wanted to avoid colluding with many academic writers in the widespread use of code words such as "critical," which hide the actual political agendas I assume such writers share with me—namely antiracism, antisexism, anti-elitism, anti-heterosexism, anti-ableism, anticlassism, and anti-neoconservatism.

I say "assume" because, while the literature on critical pedagogy charges the teacher with helping students to "identify and choose between sufficiently artic-ulated and reasonably distinct moral positions,"[7] it offers only the most abstract, decontextualized criteria for choosing one position over others, criteria such as "reconstructive action"[8] or "radical democracy and social justice."[9] To reject the term "critical pedagogy" and name the course "Media and Anti-Racist Pedago-gies" was to assert that students and faculty at UW-Madison in the spring of 1988 were faced with ethical dilemmas that called for political action. While a variety of "moral assessments" and political positions existed about the situation on campus, this course would attempt to construct a classroom practice that would act *on the side* of antiracism. I wanted to be accountable for naming the political agenda behind this particular course's critical pedagogy.

Thinking through the ways in which our class's activities could be understood as political was important, because while the literature states implicitly or explic-itly that critical pedagogy is political, there have been no sustained research at-tempts to explore whether or how the practices it prescribes actually alter specific power relations outside or inside schools. Further, when educational researchers advocating critical pedagogy fail to provide a clear statement of their political agendas, the effect is to hide the fact that as critical pedagogues, they are in fact seeking to appropriate public resources (classrooms, school supplies, teacher/ professor salaries, academic requirements and degrees) to further various "pro-gressive" political agendas that they believe to be for the public good—and therefore deserving of public resources. But however good the reasons are for choosing the strategy of subverting repressive school structures from within, it has necessitated the use of code words such as "critical," "social change," "revi-talized public sphere," and a posture of invisibility. As a result, the critical edu-cation "movement" has failed to develop a clear articulation of the need for its existence, its goals, priorities, risks, or potentials. As Liston and Zeichner argue, debate within the critical education movement itself over what constitutes a rad-ical or critical pedagogy is sorely needed.[10]

By prescribing moral deliberation, engagement in the full range of views pres-ent, and critical reflection, the literature on critical pedagogy implies that stu-dents and teachers can and should engage each other in the classroom as fully rational subjects. According to Valerie Walkerdine, schools have participated in producing "self-regulating" individuals by developing in students the capacity for engaging in rational argument. Rational argument has operated in ways that set up as its opposite an irrational Other, which has been understood historically as the province of women and other exotic Others. In schools, rational deliberation, reflection, and consideration of all viewpoints has become a vehicle for regulating conflict and the power to speak, for transforming "conflict into rational argument by means of universalized capacities for language and reason."[11] But both students and professor entered C&I 607 with investments of privilege and struggle already made in favor of some ethical and political positions concerning racism and against other positions. The context in which this course was developed highlighted that fact. The demands that the Minority Student Coalition delivered to the administration were not written in the spirit of engaging in rationalist, analytical debates with those holding other positions. In a racist society and its institutions, such debate has not and cannot be "public" or "democratic" in the sense of including the voices of all affected parties and affording them equal weight and legitimacy. Nor can such debate be free of conscious and unconscious concealment of interests, or assertion of interests which some participants hold as non-negotiable no matter what arguments are presented.

As Barbara Christian has written, ". . . what I write and how I write is done in order to save my own life. And I mean that literally. For me literature is a way of knowing that I am not hallucinating, that whatever I feel/know *is*."[12] Christian is an African-American woman writing about the literature of African-American women, but her words are relevant to the issues raised by the context of C&I 607. I understood the words written by the Minority Student Coalition and spoken by other students/professors of difference[13] on campus to have a similar function: they serve as a reality check for survival. It is inappropriate to respond to such words by subjecting them to rationalist debate about their validity. Words spoken for survival come already validated in a radically different arena of proof and carry no option or luxury of choice. (This is not to say, however, that the positions of students of color, or of any other group, were to be taken up unproblematically—an issue I will address below).

I drafted a syllabus and circulated it for suggestions and revisions to students I knew to be involved in the Minority Student Coalition, and to colleagues who shared my concerns. The goal of "Media and Anti-Racist Pedagogics," as stated in the revised syllabus, was to define, organize, carry out, and analyze an educational initiative on campus that would win semiotic space for the marginalized discourses of students against racism. Campus activists were defining these discourses and making them available to other groups, including the class, through documents, demonstrations, discussions, and press conferences.

The syllabus also listed the following assumptions underlying the course:

1. Students who want to acquire knowledge of existing educational media theory and criticism for the purposes of guiding their own educational

practice can best do so in a learning situation that interrelates theory with concrete attempts at using media for education.

2. Current situations of racial and sexual harassment and elitism on campus and in the curriculum demand meaningful responses from students and faculty, and responses can be designed in a way that accomplishes both academic and political goals.

3. Often, the term "critical education" has been used to imply, but also to hide positions and goals of anti-racism, anti-classism, anti-sexism, and so forth. Defining this course as one that explores the possibility of using media to construct anti-racist pedagogies asserts that these are legitimate and imperative goals for educators.

4. What counts as an appropriate use of media for an anti-racist pedagogy cannot be specified outside of the contexts of actual educational situations; therefore student work on this issue should be connected to concrete initiatives in actual situations.

5. Any anti-racist pedagogy must be defined through an awareness of the ways in which oppressive structures are the result of *intersections* between racist, classist, sexist, ableist, and other oppressive dynamics.

6. Everyone who has grown up in a racist culture has to work at unlearning racism—we will make mistakes in this class, but they will be made in the context of our struggle to come to grips with racism.

Naming the political agenda of the course to the extent that I did seemed relatively easy. I was in the fourth year of a tenure-track position in my department, and felt that I had "permission" from colleagues to pursue the line of research and practice out of which this course had clearly grown. The administration's response to the crisis on campus gave further "permission" for attempts to alleviate racism in the institution. However, the directions in which I should proceed became less clear once the class was under way. As I began to live out and interpret the consequences of how discourses of "critical reflection," "empowerment," "student voice," and "dialogue" had influenced my conceptualization of the goals of the course and my ability to make sense of my experiences in the class, I found myself struggling against (struggling to unlearn) key assumptions and assertions of current literature on critical pedagogy, and straining to recognize, name, and come to grips with crucial issues of classroom practice that critical pedagogy cannot or will not address.

From critical rationalism to the politics of partial narratives

The students enrolled in "Media and Anti-Racist Pedagogies" included Asian American, Chicano/a, Jewish, Puerto Rican, and Anglo-European men and women from the United States, as well as Asian, African, Icelandic, and Canadian international students. It was evident after the first class meeting that all of us agreed, but with different understandings and agendas, that racism was a problem on campus that required political action. The effects of the diverse social positions and political ideologies of the students enrolled, my own position and experiences as a woman and a feminist, and the effects of the course's context on the form and content of our early class discussions quickly threw the rationalist assumptions underlying critical pedagogy into question.

These rationalist assumptions have led to the following goals: the teaching of analytic and critical skills for judging the truth and merit of propositions, and the interrogation and selective appropriation of potentially transformative moments in the dominant culture.[14] As long as educators define pedagogy against oppressive formations in these ways, the role of the critical pedagogue will be to guarantee that the foundation for classroom interaction is reason. In other words, the critical pedagogue is one who enforces the rules of reason in the classroom—"a series of rules of thought that any ideal rational person might adopt if his/her purpose was to achieve propositions of universal validity."[15] Under these conditions, and given the coded nature of the political agenda of critical pedagogy, only one "political" gesture appears to be available to the critical pedagogue. S/he can ensure that students are given the chance to arrive logically at the "universally valid proposition" underlying the discourse of critical pedagogy— namely, that all people have a right to freedom from oppression guaranteed by the democratic social contract, and that in the classroom, this proposition be given equal time vis-à-vis other "sufficiently articulated and reasonably distinct moral positions."[16]

Yet educators who have constructed classroom practices dependent upon analytic critical judgment can no longer regard the enforcement of rationalism as a self-evident political act against relations of domination. Literary criticism, cultural studies, post-structuralism, feminist studies, comparative studies, and media studies have by now amassed overwhelming evidence of the extent to which the myths of the ideal rational person and the "universality" of propositions have been oppressive to those who are not European, White, male, middle-class, Christian, ablebodied, thin, and heterosexual.[17] Writings by many literary and cultural critics, both women of color and White women who are concerned with explaining the intersections and interactions among relations of racism, colonialism, sexism, and so forth, are now employing, either implicitly or explicitly, concepts and analytical methods that could be called feminist poststructuralism.[18] While poststructuralism, like rationalism, is a tool that can be used to dominate, it has also facilitated a devastating critique of the violence of rationalism against its Others. It has demonstrated that as a discursive practice, rationalism's regulated and systematic use of elements of language constitutes rational competence "as a series of exclusions—of women, people of color, of nature as historical agent, of the true value of art." In contrast, poststructuralist thought is not bound to reason, but "to discourse, literally narratives about the world that are admittedly *partial*. Indeed, one of the crucial features of discourse is the intimate tie between knowledge and interest, the latter being understood as a 'standpoint' from which to grasp 'reality'."[19]

The literature on critical pedagogy implies that the claims made by documents, demonstrations, press conferences, and classroom discussions of students of color and White students against racism could rightfully be taken up in the classroom and subjected to rational deliberation over their truth in light of competing claims. But this would force students to subject themselves to the logics of rationalism and scientism which have been predicated on and made possible through the exclusion of socially constructed irrational Others—women, people of color, nature, aesthetics. As Audre Lorde writes, "The master's tools will never dismantle the master's house," [20] and to call on students of color to justify and explicate their claims in terms of the master's tools—tools such as rationalism, fashioned precisely to perpetuate their exclusion—colludes with the oppressor in keeping "the oppressed occupied with the master's concerns." As Barbara Christian describes it:

> The literature of people who are not in power has always been in danger of extinction or cooptation, not because we do not theorize, but because what we can even imagine, far less who we can reach, is constantly limited by societal structures. For me, literary criticism is promotion as well as understanding, a response to the writer to whom there is often no response, to folk who need the writing as much as they need anything. I know, from literary history, that writing disappears unless there is a response to it. Because I write about writers who are now writing, I hope to help ensure that their tradition has continuity and survives. [21]

In contrast to the enforcement of rational deliberation, but like Christian's promotion and response, my role in C&I 607 would be to interrupt institutional limits on how much time and energy students of color, White students, and professors against racism could spend on elaborating their positions and playing them out to the point where internal contradictions and effects on the positions of other social groups could become evident and subject to self-analysis.

With Barbara Christian, I saw the necessity to take the voices of students and professors of difference at their word—as "valid"—but not without response. [22] Students' and my own narratives about experiences of racism, ableism, elitism, fat oppression, sexism, anti-Semitism, heterosexism, and so on are partial—partial in the sense that they are unfinished, imperfect, limited; and partial in the sense that they project the interests of "one side" over others. Because those voices are partial and partisan, they must be made problematic, but not because they have broken the rules of thought of the ideal rational person by grounding their knowledge in immediate emotional, social, and psychic experiences of oppression, [23] or are somehow lacking or too narrowly circumscribed. [24] Rather, they must be critiqued because they hold implications for other social movements and their struggles for self-definition. This assertion carries important implications for the "goal" of classroom practices against oppressive formations, which I will address later.

Have we got a theory for you![25]

As educators who claim to be dedicated to ending oppression, critical pedagogues have acknowledged the socially constructed and legitimated authority
that teachers/professors hold over students.[26] Yet theorists of critical pedagogy
have failed to launch any meaningful analysis of or program for reformulating
the institutionalized power imbalances between themselves and their students, or
of the essentially paternalistic project of education itself. In the absence of such
an analysis and program, their efforts are limited to trying to transform negative
effects of power imbalances within the classroom into positive ones. Strategies
such as student empowerment and dialogue give the illusion of equality while in
fact leaving the authoritarian nature of the teacher/student relationship intact.

"Empowerment" is a key concept in this approach, which treats the symptoms
but leaves the disease unnamed and untouched. Critical pedagogies employing
this strategy prescribe various theoretical and practical means for sharing, giving, or redistributing power to students. For example, some authors challenge
teachers to reject the vision of education as inculcation of students by the more
powerful teacher. In its place, they urge teachers to accept the possibility of
education through "reflective examination" of the plurality of moral positions
before the presumably rational teacher and students.[27] Here, the goal is to give
students the analytical skills they need to make them as free, rational, and objective as teachers supposedly are to choose positions on their objective merits. I
have already argued that in a classroom in which "empowerment" is made dependent on rationalism, those perspectives that would question the political interests
(sexism, racism, colonialism, for example) expressed and guaranteed by rationalism would be rejected as "irrational" (biased, partial).

A second strategy is to make the teacher more like the student by redefining
the teacher as learner of the student's reality and knowledge. For example, in
their discussion of the politics of dialogic teaching and epistemology, Shor and
Freire suggest that "the teacher selecting the objects of study knows them *better*
than the students as the course begins, but the teacher *re-learns* the objects
through studying them with their students."[28] The literature explores only one
reason for expecting the teacher to "re-learn" an object of study through the student's less adequate understanding, and that is to enable the teacher to devise
more effective strategies for bringing the student "up" to the teacher's level of
understanding. Giroux, for example, argues for a pedagogy that "is attentive to
the histories, dreams, and experiences that . . . students bring to school. It is
only by beginning with these subjective forms that critical educators can develop
a language and set of practices"[29] that can successfully mediate differences between student understandings and teacher understandings in "pedagogically progressive" ways.[30] In this example, Giroux leaves the implied superiority of the
teacher's understanding and the undefined "progressiveness" of this type of pedagogy unproblematized and untheorized.

A third strategy is to acknowledge the "directiveness"[31] or "authoritarianism"[32] of education as inevitable, and judge particular power imbalances between teacher and student to be tolerable or intolerable depending upon "towards what and with whom [they are] directive."[33] "Acceptable" imbalances are those in which authority serves "common human interests by sharing information, promoting open and informed discussion, and maintaining itself only through the respect and trust of those who grant the authority."[34] In such cases, authority becomes "emancipatory authority," a kind of teaching in which teachers would make explicit and available for rationalist debate "the political and moral referents for authority they assume in teaching particular forms of knowledge, in taking stands against forms of oppression, and in treating students as if they ought also to be concerned about social justice and political action."[35] Here, the question of "empowerment for what" becomes the final arbiter of a teacher's use or misuse of authority.

But critical pedagogues consistently answer the question of "empowerment for what?" in ahistorical and depoliticized abstractions. These include empowerment for "human betterment,"[36] for expanding "the range of possible social identities people may become,"[37] and "making one's self present as part of a moral and political project that links production of meaning to the possibility for human agency, democratic community, and transformative social action."[38] As a result, student empowerment has been defined in the broadest possible humanistic terms, and becomes a "capacity to act effectively" in a way that fails to challenge any identifiable social or political position, institution, or group.

The contortions of logic and rhetoric that characterize these attempts to define "empowerment" testify to the failure of critical educators to come to terms with the essentially paternalistic project of traditional education. "Emancipatory authority"[39] is one such contortion, for it implies the presence of, or potential for, an emancipated teacher. Indeed, it asserts that teachers "can link knowledge to power by bringing to light and teaching the subjugated histories, experiences, stories, and accounts of those who suffer and struggle."[40] Yet I cannot unproblematically bring subjugated knowledges to light when I am not free of my own learned racism, fat oppression, classism, ableism, or sexism. No teacher is free of these learned and internalized oppressions. Nor are accounts of one group's suffering and struggle immune from reproducing narratives oppressive to another's—the racism of the women's movement in the United States is one example.

As I argued above, "emancipatory authority" also implies, according to Shor and Freire, a teacher who knows the object of study "better" than do the students. In fact I understood racism no better than my students did, especially those students of color coming into class after six months (or more) of campus activism and whole lives of experience and struggle against racism—nor could I ever hope to. My experiences with and access to multiple and sophisticated strategies for interpreting and interrupting sexism (in White middle-class contexts) do not provide me with a ready-made analysis of or language for understanding my own implications in racist structures. My understanding and experience of racism will always be constrained by my white skin and middle-class privilege. Indeed, it is impossible for anyone to be free from these oppressive formations at this historical moment. Furthermore, while I had the institutional power and authority in the classroom to enforce "reflective examination" of the plurality of moral and political positions before us in a way that supposedly gave my own assessments equal weight with those of students, in fact my institutional role as professor would always weight my statements differently from those of students.

Given my own history of white-skin, middle-class, able-bodied, thin privilege and my institutionally granted power, it made more sense to see my task as one of redefining "critical pedagogy" so that it did not need utopian moments of "democracy," "equality," "justice," or "emancipated" teachers—moments that are unattainable (and ultimately undesirable, because they are always predicated on the interests of those who are in the position to define utopian projects). A preferable goal seemed to be to become capable of a sustained encounter with currently oppressive formations and power relations that refuse to be theorized away or fully transcended in a utopian resolution—and to enter into the encounter in a way that both acknowledged my own implications in those formations and was capable of changing my own relation to and investments in those formations.

The repressive myth of the silent other

At first glance, the concept of "student voice" seemed to offer a pedagogical strategy in this direction. This concept has become highly visible and influential in current discussions of curriculum and teaching, as evidenced by its appearance in the titles of numerous presentations at the 1989 American Educational Research Association Convention. Within current discourses on teaching, it functions to efface the contradiction between the emancipatory project of critical pedagogy and the hierarchical relation between teachers and students. In other words, it is a strategy for negotiating between the directiveness of dominant educational relationships and the political commitment to make students autonomous of those relationships (how does a teacher "make" students autonomous without directing them?). The discourse on student voice sees the student as "empowered" when the teacher "helps" students to express their subjugated knowledges.[41] The targets of this strategy are students from disadvantaged and subordinated social class, racial, ethnic, and gender groups—or alienated middle-class students, without access to skills of critical analysis, whose voices have been silenced or distorted by oppressive cultural and educational formations. By speaking, in their "authentic voices," students are seen to make themselves visible and define themselves as authors of their own world. Such self-definition presumably gives students an identity and political position from which to act as agents of social change.[42] Thus, while it is true that the teacher is directive, the student's own daily life experiences of oppression chart her/his path toward self-definition and agency. The task of the critical educator thus becomes "finding ways of working with students that enable the full expression of multiple 'voices' engaged in dialogic encounter,"[43] encouraging students of different race, class, and gender positions to speak in self-affirming ways about their experiences and how they have been mediated by their own social positions and those of others.

Within feminist discourses seeking to provide both a place and power for women to speak, "voice" and "speech" have become commonplace as metaphors for women's feminist self-definitions—but with meanings and effects quite different from those implied by discourses of critical pedagogy. Within feminist movements, women's voices and speech are conceptualized in terms of self-definitions that are oppositional to those definitions of women constructed by others, usually to serve interests and contexts that subordinate women to men. But while critical educators acknowledge the existence of unequal power relations in classrooms, they have made no systematic examination of the barriers that this imbalance creates for the kind of student expression and dialogue they prescribe.

The concept of critical pedagogy assumes a commitment on the part of the professor/teacher toward ending the student's oppression. Yet the literature offers no sustained attempt to problematize this stance and confront the likelihood that the professor brings to social movements (including critical pedagogy) interests of her or his own race, class, ethnicity, gender, and other positions. S/he does not play the role of disinterested mediator on the side of the oppressed group.[44] As an Anglo, middle-class professor in C&I 607, I could not unproblematically "help" a student of color to find her/his authentic voice as a student of color. I could not unproblematically "affiliate" with the social groups my students represent and interpret their experience to them. In fact, I brought to the classroom privileges and interests that were put at risk in fundamental ways by the demands and defiances of student voices. I brought a social subjectivity that has been constructed in such a way that I have not and can never participate unproblematically in the collective process of self-definition, naming of oppression, and struggles for visibility in the face of marginalization engaged in by students whose class, race, gender, and other positions I do not share. Critical pedagogues are always implicated in the very structures they are trying to change.

Although the literature recognizes that teachers have much to learn from their students' experiences, it does not address the ways in which there are things that I as a professor could *never know* about the experiences, oppressions, and understandings of other participants in the class. This situation makes it impossible for any single voice in the classroom—including that of the professor—to assume the position of center or origin of knowledge or authority, of having privileged access to authentic experience or appropriate language. A recognition, contrary to all Western ways of knowing and speaking, that all knowings are partial, that there are fundamental things each of us cannot know—a situation alleviated only in part by the pooling of partial, socially constructed knowledges in class-rooms—demands a fundamental retheorizing of "education" and "pedagogy," an issue I will begin to address below.

When educational researchers writing about critical pedagogy fail to examine the implications of the gendered, raced, and classed teacher and student for the theory of critical pedagogy, they reproduce, by default, the category of generic "critical teacher"—a specific form of the generic human that underlies classical liberal thought. Like the generic human, the generic critical teacher, is not of course, generic at all. Rather, the term defines a discursive category predicated on the current mythical norm, namely: young, White, Christian, middle-class, heterosexual, able-bodied, thin, rational man. Gender, race, class, and other differences become only variations on or additions to the generic human—"underneath, we are all the same."[45] But voices of students and professors of difference solicited by critical pedagogy are not additions to that norm, but oppositional challenges that require a dismantling of the mythical norm and its uses as well as alternatives to it. There has been no consideration of how voices of, for example, White women, students of color, disabled students, White men against masculinist culture, and fat students will necessarily be constructed in opposition to the teacher/institution when they try to change the power imbalances they inhabit in their daily lives in schools.

Critical pedagogues speak of student voices as "sharing" their experiences and understandings of oppression with other students and with the teacher in the interest of "expanding the possibilities of what it is to be human."[46] Yet White women, women of color, men of color, White men against masculinist culture, fat people, gay men and lesbians, people with disabilities, and Jews do not speak of the oppressive formations that condition their lives in the spirit of "sharing." Rather, the speech of oppositional groups is a "talking back," a "defiant speech"[47] that is constructed within communities of resistance and is a condition of survival.

In C&I 607, the defiant speech of students and professor of difference constituted fundamental challenges to and rejections of the voices of some classmates and often of the professor. For example, it became clear very quickly that in order to name her experience of racism, a Chicana student had to define her voice in part through opposition to—and rejection of—definitions of "Chicana" assumed or taken for granted by other student/professor voices in the classroom. And in the context of protests by students of color against racism on campus, her voice had to be constructed in opposition to the institutional racism of the university's curriculum and policies—which were represented in part by my discourses and actions as Anglo-American, middle-class woman professor. Unless we found a way to respond to such challenges, our academic and political work against racism would be blocked. This alone is a reason for finding a way to express and engage with student voices, one that distances itself from the abstract, philosophical reasons implied by the literature on critical pedagogy when it fails to contextualize its projects. Furthermore, grounding the expression of and engagement with student voices in the need to construct contextualized political strategies rejects both the voyeuristic relation that the literature reproduces when the voice of the professor is not problematized, and the instrumental role critical pedagogy plays when student voice is used to inform more effective teaching strategies.

The lessons learned from feminist struggles to make a difference through defiant speech offer both useful critiques of the assumptions of critical pedagogy and starting points for moving beyond its repressive myth.[48] Within feminist movements, self-defining feminist voices have been understood as constructed collectively in the context of a larger feminist movement or women's marginalized subcultures. Feminist voices are made possible by the interactions among women within and across race, class, and other differences that divide them. These voices have never been solely or even primarily the result of a pedagogical interaction between an individual student and a teacher. Yet discourses of the pedagogy of empowerment consistently position students as individuals with only the most abstract of relations to concrete contexts of struggle. In their writing about critical pedagogy, educational researchers consistently place teachers/professors at the center of the consciousness-raising activity. For example, McLaren describes alienated middle-class youth in this way:

> . . . these students do not recognize their own self-representation and suppression by the dominant society, and in our vitiated learning environments they are not provided with the requisite theoretical constructs to help them understand why they feel as badly as they do. Because teachers lack a critical pedagogy, these students are not provided with the ability to think critically, a skill that would enable them to better understand why their lives have been reduced to feelings of meaningless, randomness, and alienation. . . .[49]

In contrast, many students came into "Media and Anti-Racist Pedagogies" with oppositional voices already formulated within various antiracism and other movements. These movements had not necessarily relied on intellectuals/teachers to interpret their goals and programs to themselves or to others.

Current writing by many feminists working from antiracism and feminist poststructuralist perspectives recognizes that any individual woman's politicized voice will be partial, multiple, and contradictory.[50] The literature on critical pedagogy also recognizes the possibility that each student will be capable of identifying a multiplicity of authentic voices in her/himself. But it does not confront the ways in which any individual student's voice is already a "teeth-gritting" and often contradictory intersection of voices constituted by gender, race, class, ability, ethnicity, sexual orientation, or ideology. Nor does it engage with the fact that the particularities of historical context, personal biography, and subjectivities split between the conscious and unconscious will necessarily render each expression of student voice partial and predicated on the absence and marginalization of alternative voices. It is impossible to speak from all voices at once, or from any one, without the traces of the others being present and inter-ruptive. Thus the very term "student voice" is highly problematic. Pluralizing the concept as "voices" implies correction through addition. This loses sight of the contradictory and partial nature of all voices.

In C&I 607, for example, participants expressed much pain, confusion, and difficulty in speaking, because of the ways in which discussions called up their multiple and contradictory social positionings. Women found it difficult to prior-itize expressions of racial privilege and oppression when such prioritizing threat-ened to perpetuate their gender oppression. Among international students, both those who were of color and those who were White found it difficult to join their voices with those of U.S. students of color when it meant a subordination of their oppressions as people living under U.S. imperialist policies and as students for whom English was a second language. Asian-American women found it difficult to join their voices with other students of color when it meant subordinating their specific oppressions as Asian-Americans. I found it difficult to speak as a White woman about gender oppression when I occupied positions of institutional power relative to all students in the class, men and women, but positions of gender oppression relative to students who were White men, and in different terms, rel-ative to students who were men of color.

Finally, the argument that women's speech and voice have not been and should not be constructed primarily for the purpose of communicating women's experi-ences to men is commonplace within feminist movements. This position takes the purposes of such speech to be survival, expansion of women's own under-standings of their oppression and strength, sharing common experiences among women, building solidarity among women, and political strategizing. Many fem-inists have pointed to the necessity for men to "do their own work" at unlearning sexism and male privilege, rather than looking to women for the answers. I am similarly suspicious of the desire by the mostly White, middle-class men who write the literature on critical pedagogy to elicit "full expression" of student voices. Such a relation between teacher/student becomes voyeuristic when the voice of the pedagogue himself goes unexamined.

Furthermore, the assumption present in the literature that silence in front of a teacher or professor indicates "lost voice," "voicelessness," or lack of social iden-tity from which to act as a social agent betrays deep and unacceptable gender, race, and class biases. It is worth quoting bell hooks at length about the fiction of the silence of subordinated groups:

Within feminist circles silence is often seen as the sexist defined "right speech of womanhood"—the sign of woman's submission to patriarchal authority. This emphasis on woman's silence may be an accurate remembering of what has taken place in the households of women from WASP backgrounds in the United States but in Black communities (and in other diverse ethnic communi-ties) women have not been silent. Their voices can be heard. Certainly for

Black women our struggle has not been to emerge from silence to speech but to change the nature and direction of our speech. To make a speech that compels listeners, one that is heard . . . Dialogue, the sharing of speech and recognition, took place not between mother and child or mother and male authority figure, but with other Black women. I can remember watching, fascinated, as our mother talked with her mother, sisters, and women friends. The intimacy and intensity of their speech—the satisfaction they received form talking to one another, the pleasure, the joy. It was in this world of woman speech, loud talk, angry words, women with tongues sharp, tender sweet tongues, touching our world with their words, that I made speech my birthright—and the right to voice, to authorship, a privilege I would not be denied. It was in that world and because of it that I came to dream of writing, to write.[51]

White women, men and women of color, impoverished people, people with disabilities, gays and lesbians, are not silenced in the sense implied by the literature on critical pedagogy. They are not talking in their authentic voices, or they are declining/refusing to talk at all, to critical educators who have been unable to acknowledge the presence of knowledges that are challenging and most likely inaccessible to their own social positions. What they/we say, to whom, in what context, depending on the energy they/we have for the struggle on a particular day, is the result of conscious and unconscious assessments of the power relations and safety of the situation.

As I understand it at the moment, what got said—and how—in our class was the product of highly complex strategizing for the visibility that speech gives without giving up the safety of silence. More than that, it was a highly complex negotiation of the politics of knowing and being known. Things were left unsaid, or they were encoded, on the basis of speakers' conscious and unconscious assessments of the risks and costs of disclosing their understandings of themselves and of others. To what extent had students occupying socially constructed positions of privilege at a particular moment risked being known by students occupying socially constructed positions of subordination at the same moment? To what extent had students in those positions of privilege relinquished the security and privilege of being the knower?[52]

As long as the literature on critical pedagogy fails to come to grips with issues of trust, risk, and the operations of fear and desire around such issues of identity and politics in the classroom, their rationalistic tools will continue to fail to loosen deep-seated, self-interested investments in unjust relations of, for example, gender, ethnicity, and sexual orientation.[53] These investments are shared by both teachers and students, yet the literature on critical pedagogy has ignored its own implications for the young, White, Christian, middle-class, heterosexual, able-bodied man/pedagogue that it assumes. Against such ignoring Mohanty argues that to desire to ignore is not cognitive, but performative. It is the incapacity or refusal "to acknowledge one's own implication in the information."[54] [Learning] involves a necessary implication in the radical alterity of the unknown, in the desire(s) not to know, in the process of this unresolvable dialectic."[55]

From dialogue to working together across differences

Because student voice has been defined as "the measures by which students and teacher participate in dialogue,"[56] the foregoing critique has serious consequences for the concept of "dialogue" as it has been articulated in the literature on critical pedagogy. Dialogue has been defined as a fundamental imperative of critical pedagogy and the basis of the democratic education that insures a democratic state. Through dialogue, a classroom can be made in to a public sphere, a locus of citizenship in which:

> Students and teachers can engage in a process of deliberation and discussion aimed at advancing the public welfare in accordance with fundamental moral judgments and principles. . . . School and classroom practices should, in some manner, be organized around forms of learning which serve to prepare students for responsible roles as transformative intellectuals, as community members, and as critically active citizens outside of schools.[57]

Dialogue is offered as a pedagogical strategy for constructing these learning conditions, and consists of ground rules for classroom interaction using language. These rules include the assumptions that all members have equal opportunity to speak, all members respect other members' rights to speak and feel safe to speak, and all ideas are tolerated and subjected to rational critical assessment against fundamental judgments and moral principles. According to Henry Giroux, in order for dialogue to be possible, classroom participants must exhibit "trust, sharing, and commitment to improving the quality of human life." While the specific form and means of social change and organization are open to debate, there must be agreement around the goals of dialogue: "All voices and their differences become unified both in their efforts to identify and recall moments of human suffering and in their attempts to overcome conditions that perpetuate such suffering."[58]

However, for the reasons outlined above—the students' and professor's asymmetrical positions of difference and privilege—dialogue in this sense was both impossible and undesirable in C&I 607. In fact, the unity of efforts and values unproblematically assumed by Giroux was not only impossible but potentially repressive as well. Giroux's formula for dialogue requires and assumes a classroom of participants unified on the side of the subordinated against the subordinators, sharing and trusting in an "us-ness" against "them-ness." This formula fails to confront dynamics of subordination present among classroom participants, and within classroom participants, in the form of multiple and contradictory subject positions. Such a conception of dialogue invokes the "all too easy polemic that opposes victims to perpetrators," in which a condition for collective purpose among "victims" is the desire for home, for synchrony, for sameness.[59] Biddy Martin and Chandra Mohanty call for creating new forms of collective struggle that do not depend upon the repressions and violence needed by "dialogue" based on and enforcing a harmony of interests. They envision collective struggle that starts from an acknowledgment that "unity"—interpersonal, personal, and political—is necessarily fragmentary, unstable, not given, but chosen and struggled for—but not on the basis of "sameness."[60]

But despite early rejections of fundamental tenets of dialogue, including the usually unquestioned emancipatory potentials of rational deliberation and "unity," we remained in the grip of other repressive fictions of classroom dialogue for most of the semester. I expected that we would be able to ensure all members a safe place to speak, equal opportunity to speak, and equal power in influencing decisionmaking—and as a result, it would become clear what had to be done and why. It was only at the end of the semester that I and the students recognized that we had given this myth the power to divert our attention and classroom practices away from what we needed to be doing. Acting as if our classroom were a safe space in which democratic dialogue was possible and happening did not make it so. If we were to respond to our context and the social identities of the people in our classroom in ways that did not reproduce the oppressive formations we were trying to work against, we needed classroom practices that confronted the power dynamics inside and outside of our classroom that made democratic dialogue impossible. During the last two weeks of the semester, we reflected in class on our group's process—how we spoke to and/or silenced each other across our differences, how we divided labor, made decisions, and treated each other as visible and/or invisible. As students had been doing with each other all along, I began to have informal conversations with one or two students at a time who were extremely committed on personal, political, and academic levels to breaking through the barriers we had encountered and understanding what had happened during the semester. These reflections and discussions led me to the following conclusions.

Our classroom was not, in fact, a safe space for students to speak out or talk back about their experiences of oppression both inside and outside of the classroom. In our class, these included experiences of being gay, lesbian, fat, women of color working with men of color, white women working with men of color, and men of color working with White women and men.[61] Things were not being said for a number of reasons. These included fear of being misunderstood and/or disclosing too much and becoming too vulnerable; memories of bad experiences in other contexts of speaking out; resentment that other oppressions (sexism, heterosexism, fat oppression, classism, anti-Semitism) were being marginalized in the name of addressing racism—and guilt for feeling such resentment; confusion about levels of trust and commitment surrounding those who were allies to another group's struggles; resentment by some students of color for feeling that they were expected to disclose "more" and once again take the burden of doing the pedagogic work of educating White students/professor about the consequences of White middle-class privilege; and resentment by White students for feeling that they had to prove they were not the enemy.

Dialogue in its conventional sense is impossible in the culture at large, because at this historical moment, power relations between raced, classed, and gendered students and teachers are unjust. The injustice of these relations, and the way in which those injunctions distort communication, cannot be overcome in a classroom, no matter how committed the teacher and students are to "overcoming conditions that perpetuate suffering." Conventional notions of dialogue and democracy assume rationalized, individualized subjects capable of agreeing on universalizable "fundamental moral principles" and "quality of human life" that become self-evident when subjects cease to be self-interested and particularistic about group rights. Yet social agents are not capable of being fully rational and disinterested; and they are subjects split between the conscious and unconscious and among multiple social positionings. Fundamental moral and political principles are not absolute and universalizable, waiting to be discovered by the disinterested researcher/teacher; they are "established intersubjectively by subjects capable of interpretation and reflection."[62] Educational researchers attempting to construct meaningful discourses about the politics of classroom practices must begin to theorize the consequences for education of the ways knowledge, power and desire are mutually implicated in each other's formations and deployments.

By the end of the semester, participants in the class agreed that commitment to rational discussion about racism in a classroom setting was not enough to make that setting a safe place for speaking out and talking back. We agreed that a safer space required high levels of trust and personal commitment to individuals in the class, gained in part through social interactions outside of class—potlucks, field trips, participation in rallies and other gatherings. Opportunities to know the motivations, histories, and personal stakes of individuals in the class should have been planned early in the semester.[63] Furthermore, White students/professor should have shared the burden of educating themselves about the consequences of their White-skin privilege, and to facilitate this, the curriculum should have included significant amounts of literature, films, and videos by people of color and White people against racism—so that the students of color involved in the class would not always be looked to as "experts" in racism or the situation on the campus.

Because all voices within the classroom are not and cannot carry equal legitimacy, safety, and power in dialogue at this historical moment, there are times when the inequalities must be named and addressed by constructing alternative ground rules for communication. By the end of the semester, participants in C&I 607 had begun to recognize that some social groups represented in the class had had consistently more speaking time than others. Women, international students for whom English was a second language, and mixed groups sharing ideological and political languages and perspectives began to have very significant interactions outside of class. Informal, overlapping affinity groups formed and met un-officially for the purpose of articulating and refining positions based on shared oppressions, ideological analyses, or interests. They shared grievances about the dynamics of the larger groups and performed reality checks for each other. Because they were "unofficial" groups constituted on the spot in response to specific needs or simply as a result of casual encounters outside of the classroom, alliances could be shaped and reshaped as strategies in context.

The fact that affinity groups did form within the larger group should not be seen as a failure to construct a unity of voices and goals—a possibility unproblematically assumed and worked for in critical pedagogy. Rather, affinity groups were necessary for working against the way current historical configurations of oppressions were reproduced in the class. They provided some participants with safer home bases from which they gained support, important understandings, and a language for entering the larger classroom interactions each week. Once we acknowledged the existence, necessity, and value of these affinity groups, we began to see our task not as one of building democratic dialogue between free and equal individuals, but of building a coalition among the multiple, shifting, intersecting, and sometimes contradictory groups carrying unequal weights of legitimacy within the culture and the classroom. Halfway through the semester, students renamed the class Coalition 607.

At the end of the semester, we began to suspect that it would have been appropriate for the large group to experiment with forms of communication other than dialogue. These could have brought the existence and results of affinity group interactions to bear more directly on the larger group's understandings and practices. For example, it seemed that we needed times when one affinity group (women of color, women and men of color, feminists, White men against masculinist culture, White women, gays, lesbians) could "speak out" and "talk back" about their experience of Coalition 607's group process or their experience of racial, gender, or other injustice on the campus, while the rest of the class listened without interruption. This would have acknowledged that we were not interacting in class dialogue solely as individuals, but as members of larger social groups, with whom we shared common and also differing experiences of oppression, a language for naming, fighting, and surviving that oppression, and a shared sensibility and style. The differences among the affinity groups that composed the class made communication within the class a form of cross-cultural or cross-subcultural exchange, rather than the free, rational, democratic exchange between equal individuals implied in critical pedagogy literature.

But I want to emphasize that this does not mean that discourses of students of difference were taken up and supported unconditionally by themselves and their allies. There had been intense consciousness-raising on the UW-Madison campus between African-American students, Asian-American students, Latino/a, Chicano/a students, Native American students, the men and women of color, about the different forms racism had taken across the campus, depending on ethnicity and gender—and how no single group's analysis could be adopted to cover all other students of color.

Early in the semester, it become clear to some in Coalition 607 that some of the anti-racism discourses heard on campus were structured by highly problematic gender politics, and White women and women of color could not adopt those discourses as their own without undercutting their own struggles against sexism on campus and in their communities. We began to define coalition-building not only in terms of what we shared—a commitment to work against racism—but in terms of what we did not share—gender, sexual orientation, ethnicity, and other differences. These positions gave us different stakes in, experiences of, and perspectives on, racism. These differences meant that each strategy we considered for fighting racism on campus had to be interrogated for the implications it held for struggles against sexism, ableism, elitism, fat oppression, and so forth.

We agreed to a final arbiter of the acceptability of demands/narratives by students of color and our class's actions on campus. Proposals would be judged in light of our answers to this question: To what extent do our political strategies and alternative narratives about social difference succeed in alleviating campus racism, while at the same time managing *not to undercut* the efforts of the other social groups to win self-definition?

A pedagogy of the unknowable

Like the individual students themselves, each affinity group possessed only partial narratives of its oppressions—partial, in that they were self-interested and predicated on the exclusion of the voices of others—and also in the sense that the meaning of an individual's or group's experience is never self-evident or complete. No one affinity group could ever "know" the experiences and knowledges of another, nor the social positions that were not their own. Nor can social subjects who are split between the conscious and unconscious, and cut across by multiple, intersecting, and contradictory subject positions, ever fully "know" their own experiences. As a whole, Coalition 607 could never know with certainty whether the actions it planned to take on campus would undercut the struggle of other social groups, or even that of its own affinity groups. Realizing that there are partial narratives that some social groups or cultures have and others can never know, but that are necessary to human survival, is a condition to embrace and use as an opportunity to build a kind of social and educational interdependency that recognizes differences as "different strengths" and as "forces for change." In the words of Audre Lorde, "Difference must be not merely tolerated, but seen as a fund of necessary polarities between which our creativity can spark like a dialectic. Only then does the necessity for interdependency become unthreatening."[64]

In the end, Coalition 607 participants made an initial gesture toward acting out the implications of the unknowable and the social, educational, and political interdependency that it necessitates. The educational interventions against racism that we carried out on campus were put forth as Coalition 607's statement about its members' provisional, partial understanding of racial oppression on the UW-Madison campus at the moment of its actions. These statements were not offered with the invitation for audiences to participate in dialogue, but as a speaking out from semiotic spaces temporarily and problematically controlled by Coalition 607's students. First, we took actions on campus by interrupting business-as-usual (that is, social relations of racism, sexism, classism, Eurocentrism as usual) in the public spaces of the library mall and administrative offices. (The mall is a frequent site for campus protests, rallies, and graffiti, and was chosen for this reason). These interruptions consisted of three events.

At noon on April 28, 1988, a street theater performance on the library mall, "Meet on the Street," presented an ironic history of university attempts to coopt and defuse the demands of students of color from the 1950s through the 1980s. The affinity group that produced this event invited members of the university and Madison communities who were not in the class to participate. That night, after dark, "Scrawl on the Mall" used overhead and movie projectors to project towering images, text, and spontaneously written "graffiti" on the white walls of the main campus library. Class members and passersby drew and wrote on transparencies for the purpose of deconstructing, defacing, and transforming racist discourses and giving voice to perspectives and demands of students of color and White students against racism. For example, students projected onto the library a page from the administration's official response to the Minority Student Coalition demands, and "edited" it to reveal how it failed to meet those demands. Throughout the semester, a third group of students interrupted business-as-usual in the offices of the student newspaper and university administrators by writing articles and holding interviews that challenged the university's and the newspaper's response to the demands by students of color.

These three events disrupted power relations, however temporarily, within the contexts in which they occurred. Students of color and White students against racism opened up semiotic space for discourses normally marginalized and silenced within the everyday uses of the library mall and administrators' offices. They appropriated means of discourse production—overhead projectors, microphones, language, images, newspaper articles—and controlled, however problematically, the terms in which students of color and racism on campus would be defined and represented within the specific times and spaces of the events. They made available to other members of the university community, with unpredictable and uncontrollable effects, discourses of antiracism that might otherwise have remained unavailable, distorted, more easily dismissed, or seemingly irrelevant. Thus students engaged in the political work of changing material conditions within a public space, allowing them to make visible and assert the legitimacy of their own definitions, in their own terms, of racism and anti-racism on the UW campus.

Each of the three actions was defined by different affinity groups according to different priorities, languages of understanding and analysis, and levels of comfort with various kinds of public action. They were "unified" through their activity of mutual critique, support, and participation, as each group worked through, as much as possible, ways in which the others supported or undercut its own understandings and objectives. Each affinity group brought its proposal for action to the whole class, to assess the ways that action might affect the other groups' self-definitions, priorities, and plans for action. Each group asked the others for various types of labor and support to implement its proposed action. During these planning discussions, we concluded that the results of our interventions would be unpredictable and uncontrollable, and dependent upon the subject positions and changing historical contexts of our audiences on the mall and in administrative offices. Ultimately, our interventions and the process by which we arrived at them had to make sense—both rationally and emotionally—to *us*, however problematically we understand "making sense" to be a political action. Our actions had to make sense as interested interpretations and constant rewritings of ourselves in relation to shifting interpersonal and political contexts. Our interpretations had to be based on attention to history, to concrete experiences of oppression, and to subjugated knowledges.[65]

Conclusion

For me, what has become more frightening than the unknown or unknowable, are social, political, and educational projects that predicate and legitimate their actions on the kind of knowing that underlies current definitions of critical pedagogy. In this sense, current understandings and uses of "critical," "empowerment," "student voice," and "dialogue" are only surface manifestations of deeper contradictions involving pedagogies, both traditional and critical. The kind of knowing I am referring to is that in which objects, nature, and Others are seen to be known or ultimately knowable, in the sense of being "defined, delineated, captured, understood, explained, and diagnosed" at a level of determination never accorded to the "knower" herself or himself.[66]

The experience of Coalition 607 has left me wanting to think through the implications of confronting unknowability. What would it mean to recognize not only that a multiplicity of knowledges are present in the classroom as a result of the way difference has been used to structure social relations inside and outside the classroom, but that these knowledges are contradictory, partial, and irreducible? They cannot be made to "make sense"—they cannot be known, in terms of the single master discourse of an educational project's curriculum or theoretical framework—even that of critical pedagogy. What kinds of classroom practice are made possible and impossible when one affinity group within the class has lived out and arrived at a currently useful "knowledge" about a particular oppressive formation on campus, but the professor and some of the other students can never know or understand that knowledge in the same way? What practice is called for when even the combination of all partial knowledges in a classroom results in yet another partial knowing, defined by structuring absences that mark the "terror and loathing of any difference?"[67] What kinds of interdependencies between groups and individuals inside and outside of the classroom would recognize that every social, political, or educational project the class takes up locally will already, at the moment of its definition, lack knowledges necessary to answer broader questions of human survival and social justice? What kind of educational project could redefine "knowing" so that it no longer describes the activities of those in power "who started to speak, to speak alone and for everyone else, on behalf of everyone else?"[68] What kind of educational project would redefine the silence of the unknowable, freeing it from "the male-defined context of Absence, Lack, and Fear," and make of that silence "a language of its own" that changes the nature and direction of speech itself?[69]

Whatever form it takes in the various, changing, locally specific instances of classroom practices, I understand a classroom practice of the unknowable right now to be one that would support students/professor in the never-ending "moving about" Trinh Minh-Ha describes:

> After all, she is this Inappropriate/d Other who moves about with always at least two/four gestures: that of affirming "I am like you" while pointing insistently to the difference; and that of reminding "I am different" while unsettling every definition of otherness arrived at.[70]

In relation to education, I see this moving about as a strategy that affirms "you know me/I know you" while pointing insistently to the interested partialness of those knowings; and constantly reminding us that "you can't know me/I can't know you" while unsettling every definition of knowing arrived at. Classroom practices that facilitate such moving about would support the kind of contextually, politically and historically situated identity politics called for by Alcoff, hooks, and others.[71] That is, one in which "identity" is seen as "nonessentialized and emergent from a historical experience"[72] as a necessary stage in a process, a starting point—not an ending point. Identity in this sense becomes a vehicle for multiplying and making more complex the subject positions possible, visible, and legitimate at any given historical moment, requiring disruptive changes in the way social technologies of gender, race, ability, and so on define Otherness and use it as a vehicle for subordination.

Gayatri Spivak calls the search for a coherent narrative "counterproductive" and asserts that what is needed is "persistent critique"[73] of received narratives and a priori lines of attack. Similarly, unlike post-liberal or post-Marxist movements predicated on repressive unities, Minh-ha's "moving about" refuses to reduce profoundly heterogeneous networks of power/desire/interest to any one a priori, coherent narrative. It refuses to know and resist oppression from any a priori line of attack, such as race, class, or gender solidarity.

But participants in Coalition 607 did not simply unsettle every definition of knowing, assert the absence of a priori solidarities, or replace political action (in the sense defined at the beginning of the chapter) with textual critique. Rather, we struggled, as S. P. Mohanty would have us do, to "develop a sense of the profound *contextuality* of meanings [and oppressive knowledges] in their play and their ideological effects."[74]

Our classroom was the site of dispersed, shifting, and contradictory contexts of knowing, that coalesced differently in different moments of student/professor speech, action, and emotion. This situation meant that individuals and affinity groups constantly had to change strategies and priorities of resistance against oppressive ways of knowing and being known. The antagonist became power itself as it was deployed within our classroom—oppressive ways of knowing and oppressive ℄nowledges.

This position, informed by post-structuralism and feminism, lets no one off the hook, including critical pedagogues. We cannot act as if our membership in or alliance with an oppressed group exempts us from the need to confront the "grey areas which we all have in us."[79] As Minh-ha reminds us, "There are no social positions exempt from becoming oppressive to others. . . . any group—any position—can move into the oppressor role,"[76] depending upon specific historical contexts and situations. Or as Mary Gentile puts it, "everyone is someone else's 'Other'."[77]

Various groups struggling for self-definition in the United States have identified the mythical norm deployed for the purpose of setting the standard of humanness against which Others are defined and assigned privilege and limitations. At this moment in history, that norm is young, White, heterosexual, Christian, able-bodied, thin, middle-class, English-speaking, and male. Yet, as Gentile argues no individual embodies, in the essentialist sense, this mythical norm.[78] Even individuals who most closely approximate it experience a dissonance. As someone who embodies some but not all of the current mythical norm's socially constructed characteristics, my colleague Albert Selvin wrote in response to the first draft of this article: "I too have to fight to differentiate myself from a position defined for me—whose terms are imposed on me—which limits and can destroy me—which does destroy many White men or turns them into helpless agents. . . . I as a White man/boy was not allowed—by my family, by society—to be anything *but* cut off from the earth and the body. That condition is not/was not an essential component or implication of my maleness.[79]

To assert multiple perspectives in this way is not to draw attention away from the distinctive realities and effects of the oppression of any particular group. It is not to excuse or relativize oppression by simply claiming, "we are all oppressed." Rather, it is to clarify oppression by preventing "oppressive simplifications,"[80] and insisting that it be understood and struggled against contextually. For example, the politics of appearance in relation to the mythical norm played a major role in our classroom. Upon first sight, group members tended to draw alliances and assume shared commitments because of the social positions we presumed others to occupy (radical, heterosexual, anti-racist person of color, and so on). But not only were these assumptions often wrong, at times they denied ideological and personal commitments to various struggles by people who appeared outwardly to fit the mythical norm.

The terms in which I can and will assert and unsettle "difference" and unlearn my positions of privilege in future classroom practices are wholly dependent on the Others/others whose presence—with their concrete experiences of privileges and oppressions, and subjugated or oppressive knowledges—I am responding to and acting with in any given classroom. My moving about between the positions of privileged speaking subject and Inappropriate/d Other cannot be predicted, prescribed, or understood beforehand by any theoretical framework or methodological practice. It is in this sense that a practice grounded in the unknowable is profoundly contextual (historical) and interdependent (social). This reformulation of pedagogy and knowledge removes the critical pedagogue from two key discursive positions s/he has constructed for her/himself in the literature— namely, origin of what can be known and origin of what should be done. What remains for me is the challenge of constructing classroom practices that engage with the discursive and material spaces that such a removal opens up. I am trying to unsettle received definitions of pedagogy by multiplying the ways in which I am able to act on and in the university both as the Inappropriate/d Other and as the privileged speaking/making subject trying to unlearn that privilege.

This semester, in follow-up to Coalition 607, Curriculum and Instruction 800 is planning, producing, and "making sense" of a day-long film and video event combatting oppressive knowledges and ways of knowing in the curriculum, pedagogy, and everyday life at UW-Madison. This time, we are not focusing on any one formation (race *or* gender *or* ableism). Rather, we are engaging with each other and working against oppressive social formations on campus in ways that try to "find a commonality in the experience of difference without compromising its distinctive realities and effects."[81]

Right now, the classroom practice that seems most capable of accomplishing this is one that facilitates a kind of communication across differences that is best represented by this statement: "If you can talk to me in ways that show you understand that your knowledge of me, the world, and 'the Right thing to do' will always be partial, interested, and potentially oppressive to others, and if I can do the same, then we can work together on shaping and reshaping alliances for constructing circumstances in which students of difference can thrive."

This chapter is a revised version of a paper presented at the Tenth Conference on Curriculum Theory and Classroom Practice, Bergamo Conference Center, Dayton, Ohio, October 26–29, 1988. It was part of a symposium entitled "Reframing the Empirical 'I/Eye': Feminist, Neo-Marxist, and Post-Structuralist Challenges to Research in Education."

I want to thank Mimi Orner, recent Ph.D. graduate in the Department of Curriculum and Instruction, UW-Madison, for her insights and hours of conversations about the meanings of C&I 607. They have formed the backbone of this chapter.

Notes

1. By "critique," I do not mean a systematic analysis of the specific articles or individual authors' positions that make up this literature, for the purpose of articulating a "theory" of critical pedagogy capable of being evaluated for its internal consistency, elegance, powers of prediction, and so on. Rather, I have chosen to ground the following critique in my interpretation of my experiences in C&I 607. That is, I have attempted to place key discourses in the literature on critical pedagogy *in relation to* my interpretation of my experience in C&I 607—by asking which interpretations and "sense making" those discourses facilitate, which do they silence and marginalize, and what interests do they appear to serve.

2. By "the literature on critical pedagogy," I mean those articles in major educational journals and special editions devoted to critical pedagogy. For the purpose of this article, I systematically reviewed more than thirty articles appearing in journals such as *Harvard Educational Review, Curriculum Inquiry, Educational Theory, Teachers College Record, Journal of Curriculum Theorizing,* and *Journal of Curriculum Studies* between 1984 and 1988. The purpose of this review was to identify key and repeated claims, assumptions, goals, and pedagogical practices that currently set the terms of debate within this literature. "Critical pedagogy" should not be confused with "feminist pedagogy," which constitutes a separate body of literature with its own goals and assumptions.

3. Some of the more representative writing on this point can be found in Michelle Fine, "Silencing in the public schools," *Language Arts, 64* (1987), 157–174; Henry Giroux, "Radical pedagogy and the politics of student voice," *Interchange, 17* (1986), 48–69; and Roger Simon, "Empowerment as a pedagogy of possibility," *Language Arts, 64* (1987), 370–382.

4. See Henry A. Giroux and Peter McLaren, "Teacher education and the politics of engagement: The case for democratic schooling," *Harvard Educational Review, 56* (1986), 213–238; and Ira Shor and Paulo Freire, "What is the 'dialogical method' of teaching?" *Journal of Education, 169* (1987), 11–31.

5. Shor and Freire, "What is the 'Dialogical Method'?" and Henry A. Giroux, "Literacy and the pedagogy of voice and political empowerment," *Educational Theory, 38* (1988), 61–75.

6. Daniel P. Liston and Kenneth M. Zeichner, "Critical pedagogy and teacher education," *Journal of Education, 169* (1987), 117–137.

7. Ibid., p. 120.

8. Ibid., p. 127.

9. Giroux, "Literacy and the pedagogy of voice," p. 75.

10. Liston and Zeichner, op. cit., p. 128.

11. Valerie Walkerdine, "On the regulation of speaking and silence: Subjectivity, class, and gender in contemporary schooling," in Carolyn Steedman, Cathy Urwin, and Valerie Walkerdine (Eds.), *Language gender and childhood.* (London: Routledge and Kegan Paul, 1985) p. 205.

12. Barbara Christian, "The race for theory," *Cultural Critique, 6* (Spring, 1987), 51–63.

13. By the end of the semester, many of us began to understand ourselves as inhabiting intersections of multiple, contradictory, overlapping social positions not reducible either to race, or class, or gender, and so on. Depending upon the moment and the context, the degree to which any one of us "differs" from the mythical norm (see conclusion) varies along multiple axes, and so do

the consequences. I began using the terms "students of difference," "professor of difference," to refer to social positionings in relation to the mythical norm (based on ability, size, color, sexual preference, gender, ethnicity, and so on). This reminded us of the necessity to reconstruct how, within specific situations, particular socially constructed differences from the mythical norm (such as color) get taken up as vehicles for institutions such as the university to act out and legitimate oppressive formations of power. This enabled us to open up our analysis of racism on campus for the purpose of tracing its relations to institutional sexism, ableism, elitism, anti-Semitism, and other oppressive formations.

14. Giroux and McLaren, "Teacher education and the politics of engagement," p. 229.

15. Stanley Aronowitz, "Postmodernism and Politics," *Social Text, 18* (Winter, 1987/1988), p. 99–115.

16. Liston and Zeichner, "Critical Pedagogy," p. 120.

17. For an excellent theoretical discussion and demonstration of the explanatory power of this approach, see Julian Henriques, Wendy Hollway, Cathy Urwin, Couze Venn, and Valerie Walkerdine, *Changing the subject: Psychology, social regulation, and subjectivity* (New York: Methuen, 1984); Gloria Anzaldua, *Borderlands/La Frontera: The New Mestiza* (San Francisco: Spinster/Aunt Lute, 1987); Theresa de Lauretis, ed., *Feminist studies/critical studies* (Bloomington: Indiana University Press, 1986); Hal Foster, ed., *Discussions in contemporary culture,* (Seattle: Bay Press, 1987); Chris Weedon, *Feminist practice and poststructuralist theory* (New York: Basil Blackwell, 1987).

18. Weedon, *Feminist practice and poststructuralist theory,* pp. 40–41.

19. Aronowitz, "Postmodernism and Politics," p. 103.

20. Audre Lorde, *Sister outsider* (New York: The Crossing Press, 1984), p. 112.

21. Christian, "The race for theory," p. 63.

22. For a discussion of the thesis of the "epistemic privilege of the oppressed," see Uma Narayan, "Working together across difference: Some considerations on emotions and political practice," *Hypatia, 3* (Summer, 1988), 31–47.

23. For an excellent discussion of the relation of the concept of "experience" to feminism, essentialism, and political action, see Linda Alcoff, "Cultural feminism versus post-structuralism: The identity crisis in feminist theory, *Signs, 13*(Spring, 1988), 405–437.

24. Narayan, "Working together across difference," pp. 31–47.

25. This subtitle is borrowed from Maria C. Lugones and Elizabeth V. Spelman's critique of imperialistic, ethnocentric, and disrespectful tendencies in White feminists' theorizing about women's oppression, "Have we got a theory for you! Feminist theory, cultural imperialism, and the demand for 'the woman's voice,'" *Woman's Studies International forum* (1983), 573–581.

26. Nicholas C. Burbules, "A theory of power in education, *Educational Theory, 36* (Spring, 1986), 95–114; Giroux and McLaren, "Teacher education and the politics of engagement," pp. 224–227.

27. Liston and Zeichner, "Critical pedagogy and teacher education," p. 120.

28. Shor and Freire, "What is the 'dialogical method' of teaching?," p. 14.

29. Giroux, "Radical pedagogy", p. 64.

30. Giroux, "Radical pedagogy," p. 66.

31. Shor and Freire, "What is the 'dialogical method' of teaching?," p. 22.

32. Burbules, "A theory of power in education"; and Giroux and McLaren, "Teacher education and the politics of engagement," pp. 224–227.

33. Shor and Freire, "What is the 'dialogical method' of teaching?," p. 23.

34. Burbules, "A theory of power in education," p. 108.

35. Giroux and McLaren, "Teacher education and the politics of engagement," p. 226.

36. Walter C. Parker, "Justice, social studies, and the subjectivity/structure problem," *Theory and Research in Social Education, 14* (Fall, 1986), p. 227.

37. Simon, "Empowerment as a pedagogy of possibility," p. 372.

38. Giroux, "Literacy and the pedagogy of voice," pp. 68–69.

39. Giroux and McLaren, "Teacher education and the politics of engagement," p. 225.

40. Ibid., p. 227.

41. Shor and Freire, "What is the 'dialogical method' of teaching?" p. 30; Liston and Zeichner, "Critical pedagogy," p. 122.

42. Simon, "Empowerment as a pedagogy of possibility," p. 380.

43. Simon, "Empowerment as a pedagogy of possibility," p. 375.

44. Aronowitz, "Postmodernism and politics," p. 111.

45. Alcoff, "Cultural feminism versus post-structuralism," p. 420.

46. Simon, "Empowerment as a pedagogy of possibility," p. 372.

47. bell hooks, "Talking back," *Discourse, 8* (Fall/Winter, 1986/1987), p. 123–128.

48. bell hooks, "Pedagogy and Political Commitment: A Comment" in *Talking back: Thinking feminist, thinking Black* (Boston: South End Press, 1989), pp. 98–104.

49. Peter McLaren, *Life in schools,* (New York: Longman, 1989), p. 18.

50. Alcoff, "Cultural feminism versus post-structuralism"; Anzaldua, *Borderlands/La Frontera;* de Lauretis, *Feminist studies/ critical studies;* Hooks, *Talking back;* Trihn T. Minh-ha, *Woman, native, Other* (Bloomington: Indiana University Press, 1989); Weedon, *Feminist practice and poststructuralist theory.*

51. hooks, *Talking back,* p. 124.

52. Susan Hardy Aiken, Karen Anderson, Myra Dinerstein, Judy Lensink and Patricia Mac-Corquodale, "Trying transformations: Curriculum integration and the problem of resistance," *Signs, 12* (Winter 1987), 225–275.

53. Ibid., p. 263.

54. Shoshana Felman, "Psychoanalysis and education: Teaching terminable and interminable." *Yale French Studies, 63* (1982), 21–44.

55. S. P. Mohanty, "Radical teaching, radical theory: The ambiguous politics of meaning," in *Theory in the classroom,* ed. Cary Nelson (Urbana: University of Illinois Press, 1986), p. 155.

56. Giroux & McLaren, "Teacher education and the politics of engagement," p. 235.

57. Ibid., p. 237.

58. Giroux "Literacy and the pedagogy of voice," p. 72.

59. Biddy Martin and Chandra Talpade Mohanty, "Feminist politics: What's home got to do with it?" in *Feminist Studies/Critical studies,* ed. Theresa de Lauretis (Bloomington: Indiana University Press, 1986), pp. 208–209.

60. Ibid., p. 208.

61. Discussions with students after the semester ended and comments from students and colleagues on the draft of this article have led me to realize the extent to which some international students and Jews in the class felt unable or not safe to speak about experiences of oppression inside and outside of the class related to those identities. Anti-Semitism, economic and cultural imperialism, and the rituals of exclusion of international students on campus were rarely named and

never fully elaborated in the class. The classroom practices that reproduced these particular oppressive silences in C&I 607 must be made the focus of sustained critique in the follow-up course, C&I 800, "Race, Class, Gender, and the Construction of Knowledge in Educational Media."

62. John W. Murphy, "Computerization, postmodern epistemology, and reading the postmodern era," *Educational Theory, 38* (Spring, 1988), 175–182.

63. Lugones and Spelman (1983) assert that the only acceptable motivation for following Others into their worlds is friendship. Self-interest is not enough, because "the task at hand for you is one of extraordinary difficulty. It requires that you be willing to devote a great part of your life to it and that you be willing to suffer alienation and self-disruption . . . whatever the benefits to you may accrue from such a journey, they cannot be concrete enough for you at this time and they are not worth your while" ("Have we got a theory for you," p. 576). Theoretical or political "obligation" is inappropriate, because it puts White/Anglos "in a morally self-righteous position" and makes people of color vehicles of redemption for those in power (p. 581). Friendship, as an appropriate and acceptable "condition" under which people become allies in struggles that are not their own, names my own experience and has been met with enthusiasm by students.

64. Lorde, *Sister outsider,* p. 112.

65. Martin & Mohanty, "Feminist politics," p. 210.

66. Alcoff, "Cultural feminism versus post-structuralism," p. 406.

67. Lorde, *Sister outsider,* p. 113.

68. Trinh T. Minh-ha, "Introduction," *Discourse, 8* (Fall/Winter, 1986/1987), p. 7.

69. Minh-ha, "Introduction," p. 8.

70. Ibid., p. 9.

71. Alcoff, "Cultural feminism versus post-structuralism"; bell hooks, "The politics of radical black subjectivity," *Zeta Magazine* (April, 1989), pp. 405–436.

72. hooks, "The politics of radical black subjectivity," p. 54.

73. Gayatri Chakravorty Spivak, "Can the subaltern speak?" in *Marxism and the Interpretation of culture,* eds. Cary Nelson and Lawrence Grossberg (Urbana: University of Illinois Press, 1988), p. 272.

74. S. P. Mohanty, "Radical teaching, radical theory," p. 169.

75. Minh-ha, "Introduction," p. 6.

76. A. Selvin, personal correspondence (October 24, 1988).

77. Mary Gentile, *Film feminisms: Theory and practice,* (Westport, CT: Greenwood Press, 1985), p. 7.

78. Gentile, *Film feminisms,* p. 7.

79. A. Selvin, personal correspondence.

80. Gentile, *Film feminisms,* p. 7.

81. Ibid., p. 7.

7

Post-Critical Pedagogies: A Feminist Reading

Patti Lather

Pedagogy must itself be a text. (Ulmer, 1985, p. 52)

. . . teaching is a question of strategy. That is perhaps the only place where we
actually get any experience in strategy, although we talk a lot about it. (Spivak,
1989, p. 146)

This paper foregrounds the conflicts between the emancipatory projects and
deconstruction by attempting a constructive displacement of the emancipatory
impulse at work in the discourses of "critical pedagogy". Understanding what I
mean by such a statement entails some sense of my working definitions of at least
three terms: deconstruction, critical and pedagogy.

I frame *deconstruction* as "not a method", but a disclosure of how a text functions as desire (Derrida, in Kearney, 1984, p. 124). Rather than an exposure of
error, deconstruction is "a way of thinking . . . about the danger of what is powerful and useful. . . . You deconstructively critique something which is so useful
to you that you cannot speak another way" (Spivak, 1989, pp. 135, 151).[1] The
goal of deconstruction is neither unitary wholeness nor dialectical resolution.
The goal of deconstruction is to keep things in process, to disrupt, to keep the
system in play, to set up procedures to continuously demystify the realities we
create, and to fight the tendency for our categories to congeal (Caputo, 1987, p.
236). Deconstruction foregrounds the lack of innocence in any discourse by
looking at the textual staging of knowledge, the constitutive effects of our uses
of language. As the postmodern equivalent of the dialectic, deconstruction provides a corrective moment, a safeguard against dogmatism, a continual displacement.

As noted by Spivak, such a strategy cannot ground a politics (Harasym, 1988).
This raises many concerns regarding the politics of postmodernism/poststructur-
alism,[2] especially its undercutting of the claims to truth and justice that undergird
emancipatory efforts (e.g., Habermas, 1987; Haraway, 1988; Hartsock, 1987;
West, 1987). In a time marked by the dissolution of authoritative foundations of
knowledge, the possibilities of liberatory praxis grow increasingly problematic.
Lyotard, for example, writes that "oppositional thinking . . . is out of step with
the most vital modes of postmodern knowledge" (quoted in Schrift, 1990, p. 2).
Additionally, the "interpretive praxis" that is deconstruction includes the development of a Foucauldian awareness of the oppressive role of ostensibly libera-

tory forms of discourse (Atkins and Johnson, 1985, p. 2). In a move to "salvage praxis" (Foucault, 1984), reflexive practice is strategically privileged as a site for learning the possibilities and limits of turning critical thought into emancipatory action: "In periods when fields are without secure foundations, practice becomes the engine of innovation" (Marcus and Fischer, 1986, p. 166). This entails a reflexivity that attends to the politics of what is and is not done at a practical level in order to learn "to 'read out' the epistemologies in our various practices" (Hartsock, 1987, p. 206). Exploring whether such a salvaging of praxis is possible in a post-foundational era is a major focus of this paper.

Within the context of Frankfurt School critical theory, *critical* reason was used as the interlocutor of *instrumental* reason, the driving force behind modernism. In Poster's words, "critical theory springs from an assumption that we live amid a world of pain, that much can be done to alleviate that pain, and that theory has a crucial role to play in that process" (1989, p. 3). The various feminisms, neomarxisms and the "postmodernisms of resistance" (Hutcheon, 1988, 1989), then, become kinds of critical theories which are informed by identification with and interest in "oppositional" social movements.[3] While in practice not unknown to have *instrumental* moments, critical theories are positioned in relation to counter-hegemonic social movements and take as their charge "the self-clarification of the struggles and wishes of the age" (Marx, quoted in Fraser, 1987, p. 31). As critical practices derive their forms and meanings in relation to their changing historical conditions, positions of resistance can never be established once and for all. They must, instead, be perpetually refashioned to address adequately the shifting conditions and circumstances that ground them (Solomon-Godeau, 1988, p. 208).

I take *pedagogy* to mean that which addresses "the transformation of consciousness that takes place in the intersection of three agencies—the teacher, the learner and the knowledge they together produce" (Lusted, 1986, p. 3). According to Lusted's oft-quoted definition, pedagogy refuses to instrumentalize these relations, diminish their interactivity, or value one over another. It, furthermore, denies the teacher as neutral transmitter, the student as passive, and knowledge as immutable material to impart. Instead, the concept of pedagogy focuses attention on the conditions and means through which knowledge is produced. All pedagogies are situated—specific and contingent to the cultural fields within which they operate. Lusted sees the disattention, the "desperately undertheorized" (p. 3) nature of pedagogy as at the root of the failure of emancipatory objectives. Such a claim constructs the interactive productivity, as opposed to the merely transmissive nature of what happens in the pedagogical act, as a central issue in the struggle for a more just world.[4]

Within my definitional web, *critical pedagogy* is positioned as that which attends to practices of teaching/learning intended to interrupt particular historical, situated systems of oppression. Such pedagogies go by many names: Freirean, feminist, anti-racist, radical, empowering, liberation theology. With both overlaps and specificities within and between, each is constructed out of a combination of Frankfurt School critical theory, Gramscian counter-hegemonic practice and Freirean conscientization (Luke, this volume). It is the central claim of this paper that, too often, such pedagogies have failed to probe the degree to which "empowerment" becomes something done "by" liberated pedagogies "to" or "for" the as-yet-unliberated, the "Other", the object upon which is directed the "emancipatory" actions (Ellsworth, this volume). It is precisely this question that postmodernism frames: How do our very efforts to liberate perpetuate the relations of dominance? What follows explores that question by looking first at the discourses of emancipatory education and then at what I am presently calling "post-critical pedagogies".

The discourses of emancipatory education

> If intellectuals have to talk to one another in specialized terms, so be it. The question becomes "Does that get translated at some level into the classroom?" And if it *does*, then the barn door is open. Once you get into the undergraduate classroom successfully, then you're outside the ivory tower. You're into the culture (Lentricchia, quoted in DeCurtis, 1989, p. 8.)

Lentricchia's pedagogical strategy uses deconstruction to help students create subject positions such as "a kind of new person who's not going to be satisfied with the usual canonical things" (ibid., p. 148). In this section, I explore the problematic intersection between the emancipatory projects and deconstruction via a tracing of its inscription in the discourses of emancipatory education. With Lentricchia's argument for pedagogical intervention in mind, I first construct a necessarily partial "review of the literature" to provide an overview of that intersection. I then position it as a site of struggle by juxtaposing multiple, conflicting readings of Ellsworth's (this volume) essay, "Why Doesn't This Feel Empowering? Working Through the Repressive Myths of Critical Pedagogy."

At one level, the problematic of postmodernism is to "make of our disorders new knowledge" (Hassan, 1987, p. 81). What this might mean within the context of educational thought and practice is captured by Johnson's (1987) argument that the politics of undecidability, the unavoidable openendedness and inherent perspectivity of knowledge, "become an access route to a whole rethinking of the educational enterprise" (p. 44). Some of this work is beginning regarding pedagogy. Much of the "deconstructivist pedagogy" literature comes from the area of literary criticism and cultural studies, but work located in educational studies is emerging.[5] Ellsworth's situated problematizing of the abstract prescriptions of critical pedagogies, which I will address later, is a highly visible example, given its publication in a major educational journal and its targeting for commentary by some of the chief architects of "critical pedagogy" (Giroux, 1988; McLaren, 1988).

In terms of the ways that postmodernism is being inscribed in the discourses of emancipatory education, Britzman's (1991) exploration of a poststructural account of teacher identity brings issues of subjectivity, language and power to bear on teacher education. The postmodern focus on what makes our knowledge both possible and problematic underscores the projects of Cherryholmes (1988), Wexler (1987), and Whitson (1988). Cherryholmes' book, the first in education to have "poststructural" in the title, is especially valuable in its effort to work at an introductory level. Arguing that "much of the unfamiliarity and strangeness of poststructuralism recedes when applied to everyday life" (p. 142), Cherryholmes describes educational reform as one structural invasion after another by looking at Bloom's toxonomy, Tyler's rationale, Schwab's "The Practical 4", the relationship between textbooks, standardized tests and teaching, empirical research, and critical "emancipatory" practice.[6]

First in Britain and now globally, Stuart Hall and the cultural studies groups probe popular culture as a means to understand the formation of subjects in relations of power. A growing body of such work is developing (e.g., Roman, Christian-Smith and Ellsworth, 1988). Schooling is one of many sites looked at in the development of a non-dualistic theory of subjectivity that privileges neither the romanticized individual nor social, linguistic and cultural structures as determinants (Henriques et al., 1984). A more complex understanding of identity and citizenship is constructed via a discursive focus on networks of practices which constitute subjects in shifting, multiple, contradictory sites. Hence, identity is positioned as an effect of subjectification, rather than as a natural right or an essence which the discourses of emancipation can unfurl (Donald, 1985). As such, poststructural perspectives problematize received wisdom in social theory regarding identity, subjectivity and agency. Context and meaning in everyday life are posited as co-constructions, multiple, complex, open and changing, neither pre-given nor explainable by large-scale causal theories. They are, rather,made and re-made across a multiplicity of minor scattered practices. Agency is reconceptualized within the context of a fluid, changeable social setting, in motion via the interaction of a plurality of multiply sited, diffused agents who create "always there and always fragile systems" (Bauman, 1989, p. 51). Walkerdine has amassed a considerable body of work in this area: a deconstruction of Piaget and theories of developmental psychology (1984), the effects on girls of their contradictory positioning in primary classrooms in both dominant/subordinate and power/resistance discourse/practices (1985), and the discursive positioning of females as teachers and students in schools (1981, 1986).

A focus on the reception by students of curricular interventions done in the name of liberation is exemplified in Davies' (1989) work on pre-school student responses to feminist fairy tales. By foregrounding the ambiguities of how texts make meaning, such a focus has great implications for curriculum. Other efforts to rethink curricular issues are Doll (1989), Stephen Ball's (1990) edited collection, *Foucault and Education,* and such work as Bowers (1988), and Murphy (1988), on computers and the move away from text-based pedagogy. Henry Giroux has edited a 1988 special issue of the *Journal of Education,* "Schooling in the Postmodern Age," and co-authored, with Stanley Aronowitz, *Postmodern Education: Politics, Culture and Social Criticism* (1990). Finally, the pages of *Educational Theory, Educational Foundations* and *Qualitative Studies in Education* increasingly attend to the implications of postmodernism for education.

Why doesn't this feel empowering?

To explore the problems and possibilities that this emerging body of work raises for emancipatory education, I turn to Ellsworth's implosion of the canons of critical pedagogy. She places the key discourses in the literature of critical pedagogy in relation to her interpretation of her experience of teaching a university-level anti-racism course, and then examines the discourses within which critical pedagogues are caught up. Problematizing the concepts of empowerment, student voice, dialogue and the term "critical" itself, she asks which interpretations and 'sense making' these discourses facilitate, which do they silence and marginalize, and what interests do they serve?

Rooted in her own experience of the limits of the prescriptions of critical pedagogy, she suggests a movement from "dialogue" to "working together across differences" (p. 106), from a concept of an eventually unified dialogue to the construction of "strategies in context" (p. 109) for dealing with the unsaid and unsayable present within classrooms. There "all voices . . . are not and cannot carry equal legitimacy, safety, and power" given present social structures. As she notes, this problematizes the concept of "voice" so evident in liberatory discourse in education.[7] "Pluralizing the concept as 'voices' implies correction through addition. Such unproblematic pluralizing loses sight of the contradictory and partial nature of all voices" (p. 104):

> Conventional notions of dialogue and democracy assume rationalized, individualized subjects capable of agreeing on universalizable "fundamental moral principles" and "quality of human life" that become self-evident when subjects cease to be self-interested and particularistic about group rights. Yet social agents are not capable of being fully rational and disinterested; and they are subjects split between the conscious and unconscious and among multiple social positionings. (p. 108)

Ellsworth is especially interested in what she calls "the violence of rationalism against its Others" (p. 96). She shifts the focus from the effort to create a dialogical community to an effort toward "sustained encounter with currently oppressive formations and power relations." This encounter "owned up to my own implications in those formations and was capable of changing my own relation to and investments in those formations" (p. 100). Unsettling received definitions, multiplying subject positions, unlearning our own privileges, "profoundly contextual (historical) and interdependent (social)" (p. 115), such a pedagogy has no prescriptions. Moving out of the position of "master of truth and justice" (Foucault, 1977, p. 12), Ellsworth conceptualizes her task as "the challenge of constructing classroom practices that engage with the discursive and material spaces that such a removal opens up" (p. 115).

In terms of exploring the intersection of postmodernism and the emancipatory projects, Ellsworth's essay and reactions to it evoke a keen sense of the complexities of doing praxis-oriented intellectual work in a post-foundational context. By positioning modernist assumptions of truth, objectivity and "correct readings" as ensnared in phallocentric and logocentric rationalities, can postmodernism begin to clear the ground and challenge the plethora of concepts that appear as givens in our debates about the possibilities and limits of emancipatory education? How can such self-reflexivity both render our basic assumptions problematic and provisional and yet still propel us to take a stand?

In raising such issues, postmodernism positions emancipatory reason as vulnerable to interrogation. It traces the collusion of oppositional intellectuals with the very cultural dominants they are opposing via the intersection of liberatory intentions and the "will to power" that underscores the privileged positions of knowing and changing. Hence, the discourses of emancipation are located as much within Foucault's "regimes of truth" as not. Additionally, rather than separating the "true" from the "false", postmodernism destabilizes assumptions of interpretive validity and shifts emphasis to the contexts in which meanings are produced.

Any exploration of the conditions of receptivity within which an intervention such as Ellsworth's is situated grows out of the postmodern assumption that audiences are fragmented and multiple in their production of any meanings that a text might have. Given congested and conflicted semiotic environments and different positionalities in the "difference crisis" that repositions centers and margins in leftist discursive practices, multiple and contradictory readings are to be expected. As an example, I will read McLaren (1988) and Giroux's (1988) readings of Ellsworth's text against time.

McLaren, admittedly ambivalent about postmodernism, frames Ellsworth in a "post-critical" position of

> . . . political inertia and moral cowardice where educators remain frozen in the zone of "dead" practice in which it is assumed that all voices are those which silence or which contain the "other" by a higher act of violence, and all passionate ethical stances are those built upon the edifices of some form of tyranny or another. Unable to speak with any certainty, or with an absolute assurance that his or her pedagogy is untainted by any form of domination, the 'post-critical' educator refuses to speak at all. (pp. 71–72)

According to McLaren, her essay is, furthermore, an attempt to "discredit" selected critical educators via the assumedly inadequate "proof" of her account of her own teaching and the use of "decontextualized quotes" to represent theorists' positions, thereby "setting up critical pedagogy to fail from the very beginning." This "woeful misreading of the tradition she so cavalierly indicts" is full of "distortions, mystifications, and despair" based on her "self-professed lack of pedagogical success" and "her inability to move beyond her own self-doubt", thereby "hold[ing] her voice hostage" and "using theory as a scapegoat for failed practice" (p. 72).

Giroux positions Ellsworth's piece as "a liberal call to harmonize and resolve differences" (p. 170). Conversely, her view of differences as "merely antagonistic" results in "separatism [a]s the only valid political option for any kind of pedagogical and political action . . . a crippling form of political disengagement" (p. 177). An "attempt to delegitimate the work of other critical educators" (p. 177), he positions her as

> . . . claiming rather self-righteously the primacy and singularity of her own ideological reading of what constitutes a political project . . . degrad[ing] the rich complexity of theoretical and pedagogical processes that characterize the diverse discourses in the field of critical pedagogy. In doing so, she succumbs to the familiar academic strategy of dismissing others through the use of strawman tactics and excessive simplifications which undermine not only the strengths of her own work, but also the very nature of social criticism itself. This is "theorizing" as a form of "bad faith," a discourse imbued with the type of careerism that has become all too characteristic of many left academics. (p. 178)

Across McLaren and Giroux's readings, I present two of my own readings of Ellsworth. The first focuses on the textual practices that she uses to locate her intervention. The second reading offers a construction of both how she evokes ways to work with rather than be paralyzed by the loss of Cartesian stability and unity (Weedon, 1987), and what the material consequences of her project might be. Foregrounding the reductiveness of the interpretive act, I propose my readings across these complex, shifting and polyvalent fields as neither "correct" nor final. Like Lanser (1989) in her reading of the political unconscious inscribed in white academic feminist readings of Gilman's "The Yellow Wallpaper," I call on Adrienne Rich in order to frame my readings as evocations to look beyond old critical premises and toward continuing revision:

> How can I fail to love
> > your clarity and fury
> How can I give you
> > all your due
> > > take courage from your courage
> honor your exact
> > > legacy as it is
> recognizing
> > as well
> > > that it is not enough?
> > > (Rich, in Lanser, 1989, p. 436)

In terms of textual performativity in her essay, Ellsworth's move is to clear a space from which to articulate her own difference within a field of competing discourses. Using self-reflexive experience as a basis for knowing, she operates out of what Hutcheon (1989) calls "a very feminist awareness of the value of experience and the importance of its representation in the form of 'life-writing'—however difficult or even falsifying that process might turn out to be" (p. 167). Self-consciously positioning herself as an alternative to the presumed dominant, she sets herself both within and against the political terrain where Enlightenment discourses function and have their effectivity. Inserting herself into a largely unexplicated but privileged field of feminist pedagogy, she does battle with other texts according to her own ground rules, texts which precede and surround the "intertextual arena" that she creates (Collins, 1989). Intensifying differences as a way to clear such a space, she tends to "a counter-cultural Salvation Army beating its moral drum about the wickedness of the dominant" (Collins, p. 122). Her seizing of a moral high ground and her demonizing of critical pedagogy's "repressive myths" perpetuate monolithic categories of dominant/dominated, thereby intensifying the conflictive nature of the semiotic environment. A way out of this might have been to foreground how her construction of herself as a privileged alternative inscribes as well as subverts, in essence deconstructing her own strategies of self-legitimation. Such a move would have added another textual dimension to the Foucauldian suspicion of every operation that seeks to center a subject who is in a position to know, a suspicion that is at the heart of her project.

Shifting from textual practices to her positioning of the realms of pedagogy as a powerful site for liberatory intervention, Ellsworth's work displaces the totalizing desire to establish foundations with a move toward self-critique. This move is premised on her acknowledgment of the profound challenge that poststructural theories of language and subjectivity offer to our capacity to know the "real" via the mediations of critical pedagogy. Primary in this move is her decentering of the "transformative intellectual" (Aronowitz and Giroux, 1985) as the origin of what can be known and done. To multiply the ways in which we can interrupt the relations of dominance requires deconstructing such vanguardism. Britzman's (1989) questions evoke this reflexive process: "What kinds of practices are possible once vulnerability, ambiguity, and doubt are admitted? What kinds of power and authority are taken up and not admitted?" (p. 17). Deconstructing vanguardism means asking ourselves hard questions about how our interventionary moves render people passive, "positioned as potential recipients of predefined services rather than as agents involved in interpreting their needs and shaping their life-conditions" (Fraser, 1989, p. 174).

Rather than attacking the work of others, Ellsworth's project can be read as an example of how deconstruction can serve to problematize critical pedagogy in ways that *resituate* our emancipatory work as opposed to destroy it. Making the workings of pedagogy more apparent, her project demonstrates how deconstructing our own practices can animate and expand our sense of the structure of possibilities in regards to change-oriented practices. Ellsworth also begins to give a feel for the political possibilities of the multiply-sited subject of poststructuralist theory, a subject characterized by heterogeneity, irreducible particularities, and incalculable differences. Her focus on different differences or Derrida's différance, the condition of differences *and* identity (Grosz, 1989, p. 31), is radically other than the separatism of which Giroux accuses her. Rather than speaking to Ellsworth's intervention as "a crippling form of political disengagement" (p. 177), I read his accusation as saying more about his own continued investments in the liberal struggle for equality and identity politics via the mediations of critical pedagogy.

Against the inertia and moral cowardice that McLaren speaks of, I position Ellsworth's intervention as an act of courage in taking on such dominant architects of critical pedagogy. This seems especially so given the vitriol she has evoked, e.g., McLaren's reading of Ellsworth's openness and uncertainties regarding her pedagogical strategies as "a scapegoat for failed practice." Instead of "dead" or "failed" practice, I read her as positioning herself "always in the position of beginning again" (Foucault, 1984, p. 47) within the context of both the foregrounding of limits that is postmodernism and the embodied reflexivity that characterizes feminist pedagogy. In regards to Giroux's pronouncements about the effects of her self-reflexive decentering, I read his statements about "careerism" and the undermining of "the very nature of social criticism itself" (p. 178) as ironically repositioning himself and the other (largely male) architects of critical pedagogy at the center of her discourse. She is reduced to the "Young Turk", the "daughter" out to displace her fathers. Disrupting any notion of a privileged, unproblematic position from which to speak, she seems to have unleashed "the virulence and the power invested in logocentric thought" (Grosz, 1989, p. 34).

McLaren and Giroux worry much about the nihilism assumed to undergird postmodernism's suspicion of claims to truth, the will to knowledge and the primacy of reason. I share Derrida's suspicion of the nihilism charge often levelled against postmodernism as "not just a simplification; it is symptomatic of certain political and instrumental interests" (in Kearney, 1984, p. 124). Ellsworth's project belies the spectre of such nihilism. Like most of the work mentioned in this section, her project demonstrates how postmodernism has much to offer those of us who do our work in the name of emancipation, constructing the material for struggle present in the stuff of our daily lives to which we all have access.

Such a reading of the incursion of postmodernism into the discourses of liberatory education foregrounds my position that there is nothing in postmodernism that makes it intrinsically reactionary. The postmodern moment is an open-ended construction that is contested, incessantly perspectival and multiply-sited. Framing reactions to Ellsworth as disparate, full of unresolvable tensions, and necessarily partial, I have used what Collins (1989) terms "juxtaposition as interrogation" (p. 140) in order to foreground what is at stake in our interpretive practices.

Such deconstructive textual strategy embodies how postmodernism imposes a severe reexamination of the thought of the Enlightenment. It also enacts how it is being inscribed by those who want to critically preserve the emancipatory impulse within a framework sympathetic to postmodernism's resituating of that impulse (Peters, 1989). I now turn to the difficulties of a position that seeks to use postmodernism to both problematize and advance emancipatory pedagogy. My focus in this final section is on the relationship of the self-proclaimed discourses of feminist and critical pedagogies.

Post-critical pedagogies

> It is the early 1970's. Picture a room of male marxists around a table, debating the role of feminism in the struggle, deciding that it is, in fact, important. They go to the door, having decided to invite in the feminists. In the meantime, the feminists break through the window and shit on the table (Paraphrase of a story told by Stuart Hall at the Cultural Studies Now and in the Future Conference, University of Illinois, April, 1990).

The relationship between feminist pedagogy and the largely male inscribed liberation models of critical pedagogy is generally unexamined. Until very recently, what small attention there had been often called for feminism as the practice, Marxism as the theory (e.g., Lather, 1984). Rather than such a "handmaiden" positioning of Marxism and feminism, much more likely today are calls for serious skepticism of and critical attention to those contemporary education narratives that claim to be emancipatory. Luke, for example, positions radical pedagogy as an "exemplary text" of masculinist epistemology (this volume p. 45). Ellsworth (this volume) brings a feminist suspicion to the largely male discourses of "critical pedagogy". And Gore (this volume) follows the counter-canonical Foucauldian tenet that "nothing is innocent", as she places feminist as well as critical pedagogies under suspicion.

Rather than positioning liberatory pedagogies as logical unfoldings toward a desired goal, such work explores their contradictions and contingencies, their tensions, and internal resistances to their own "forward" movement. Foregrounded are the exclusions, limitations and constraints placed on practice, including the inevitable collusion of liberatory pedagogues with that to which they are opposed. In my own work, for example, I have tried to turn the gaze upon myself as well as others, as I look at the sins of imposition that we commit in the name of liberation (Lather, 1988a, 1991).

One reading of Hall's story is that the object of the noxious waste left by feminists is the male movement of inclusion into the site of "critical pedagogy", a site men have constructed to serve themselves. Refusing the invitation, feminists left to create the discourses of feminist pedagogy, thereby contributing to the "difference crisis" which challenges the status of Marxism as the center of leftist discursive practices and forms of cultural struggle that hope to make a difference. Now, spurred on by deconstruction, feminists return to the site of "critical pedagogy" in order to reconfigure the relationship between feminist and masculinist discourses of liberatory pedagogy.

The relationship of feminism and Marxism so pungently evoked in Hall's story is reconfigured in postmodernism as Other to dutiful wife/daughter/handmaid. Kroker and Cook, in my favorite example of this reconfiguration, have termed feminism *"the quantum physics of postmodernism"* (1986, p. 22, original emphasis). I have thought much about what this might mean. I shall only briefly rehearse here a line of argument more fully developed elsewhere (Lather, 1991). This argument, of course, is deeply inscribed with my own investments of privilege and struggle.

Feminism displaces the articulation of postmodernism from the site of the fathers and opens up the possibility of a heteroglot articulation premised on multiplicities and particularities. Full of contestatory and contradictory theories and practices "while still producing solidarity and concerted action" (Smith, 1988, p. 155), feminism is, at this particular historical juncture in western academic culture, "the paradigmatic political discourse of postmodernism" (Kipnis, 1988, p. 60). Such a claim can be advanced on three grounds: feminism's tendency toward practice-based theorizing that interrupts the "theoreticism" of Marxism, its relegation of practice to an object of theory (Reiss, 1988); feminism's disruption of the "death of the subject" postulated by poststructuralism (Hartsock, 1987); and, finally, feminism's long-running practices of self-reflexivity which both render basic assumptions partial and provisional and yet, never the less, act in and on the world, refusing the political surrender, the Nietzschean anger assumed by so many, in some interestingly gendered ways, to be attendant upon "the postmodern turn" (Hassan, 1987; Riley, 1988).

While both feminist and Marxist thought share aspirations to be theories in the service of a politics, my argument for foregrounding feminist thought and practice in the inscribing of postmodernism displaces the hegemony of Marxism over Left discourse/practices. In doing so, it is important to not set up a false and problematic "male" system beneath which is a true "female" essence recuperable via "correct" practices. In developing counter-practices, the multiplicity of minor scattered practices that make up the fabric of our lives, feminism is no more "the angel in the house of critical theory" (Scholes, quoted in Fuss, 1989, p. 80) than are male practices. Feminism is, however, doubly positioned both within and against the discourses of the fathers, inscribed in logocentrism, patriarchal rationality and imperialistic practices even as it struggles to transform such practices. A stunning example is Lanser's (1988) deconstruction of the layers of racial politics in white feminist readings of Gilman's "The Yellow Wallpaper." Positioning herself both within and against the standard feminist readings of the story, Lanser demonstrates how our readings are both transformative and limiting, inevitably fixed and reductive of possibilities. Most impressive to me, she does so in a way that is respectful of the difficulties of such work, that loves the "clarity" and "fury" and "courage" of such work, but pushes against it from within as she demonstrates "that it is not enough" (p. 436). As such, feminism has much to offer in the development of practices of self-interrogation and critique, practice-based theorizing and more situated and embodied discourses about pedagogy.

If deconstruction is about probing the limits of what we cannot think without, deconstructing "critical" is as necessary to critical pedagogies as deconstructing "woman" is to any "forwarding" movement of feminism (Riley, 1988). In the "difference crisis" that repositions centers and margins in leftist discursive practices, what might the sign of "post-critical" mean?

McLaren's fixing of the term as political quietude and "dead" practice (1988, pp. 1–71) is symptomatic of the tenuous relationship of many leftist intellectuals with deconstruction. Much more comfortable with practices of ideology critique, with its binary logic which demonizes some "Other" and positions itself as innocent, many find unnerving the "new canon" (Rajchman, 1985) of deconstructive self-reflexivity: " 'There are no social positions exempt from becoming oppressive to others. . . . any group—any position—can move into the oppressor role' . . . 'everyone is someone else's 'Other' ' " (Minh-ha and Gentile, respectively, quoted in Ellsworth, this volume, p. 114).

Perhaps the need to look beyond old critical premises and toward continuing revision might be more palatable if displayed under the sign of (post)critical—a textual display of the continued centrality of critical reason, as defined at the beginning of this essay. Practices of pedagogy that work against systems of oppression are more, not less, needed in a world marked by growing global maldistribution of power and resources. In translating critical theory into a pedagogical agenda, (post)critical foregrounds movement beyond the sedimented discursive configurations of essentialized, romanticized subjects with authentic needs and real identities, who require generalized emancipation from generalized social oppression via the mediations of liberatory pedagogues capable of exposing the "real" to those caught up in the distorting meaning systems of late capitalism.

Within (post)critical practices of pedagogy, emancipatory space is problematized via deconstruction of the Enlightenment equation of knowing, naming and emancipation. Especially placed under suspicion are the philosophies of presence, which assume the historical role of self-conscious human agency and the vanguard role of critical intellectuals. Addressing the impasse between idealist voluntarism and structuralist fatalism, theories of the irreducibly necessary subject are reinscribed in postmodern discourses via a problematizing of "a metaphysics of human agency . . . an inflated conception of the powers of human reason and will" (Fay, 1987, pp. 26,9). In an especially important move, feminist postmodernism refuses both Althusser's "process without a subject" and poststructuralism's fractured, fragmented subject. Neither the romanticized individual nor the pawn of social determinants, the subject of contemporary feminism is theorized in ways that offer hope for sustained contestation and resistance (for more on identity politics, consciousness and agency, see Lather, 1989). I conclude with some thoughts on the possibilities for post-critical intellectuals.

To abandon crusading rhetoric, and begin to think outside of a framework which sees the "other" as the problem for which they are the solution, is to shift the role of critical intellectuals. This shift entails a move away from positions of either universalizing spokespeople for the disenfranchised, or cultural workers who struggle against the barriers which prevent people from speaking for themselves. This postmodern re-positioning of critical intellectuals has to do with struggling to decolonize the space of academic discourse that is accessed by our privilege, to open that space up in a way that contributes to the production of a politics of difference. Such a politics recognizes the paradox, complexity and complicity at work in our efforts to understand and change the world. Hence, perhaps the subtext of what Foucault (1980) and Lyotard (1984) are saying about the end of the great metanarratives of emancipation and enlightenment is that *who speaks* is more important than *what is said* (Said, 1986, p. 153, original emphasis). Their pronouncements may have more to do with the end of some speaking for others than the end of liberatory struggle.

Conclusion

Rather than epistemologically constituted domains of norms, I have positioned both feminist and critical pedagogies as historically produced and situated sites from which to ask questions about the relationship of feminism and marxism in a post-foundational context. From my own marked position of feminism, I have tried to construct a non-agonistic narrative which proceeds otherwise than by thinking via oppositions (de Lauretis, 1989). In a place where there is no innocent discourse of liberation, my hope has been to use both our internal contradictions and our differences across one another to refigure community, to include ways of disagreeing productively among ourselves, as we struggle to use postmodernism to both problematize and advance emancipatory pedagogy.

Notes

This paper is reprinted with permission from James Nicholas Publishers and originally appeared in *Education and Society, 9*(2), 1991, pp. 100–111, and in Peter McLaren (Ed.), *Postmodernity and Pedagogy*, James Nicholas Publishers, Albert Park, Australia, in press.

1. While impossible to freeze conceptually, deconstruction can be broken down into three steps: 1) identify the binaries, the oppositions that structure an argument; 2) reverse/displace the dependent term from its negative position to a place that locates it as the very condition of the positive term; and 3) create a more fluid and less coercive conceptual organization of terms which transcends a binary logic by simultaneously being both and neither of the binary terms (Grosz, 1989, p. xv).

    This somewhat linear definition is deliberately placed in the endnotes in order to displace the desire to domesticate deconstruction as it moves across the many sites of its occurrence, e.g., the academy, architecture, and the arts.

2. While suspicious of the desire for definitions which analytically "fix" complex, contradictory and relational constructs, I generally use the term *postmodern* to mean the shift in material conditions of advanced monopoly capitalism brought on by the micro-electronic revolution in information

technology, the growth of multinational capitalism and the global uprising of the marginalized. This conjunction includes movements in art, architecture, and the practices of everyday life. I generally use *poststructural* to mean the working out of cultural theory within that context, but I also sometimes use the terms interchangeably. For a more extensive wrestling with these definitions, see Lather, 1991.

3. "Oppositional" is a problematic term on many levels, subscribing as it does to a binary logic of opposites. Nancy Fraser, however, has come up with a relational definition rather than a definition statically grounded in binaries. She defines oppositional as "forms of needs talk, which arise when needs are politicized 'from below' " (1989, p. 171).

   Another problematic term in this sentence is "postmodernisms of resistance". Calinescu (1987) warns that the tendency to construct "a bad reactionary" postmodernism" and "a good, resistant, anticapitalist variety" reproduces the very binaries to which postmodernism is purportedly other than (p. 292).

4. The centrality of pedagogy in postmodern discursive practices can be explored by contrasting the title of a 1987 conference, "Postmodernism: Text, Politics, Instruction" (sponsored by the University of Kansas and the International Association for Philosophy and Literature), with the complete lack of attention to issues of teaching and learning in the conference program. A recent "turn to pedagogy" in cultural studies is evident in such work as Henricksen and Morgan (1990), Morton and Zavarzadeh (1991), and a special issue of *Strategies: A Journal of Theory, Culture and Politics* on "Pedagogical Theories/Educational Practices" (2, 1989).

5. For examples of poststructuralist discourse on pedagogy, in addition to note #4, from literary criticism and cultural studies: Atkins and Johnson, 1985; Zavarzadeh and Morton, 1986–87; Naidus, 1987; Nelson, 1986. From educational studies: Orner and Brennan, 1989; Giroux, 1988; McLaren, 1988; Maher and Tetreault, 1989; Brodkey, 1987; Lewis, 1990; Miller, 1990; Berlak, 1990; Bromley, 1989; Lather, 1990.

6. Cherryholmes' book ignores what Newton, 1988, terms "the mother roots" of poststructuralism. For a review, see Lather, 1988b.

7. The concept of "voice" is also problematized in Morton and Zavarzadeh, 1988–89 and, especially, London, 1990, who draws on feminist theory, cultural criticism, cultural ethnography and narrative theory to challenge traditional assumptions about voice as a reliable marker of individuality, originality and self-identity.

References

Aronowitz, Stanley and Giroux, Henry (1985) Radical education and transformative intellectuals. *Canadian Journal of Political and Social Theory, 9*(3), 48–63.

Aronowitz, Stanley and Giroux, Henry (1990) *Postmodern education: Politics, culture and social criticism*. Minneapolis: University of Minnesota Press.

Atkins, G. Douglas and Johnson, Michael L. (1985) *Writing and reading differently: Deconstruction and the teaching of composition and literature*. Lawrence, Kansas: University of Kansas Press.

Ball, Stephen (Ed.) (1990) *Foucault and education*. London: Routledge.

Bauman, Zygmunt (1989) Sociological responses to post-modernity. *Thesis Eleven, 23*, 35–63.

Berlak, Ann (April, 1990) Experiencing teaching: Viewing and re-viewing education 429. Paper presented at the annual meeting of the American Educational Research Association, Boston.

Bowers, C. A. (1988) *The cultural dimensions of educational computing: Understanding the non-neutrality of technology*. New York: Teacher's College Press.

Britzman, Deborah (Feb., 1989) The terrible problem of "knowing thyself": Toward a poststructural account of teacher identity. Paper presented at the Ethnography and Education Research Forum, University of PA.

Britzman, Deborah (1991) *Practice makes practice: A critical study of learning to teach.* Albany: State University of New York Press.

Brodkey, Linda (1987) Postmodern pedagogy for progressive educators: An essay review. *Journal of Education, 196*(3), 138–143.

Bromley, Hank (1989) Identity politics and critical pedagogy. *Educational Theory, 39*(3), 207–223.

Calinescu, Matei (1987) *Five faces of modernity: Modernism, avant-garde, decadence, kitsch and postmodernism.* Durham, N.C.: Duke University Press.

Caputo, John (1987) *Radical hermeneutics: Repetition, deconstruction, and the hermeneutic project.* Bloomington, Indiana: University of Indiana Press.

Cherryholmes, Cleo (1988) *Power and criticism: Poststructural investigations in education.* New York: Teacher's College Press.

Collins, Jim (1989) *Uncommon cultures: Popular culture and post-modernism.* New York: Routledge.

Davies, Bronwyn (1989) *Frogs and snails and feminist tales.* Sydney: George Allen and Unwin.

DeCurtis, Anthony (March 23, 1989) Postmodern romance: What the kids who really read are really reading. *Rolling Stone, 146,* 5–6.

de Lauretis, Teresa (1989) The essence of the triangle or, taking the risk of essentialism seriously: Feminist theory in Italy, the U.S., and Britain. *differences, 1*(2), 3–37.

Doll, William E. Jr. (1989) Foundations for a post-modern curriculum. *Journal of Curriculum Studies, 21*(3), 243–253.

Donald, James (1985) Beacons of the future: Schooling, subjection and subjectification. In Veronica Beechey and James Donald (Eds.), *Subjectivity and Social Relations.* Milton Keynes: Open University Press, 214–249.

Fay, Brian (1987) *Critical social science.* Ithaca, N.Y.: Cornell University Press.

Foucault, Michel (1977) The political function of the intellectual. *Radical Philosophy, 17,* 12–14.

Foucault, Michel (1980) *Power/knowledge: Selected interviews and other writings, 1972–1977.* Colin Gordon (Ed.) and Gordon et al. (Trans.). New York: Pantheon.

Foucault, Michel (1984) What is enlightenment? In Paul Rabinow (Ed.) *The Foucault Reader.* New York: Pantheon, 32–50.

Fraser, Nancy (1987) What's critical about critical theory? The case of Habermas and gender. In Seyla Benhabib and D. Cornell (Eds.) *Feminism as critique.* Minneapolis: University of Minnesota Press, 31–55.

Fraser, Nancy (1989) *Unruly practices: Power, discourse and gender in contemporary social theory.* Minneapolis: University of Minnesota Press.

Fuss, Diana (1989) Reading like a feminist. *differences, 1*(2), 7–92.

Giroux, Henry (1988) Border pedagogy in the age of postmodernism. *Journal of Education, 170*(3), 162–181.

Gore, Jennifer (April, 1990) The struggle for pedagogies: Critical and feminist discourses as "regimes of truth". Paper presented at the annual meeting of the American Educational Research Association, Boston.

Grosz, Elizabeth (1989) *Sexual subversions: Three French feminists.* Sydney: Allen and Unwin.

Habermas, Jurgen (1987) *The philosophical discourse of modernism.* Cambridge: Mass., M.I.T. Press.

Harasym, Sarah (1988) Practical politics of the open end: An interview with Gayatri Spivak. *Canadian Journal of Political and Social Theory, 12*(1–2), 51–69.

Haraway, Donna (1988) Situated knowledges: The science question in feminism and the privilege of partial perspective. *Feminist Studies, 14*(3), 575–599.

Hartsock, Nancy (1987) Rethinking modernism: minority vs. majority theories. *Cultural Critique, 7*, 187–206.

Hassan, Ihab (1987) *The postmodern turn: Essays in postmodern theory and culture.* Columbus, Ohio: The Ohio State University Press.

Henricksen, Bruce and Morgan, Thais (Eds.) (1990) *Reorientations: Critical theories and pedagogies.* Urbana: University of Illinois Press.

Henriques, Julian, Holloway, Wendy, Unwin, Cathy, Venn, Couze, and Walkerdine, Valerie (Eds.) (1984) *Changing the subject: Psychology, social regulation and subjectivity.* London: Methuen.

Hutcheon, Linda (1988) A postmodern problematics. In Robert Merrill (Ed.), *Ethics/Aesthetics: Postmodern positions.* Washington, D.C.: Maisonneuve Press, 1–10.

Hutcheon, Linda (1989) *The politics of postmodernism.* London: Routledge.

Johnson, Barbara (1987) *A world of difference.* Baltimore: Johns Hopkins University Press.

Kearney, Richard (1984) *Dialogues with contemporary continental thinkers: The phenomenological heritage.* Manchester: Manchester University Press.

Kipnis, Laura (1988) Feminism: The political conscience of postmodernism? In Andrew Ross (Ed.), *Universal abandon: The politics of postmodernism.* Minneapolis, University of Minnesota Press, 149–166.

Kroker, Arthur and Cook, David (1986) *The postmodern scene: Excremental culture and hyperaesthetics.* New York: St. Martin's Press.

Lather, Patti (1984) Critical theory, curricular transformation and feminist mainstreaming. *Journal of Education, 66*(1), 49–62.

Lather, Patti (1988a) Feminist perspectives on empowering research methodologies. *Women's Studies International Forum, 11*(6), 569–581.

Lather, Patti (1988b) Pretext: Unmasking the politics of educational thought and practice. Review of *Power and criticism: Poststructural investigations in education* by Cleo Cherryholmes, *Journal of Curriculum Theorizing, 8*(4), 127–134.

Lather, Patti (1989) Postmodernism and the politics of enlightenment. *Educational Foundations, 3*(3), 7–28.

Lather, Patti (April, 1990) Staying dumb? Student resistance to liberatory curriculum. Paper presented at the annual meeting of the American Educational Research Association, Boston.

Lather, Patti (1991) *Getting smart: Feminist research and pedagogy with/in the postmodern.* New York: Routledge.

Lanser, Susan S. (1989) Feminist criticism, "The Yellow Wallpaper," and the politics of color in America. *Feminist Studies, 15*(3), 415–441.

Lewis, Magda (April, 1990) Framing: Women and silence: Disrupting the hierarchy of discursive practices. Paper presented at the annual meeting of the American Educational Research Association, Boston.

London, Bette (1990) *The appropriated voice: Narrative authority in Conrad, Forster, and Woolf.* Ann Arbor: University of Michigan Press.

Lusted, David (1986) Why pedagogy? *Screen, 27*(5), 2–14.

Lyotard, Jean-Francois (1984) *The postmodern conditions: A report on knowledge.* Translated by Geoff Bennington and Brian Massumi. Minneapolis: University of Minnesota Press.

Maher, Frinde and Tetreault, Mary Kay (March, 1989) Feminist teaching: Issues of mastery, voice, authority and positionality. Paper presented at the annual meeting of the American Educational Research Association, San Francisco.

Marcus, George and Fischer, Richard (1986) *Anthropology as cultural critique.* Chicago: University of Chicago Press.

McLaren, Peter (1988) Schooling the postmodern body: Critical pedagogy and the politics of enflesh-ment. *Journal of Education, 170*(3), 53–83.

Miller, Janet (1990) *Creating spaces and finding voices: Teachers collaborating for empowerment.* New York: State University of New York Press.

Morton, Donald and Zavarzadeh, Mas'ud (1988–89) The cultural politics of the fiction workshop. *Cultural Critique, 11,* 155–173.

Morton, Donald and Zavarzadeh, Mas'ud (Eds.) (1991) *Texts for Change: Theory/Pedagogy/Politics.* Urbana: University of Illinois Press.

Murphy, John W. (1988) Computerization, postmodern epistemology, and reading in the postmodern era, *Educational Theory, 38*(2), 175–182.

Naidus, Beverly (1987) The artist/teacher as decoder and catalyst. *Radical Teacher* (Sept.), 17–20.

Nelson, Cary (Ed.) (1986) *Theory in the classroom.* Urbana: University of Illinois Press.

Newton, Judith (1988) History as usual? Feminism as the "new historicism". *Cultural Critique, 9,* 87–121.

Orner, Mimi and Brennan, Marie (March, 1989) Producing collectively: Power, identity and teaching. Paper presented at the annual meeting of the American Educational Research Association, San Francisco.

Peters, Michael (1989) Techno-science, rationality, and the university: Lyotard on the "postmodern condition". *Educational Theory, 39*(2), 93–105.

Poster, Marc (1989) *Critical theory and poststructuralism: In search of a context.* Ithaca: Cornell University Press.

Rajchman, John (1985) *Michel Foucault: The freedom of philosophy.* New York: Columbia University Press.

Reiss, Timothy J. (1988) *The uncertainty of analysis: Problems of truth, meaning and culture.* Ithaca: Cornell University Press.

Riley, Denise (1988) *"Am I that name?" Feminism and the category of 'women' in history.* Minneapo-lis: University of Minnesota Press.

Roman, Leslie, Christian-Smith, Linda and Ellsworth, Elizabeth (Eds.) (1988) *Becoming feminine: The politics of popular culture.* London: The Falmer Press.

Said, Edward (1986) Orientalism reconsidered. In Francis Barker, Peter Hulme, Margaret Iversen, and Diana Loxley (Eds.), *Literature, politics and theory.* London: Methuen, 210–229.

Schrift, Alan D. (1990) The becoming-postmodern of philosophy. In Gary Shapiro (Ed.), *After the future: Postmodern times and places.* Albany: State University of New York Press, 99–114.

Smith, Paul (1988) *Discerning the subject.* Minneapolis: University of Minnesota Press.

Solomon-Godeau, Abigail (1988) Living with contradictions: Critical practices in the age of supply-side aesthetics. In Andrew Ross (Ed.), *Universal abandon: The politics of postmodernism.* Min-neapolis: University of Minnesota Press, 191–213.

Spivak, Gayatri, with Rooney, Ellen (1989) In a word. Interview. *differences, 1*(2), 124–156.

Ulmer, Gregory (1985) *Applied grammatology: Post(e)-pedagogy from Jacques Derrida to Joseph Beuys.* Baltimore: Johns Hopkins University Press.

Walkerdine, Valerie (1981) Sex, power and pedagogy. *Screen Education, 38,* 14–24.

Walkerdine, Valerie (1984) Developmental psychology and child-centered pedagogy. In Julian Hen-riques, W. Holloway, C. Unwin, C. Venn and V. Walkerdine (Eds.), *Changing the subject.* Lon-don: Methuen, 153–202.

Walkerdine, Valerie (1985) On the regulation of speaking and science: sexuality, class and gender in contemporary schooling. In Carolyn Steedman, C. Urwin and V. Walkerdine (Eds.), *Language, gender and childhood*. London: Routledge and Kegan Paul, 203–242.

Walkerdine, Valerie (1986) Post-structuralist theory and everyday social practices: The family and the school. In Sue Wilkinson (Ed.), *Feminist Social Psychology: Developing theory and practice*. Milton Keynes: Open University Press, 57–76.

Weedon, Chris (1987) *Feminist practice and poststructuralist theory*. Oxford: Basil Blackwell.

West, Cornel (1987) Postmodernism and black America. *Zeta Magazine, 1*(6), 27–29.

Wexler, Philip (1987) *Social analysis of education: After the new Sociology*. New York: Routledge and Kegan Paul.

Whitson, Tony (1988) The politics of "non-political" curriculum: Heteroglossia and the discourse of "choice" and "effectiveness." In William Pinar (Ed.), *Contemporary Curriculum Discourses*. Scottsdale, Arizona: Gorsuch Scarisbrick, 279–330.

Zavarzadeh, Mas'ud and Morton, Donald (1986–87) Theory pedagogy politics: The crisis of "the subject" in the humanities. *Boundary 2, 15* (1–2).

8

Feminist Pedagogy and Emancipatory Possibilities

Jane Kenway and Helen Modra

Introduction

> . . . from a feminist perspective, the discourse of radical pedagogy constructs
> a masculinist subject which renders its emancipatory agenda for "gender" theo-
> retically and practically ineffective . . .

These words from Carmen Luke (this volume) reflect the dissatisfaction of many
feminist educators with the ways in which theorists of radical/critical pedagogy
address the issue of gender. As feminists constantly point out, it is extremely
common for such theorists to treat gender with "ominous politeness" (Rowbotham, 1980), "commatizing" it (O'Brien, 1984) or making occasional coop-
tive and burying reference to the most upmarket feminist theorists/researchers.
However, it is uncommon for them to either examine the gendered assumptions
embodied deeply and subtly in their theoretical premises or to grasp the full significance of the presence and power of gender in educational settings. Such theorists seem to believe that gentle genuflections, alone, demonstrate their gender-
sensitivity and make respectable their politics, while at the same time relieving
them of the scholarly responsibility for a careful and proper engagement with the
full range and complexity of feminist literature on and for education. As critical
pedagogy theorists claim that they are quintessentially engaged in democratizing
the education process, this failure to engage with feminism casts considerable
doubt on their authenticity. Nonetheless, we don't intend, in this paper, to con-
centrate our critical gaze on what the men have and have not done. This exercise
has been conducted more than adequately in this collection (see Luke, & Gore
this volume) and elsewhere (see Leck, 1987; O'Brien, 1984; Lather, 1984). And
besides, why should feminists constantly offer men this service? Rather, our purpose is to offer the naive spectator a general sense of the ways in which feminists
have addressed matters of pedagogy. In offering an account of this literature we
are not suggesting for a moment that it is free from difficulties, tensions and
dilemmas. Far from it. Let it be understood from the outset that there are aspects
of the field with which we are in quite profound disagreement. But developing

138

such disagreement in a sustained way is not the purpose of this particular exercise, which is to map the contours and concerns of at least some of the literature and to give a sense of its history. Nonetheless, in so doing we will allude to those issues which, to us, seem particularly problematic and which require further inquiry and analysis. Our ultimate concern, of course, is to contribute to the potential of feminist pedagogy as a "discourse of possibility", that is, to make our dreams practical and possible. The fields we have chosen to look at are the gender and schooling literature and Women's Studies. While both share an interest in changing education in order to benefit females, they differ quite dramatically in their pedagogical concerns.

Feminism and pedagogy

Let us begin by clarifying what we mean by our two central terms, feminism and pedagogy. Feminism is premised on the recognition that gender is a phenomenon which helps to shape our society. Feminists believe that women are located unequally in the social formation, often devalued, exploited and oppressed. Education systems, the knowledge which they offer and the practices which constitute them, are seen to be complicit in this. Feminists share a commitment to a form of politics directed towards ending the social arrangements which lead women to be "other than", less than, put down, and put upon. Feminism, then, is a social theory and a social movement, but it is also a personal political practice. For feminist educators, feminism is a primary lens through which the world is interpreted and acted upon. Of course, feminism is not a monolithic discourse. There are, in fact, many feminisms informed by various social theories and research traditions and motivated by somewhat different social, political and educational projects, each experiencing their own theoretical and practical problems (see Tong, 1990). While feminism is certainly driven by a vision of a world which might be otherwise, the vision depends on the type of feminism which is being espoused. For instance, while liberal feminists might aspire to a world in which women have equal access to current social benefits and so develop an educational agenda premised on notions of "access and success" and equality with men, socialist feminists are concerned about the exploitative practices by which such benefits are produced and their effects for women as gendered and classed social beings. Thus their educational project is directed towards ending education's complicity in reproducing the complex, intersecting social relationships which are class and gender. Sometimes race and ethnicity are also encompassed in their agenda. Radical feminism is more separatist in its imaginings. It associates much social injustice and oppression with masculinity, and identifies and promotes the positive dimensions of women's "nature" and experience—the nurturant, integrative, empathic, passionate and the imaginative. Radical feminists believe that women's growth is best encouraged within a distinctively women's educational culture—premised on such characteristics. Other feminists offer other visions.

In contrast, the term "pedagogy" is "desperately undertheorised" (Lusted, 1986, p. 3). It is a term little used by teachers and much used by academics talking about the components of the act of classroom teaching. Often such discussion rests upon an instrumental, transmission model of teaching which fails to make problematic either the learner, teacher or knowledge, or the relationship between them. Certainly the common conception of pedagogy is blind to the ways in which broader social relationships are embodied in the teaching/learning process. It is this blindness which has prompted the notions of critical, radical and feminist pedagogy—or liberatory pedagogy, which subsumes them all. As it is not appropriate that we develop a theoretical account of pedagogy here we will draw from Lusted (1986) who argues that the concept must be concerned with what is taught, how it is taught and how it is learned and, more broadly, with the nature of knowledge and learning. Lusted argues for a understanding of pedagogy which recognizes that knowledge is produced, negotiated, transformed and realized in the *interaction* between the teacher, the learner, and the knowledge itself. Such an understanding is a useful starting point for a discussion of feminist pedagogy, as it encompasses many dimensions of the teaching/learning process about which feminists have expressed concern. Further, we agree with Roger Simon that to speak adequately about teaching and learning, "what is required is a discourse about practice that references not only what we as educators might actually do; but as well, the social visions such practices would support" (Simon, 1988, p. 2). Like him, we see that pedagogy is a term that can bear, better than can "teaching", the burdens of possibility as well as of critique.

Gender and schooling

One body of literature from which we might develop a notion of feminist pedagogy is that on gender and school education, more particularly, that on the schooling of girls. This literature is produced by feminist academics (most of whom are located in Faculties of Education), feminist teachers, curriculum developers located in educational bureaucracies, and policy makers. Many varieties of feminism inform the work of this disparate group, and although liberal feminism has been the dominant tendency, the recent trend has been more towards a rather unselfconscious and uncritical eclecticism. Although the gender and schooling literature rarely uses the term "feminist pedagogy", if one accepts Lusted's definition, and if one considers this literature as a whole, then feminist pedagogy is largely what it is about. While it may emphasize some aspects more than others, and although it does not theorize the interactions between text, teacher and learner as much as it might, it is, nonetheless, concerned with all the dimensions of the teaching/learning process, the curriculum as text and the curriculum in use as teacher, text and students interact to produce both intended and unintended learnings.

In discussing the gender and schooling literature, it is important to note at the outset that its pedagogical project has a number of different dimensions which include, but go beyond, what happens to students—and girls in particular—in classrooms. Its broadest purpose is to educate the educational community (including parents). It does this in three primary ways: first, by documenting and demonstrating the inequitable distribution of educational benefits between girls and boys, and second, by exploring and explaining the various complex and subtle ways in which the different dimensions of schooling are caught up in producing and so reproducing both gender differences and gender inequalities. A third dimension involves the development and "dissemination" of alternative forms of nondiscriminatory and empowering pedagogy, which may challenge schooling's complicity in reproducing gendered inequality. Because the pedagogical movement involves the recognition of inequitable difference, the act of critique and the construction of alternatives, we will allude to each, where possible, in the following discussion of feminist pedagogy and schooling. Let us now, then, consider what gender workers in and for schools have to say on the text, the teacher and the learner and the interaction between them.

The curriculum

Dominating discussion on gender and schooling is the curriculum, often conceived as syllabus, course guide, or framework with associated textbooks. Feminists' ideology critique of all school subjects at all school levels has exposed this curriculum as heavily gender-inflected, either misrecognizing and misrepresenting, or neglecting and denying—but either way, undervaluing—the social contributions and cultural experiences of girls and women generally and working-class and minority racial and ethnic women in particular.

While much of this critique has focused on language and on the biased and selective nature of the foci and emphases of content and teaching/learning activities, there is a growing body of work which highlights the academic and social values upon which school curricula are premised. Feminists have demonstrated that the knowledge hierarchies of the school curriculum as a whole, its preference for the male-identified "hard" academic subjects and its denigration of the female-identified "soft" subjects, favor the concerns and interests of males. To be more precise, the school subjects which emphasize the rational, and impersonal, autonomy, predictability and control are much more highly valued than those associated with the artistic and emotional, the intersubjective and interpersonal or those associated with physicality. Bourgeois males are seen to identify most strongly with the first set of values which, it is often argued, cause girls and other class groupings of males to "select out" of such courses.

This set of recognitions has led feminist educators to develop a number of different, alternative curricula. These have been categorized in various ways, depending on the extent to which they are informed by liberal feminist or other, more radical, feminist values. The titles "Non-sexist", "Equal Opportunity", and "Girl-Friendly", have been applied to the former, more prominent, curricula and "Antisexist", "Feminist" and "Girl-Centered" to the latter. The former set is concerned, primarily, with such "quantifiable aspects of access" (Suggett, 1987, p. 70) as participation rates in nontraditional subjects and careers and resource distribution. The latter set is more concerned about the qualitative questions "Access to what?" "What is worthwhile and useful knowledge for girls?" However, as time proceeds, as our knowledge of the benefits and problems of each approach develops and critical borrowing and careless eclecticism occurs, and as new feminisms based on fundamentally different sets of assumptions emerge (see Weedon, 1987), the usefulness of such categorizations dimishes. Broadly, though, it can be said that the emergent feminist pedagogical imperative in this regard has been directed towards curricular revision, in order that all school subjects become at least gender-inclusive and at best gender-expansive. The argument is that curricula should include and value the range of experiences of girls and women, while at the same time recognizing that the definitions of femininity and masculinity which are formed and promoted in school curricula should encompass a wide range of possibilities which make girls and boys not only "equally human" (Blackburn, 1982) but equally free in the public and the private sphere. To this end, as Suggett (1987) points out, curriculum developers have designed new courses (e.g., Women's Studies, Family and Work Studies), attached new units to current courses, and totally redesigned existing courses. As Suggett further explains, each approach has its own difficulties, dilemmas and rewards.

There are potential contradictions between an inclusive and expansive feminist pedagogy. While some curriculum theorists make regular mention of these (e.g., Yates, 1985), curriculum developers and policy makers have yet to address the issue (Schools Commission, 1987) and, as the tensions work themselves out at the "chalk face", the implied message remains that girls should be more like boys if they wish to get on. Undoubtedly the strongest emphasis in curriculum has been on encouraging girls' and young women's access to and success in the higher status male knowledge domains of Math, Science and Technology, in order that their post-school opportunities for work, and thus for financial autonomy, may be enhanced. This has led, in some cases, to revisions in content, process and assessment. For example, in order that girls' values, interests, and "cognitive style" may be accommodated in Science, emphasis has been placed on small group learning, discussion, cooperative problem-solving, girls' interests and social contextualization (Harding, 1985a, b).

It is worth noting, however, that the emphasis on changing the educational processes of mainstream curricula in the interests of girls is a reasonably recent pedagogical development, which was preceded by a dominant and much more superficial emphasis on the elimination of sex stereotyping and gender bias in content. The main problem with this emphasis on content was that it continued to position girls as passive recipients of others' knowledge, thus still denying them a sense of agency. Further, it posited a rather naive correspondence between the text (curriculum), its delivery by the teacher and its reception by the student. Feminist post-structuralist theory has highlighted both the ambiguous ways in which texts make meaning and the highly subjective ways in which people "read". As teacher, student and knowledge interact, knowledge is produced, negotiated and transformed. Thus the best-intentioned author of non- or anti-sexist material has no guarantee that it will be read as intended. This point is vividly demonstrated in Bronwyn Davies' discussion of pre-school students' responses to feminist fairy stories (1987). Nonetheless, the enthusiasm for "process" finds its inspiration not in post-structuralism but in three other, separate bodies of thinking: feminist object relations theory (which we will return to), negotiated curriculum theory (Boomer, 1982) and critical pedagogy. Although the former is probably the most popular source, the latter are important because they represent pedagogical modes informed by radical and socialist feminism and thus, in our view, embody social visions with greater emancipatory potential.

The negotiated curriculum rests on the premise that when students are the passive recipients of knowledge which is selected by others, of teachers' assessments (premised on notions of competition for all and failure for many) and of external and remote administrative decisions, they cannot help but have a limited sense of their capacity to effect change. Involving students, individually and collectively, in the negotiation of such matters, it is believed, leads them to recognize their individual and collective capacity to act upon the world. As negotiation skills are associated with women's culture, negotiation is seen to feminise the curriculum process (Fowler, 1984). Through the negotiated curriculum, girls' self-worth is tied to their sense of empowerment and gender esteem and gender solidarity are both encouraged (Jonas, 1990). Negotiating the curriculum is also seen as one way of addressing the educational issue associated with class, ethnic and racial cultural *differences* which exist amongst girls and which have a considerable impact upon the ways in which they relate to the codes of the dominant culture which are embodied in the hegemonic curriculum. Some writers might argue that a curriculum which recognizes the commonalities and the differences amongst girls faces what Yates (forthcoming) calls "the essentialist/pluralist dilemma". Can the notion of a "women's culture" be applied to all groups of girls? Now that we have recognized difference, must we theorize anew what females have in common? Certainly there is no longer any place in feminist pedagogy for either/or thinking. What we need instead, as Lyn Yates (forthcoming) argues and demonstrates, is "sensitive, differentiated understanding".

Critical pedagogy is also concerned about the disempowering effects upon students of the conventional "top-down" power structures of schools and classrooms. It too asserts that cultural differences and their associated power relations must be acknowledged and critically addressed in schooling. Further, from this point of view, access to and control over the genres of power by disempowered groups is considered an important beginning to developing the competencies which enable such students to become critically resistant readers and writers of their social, cultural and educational environments. The emphasis is on powerfully learning powerful knowledge. To this end, students are taught to appreciate the ways in which knowledge is "historically, culturally and economically located", and "to value the role of knowledge in social action" (Suggett, 1987, p. 72).

When such thinking is applied to the education of girls, it implies the essential recognition that gender intersects with other structured social inequalities in ways which have significance for students' attachment to and achievement in curricula which are steeped in Anglo-Saxon, middle class, male values, and which thus deny multiple aspects of their home and community culture (see Kenway & Willis, 1990). However, this recognition, and the moral injunction to make school curricula all-inclusive rather than only gender-inclusive, is only the beginning to the vastly more difficult "cutting edge" task of working out what a truly inclusive curriculum looks like. This task has really only just begun, as some feminist educators seek to interrupt the dominant tendency among curriculum developers to universally apply the experiences, understandings and ambitions of white, middle-class girlhood and so to explore the curriculum implications of the commonalities and differences amongst their female students. In a sense, however, the inclusive curriculum is risky business for girls. Without some very sophisticated thinking, which includes some elements of essentialism, it threatens to become pallid and pluralist, gesturing weakly to all and serving nobody well (see further Yates, forthcoming).

The learner

When feminist school teachers and researchers make the learner problematic they, again, draw primarily from liberal feminist thinking which, in turn, draws its theories of female identity from certain "self theories" associated with social psychology and from sex role socialisation theory. The focus is primarily on girls. From this sort of position, female students are painted as lacking the ingredients which are essential to wide-ranging school success. They are seen to have low self-esteem and to take too few risks, preferring intellectual and social conformity and passivity. Such behavior is explained by those theories of socialization which emphasize the sex-stereotyping and modelling which abounds in families, schools and society, and through which girls are said to learn sex-typed behaviours. Such stereotyping, it is argued, teaches girls that only certain school subjects and choices are suited to their abilities, interests and futures. Within this formulation, feminist pedagogy has two interrelated tasks. One is to alter those aspects of the curriculum and school and classroom culture which "socialize girls" in sex-typed ways, the second is to change what is "wrong" in girls' heads by "counter-conditioning", i.e., building their self-esteem, teaching them assertiveness, and encouraging them out of gender-constrained choices through appropriate counselling.

Feminist pedagogy, from this position, sometimes tends to make the learner more problematic than the curriculum. Further, it portrays the girl as a passive victim of social forces, rather than an agent operating within constrained circumstances, and constantly threatens to slip into a deficit model of girlhood. However, associated with this way of thinking are attempts to make such male-identified subjects as Math, Science and Technology "girl friendly" (Whyte et al., 1985). But here two main dangers exist. These arise from the problem of identifying exactly what "girl friendly" means beyond, of course, the elimination of the more blatant form of sexism.

In this regard, a number of feminist educators have eagerly taken on board the notion that there are broad differences in "cognitive style", moral reasoning and ways of learning and knowing between males and females. Drawing heavily and somewhat uncritically from Harding (1985b) and Gilligan (1982) who in turn draw from such feminist object relations theorists as Chodorow (1978), the argument is put that while males have a psychic preference for autonomy, separation, certainty, control and abstraction, females are differently connected to the world through their relational and contextual preferences and their superior capacity to offer empathy and tolerate ambiguity. This type of thinking lies behind the belief that "girl friendly" pedagogy should emphasize interactive, cooperative, intuitive and holistic ways of learning. In certain senses, this argument sits comfortably with the belief of many humanist and progressive teachers that all students benefit from modes of pedagogy which harness affect and encourage group learning. However, from a feminist point of view, it has some problems. Too often in the feminist pedagogy which arises thus, definitions of girls' ways of learning and of girls' interests and motivations are developed which tap right back into the gender stereotypes from which escape is sought. As Joan Cocks (1984) argues, the line between radical feminists' arguments about women's culture and "new conservative feminism" is very fine indeed. Further, the search for "girl friendly" pedagogy often boils down to trying to identify the essential nature of girlhood.

As we implied earlier, this sort of essentialism is being challenged from a number of different directions, as matters of class, ethnicity and race become the concern of feminist teachers and researchers who increasingly recognize that students' identities cannot be reduced to one particular structural factor (see Weiner, 1988). Such recognitions have historically drawn their inspiration from socialist feminism. For instance, a number of ethnographic studies have explored the gendered dimensions of particular class cultures, their adaptations by girls and young women, and the "result" when girl culture and school culture come together. From this point of view, working-class girls are no longer depicted as schools' failures. Rather, what becomes clear is how schools have failed them by not developing forms of pedagogy which take into account the girls' "collective experiences, problems and strengths, in a framework which recognises the social and political context in which they live" (Wyn, 1990, p. 24). Weiler's study of *Women Teaching for Change: Gender, Class and Power* (1988) vividly demonstrates the difficulties which confront school teachers who seek to address the educationally compounding effects of social difference through all inclusive curricula.

Recently, the theoretical premises associated with post-structuralism, and in particular with Lacan and Foucault, have led a small number of academic feminists to move through and beyond this conceptualization of the learner (see Weedon, 1987). According to this view, students' identities are not rational and unitary; they are seen to be shifting and fragmented, multiple and contradictory, displaced and positioned as students are across the various discourses which historically and currently constitute their lives in and out of school. These may include the discourses of the youth culture industry (fashion, music, popular literature i.e., magazines, books, T.V., films for girls), which "teach" girls how to achieve pleasure and power and satisfaction through consumption, fantasy and romance. Alternatively, such discourses may include those associated with the "training" of school teachers, Piagetian psychology for instance (see Walkerdine, 1984). Such a notion is well exemplified in the work of Valerie Walkerdine. For example, her research in a nursery school shows the different discourses which male students draw upon to position the female teacher and how power accrues to and ebbs from her according to the particular discourse being brought to bear (Walkerdine, 1981). Walden and Walkerdine (1985) argue that classroom dynamics consist of discourses of domination and subordination, power and resistance, and that the extent to which girls are powerful or powerless in the classroom depends upon the positionings which are available and which they occupy. So, for example, power may accrue to primary school girls if they are positioned as "sub" teacher/mother/nurturer, but when they are positioned as sex objects by the boys they move into a position of subordination. In yet another paper, Walkerdine (1985) points to the painful psychic consequences for girls when the discourses through which they move prove too disparate and contradictory.

Such theoretical formulations and the research associated with them offer powerful new insights into the implications for girls of the curriculum, and particularly into the institutionalized "sciences of man" which have provided much of its theoretical underpinning. They also help to explain the complexity of the learner, the teacher and the teaching/learning process. Nonetheless, these have yet to be translated into suggestions for pedagogy beyond, of course, the exhortation for teachers to escape aspects of their personal, professional and institutional histories and to develop anti-sexist/racist/ethnicist/classist curricula and classroom practices.

The teacher

In focusing on teachers, what historically has caused feminist educators most concern are the ways in which the sex of the teacher is caught up in the message systems and power structures of the school. Women teachers are seen to be insufficiently represented both at the top of authority structures and in certain subject areas. In contrast, they are seen to be over-represented in lower status subjects and in those aspects and levels of schooling most associated with nurturance and domesticity. In this regard, the liberal feminist project seeks to identify and remove the structural and psychosocial barriers to women's equal representation in positions of power and authority and in the male knowledge domains. This is conceived of as an industrial, administrative and pedagogical issue, and the latter is usually couched in the language of socialization. Women in "non-traditional" arenas are seen to provide role models which demonstrate to students that men and women are equally competent, thereby challenging students' narrow views of female capacities and, in particular, girls' narrow visions of their futures.

Sometimes this type of argument expands to posit the notion that men and women have significantly different pedagogical and administrative styles. Although, again, there is a danger of slipping into the essentialist and naturalizing categorizations of female and male essences mentioned earlier, there are undoubtedly modes of pedagogy which are conventionally associated with masculinity and femininity, if not always with males and females. The former certainly include a form of power and authority which, although apparently emotionally contained, threatens constantly to spill over into symbolic and physical violence. Feminine modes of teaching tend to be associated with empathy and nurturance (see further, Connell, 1985) which in turn are thought of as particularly appropriate in early childhood education. A noticeable absence in the literature on teachers is an exploration of what it means to be a feminist teacher. The issues of power and authority over which Women's Studies teachers agonize do not seem to arise amongst feminist school teachers and researchers. Another noticeable absence is any empirical research and/or theoretical reflection on the ways in which the feminist pedagogic project for non-feminist teachers is received. The personal, cultural, institutional and professional factors which may either facilitate, alter or block the positive changes for girls which are associated with feminist pedagogy remain virtually unexamined.

The gender dynamics of schools and classrooms are another concern of feminist educators. Some researchers have pointed to the inequitable distribution of linguistic and other space in classrooms and school playgrounds. Others have pointed to the inequitable distribution and differential quality of teachers' time and attention. In allowing boys to dominate classroom resources, in setting different standards for and having different expectations of girls and boys with regard to achievement and classroom rules and speech practices (Gill & Dyer, 1987), many teachers are seen to treat their students in ways which confirm rather than challenge conventional gender identities. Feminist pedagogy directs teachers towards gender sensitivity in their interactions with students, encouraging them to monitor and change their own and their students' attitudes and behaviour. While in most instances the liberal feminist emphasis has been on teachers encouraging girls to behave in less limited ways, the radical feminist agenda insists that we make masculinity problematic—that boys and men attend to the oppressive dimensions of their attitudes and behaviour, particularly those which involve the intersection of various forms of violence/aggression/intimidation and sexuality. Recent research (e.g., Jones, 1985; Clark, 1989) has powerfully demonstrated the extent to which such matters are part of male and female teachers' and girls' and boys' experiences of the schooling system. Indeed, as Davies (1987) shows even pre-schoolers are not exempt. It is the literature on boys' and on teachers' behaviour in mixed sex classrooms which has prompted a number of feminists (e.g., Mahony, 1985) to press the not unproblematic case for single-sex spaces, classes and/or schools for girls, and it is in such work that we may see some transfer of ideas from the Women's Studies literature (for a critical discussion see Willis & Kenway, 1986). Others stress the importance of teachers developing secure and supportive school environments for girls which "explicitly state the unacceptability of practices which cause discomfort, offence, humiliation or injury and which range from so called teasing and bullying of a sexist kind, both verbal and physical, through to harassment of a more explicitly sexual nature" (Schools Commission, 1987, pp. 54, 55). In this view it is boys and men who "make trouble" for girls and women, and rather than blaming the victims, it is argued that more pedagogic effort should be directed towards educating "the boys".

Pedagogy in Women's Studies

"Women's Studies" is a name given to academic programs and/or departments within higher education and adult education which make central the experience of women, usually from a feminist perspective of one kind or another. It originated in the U.S.A. in the late 1960s as the Women's Liberation Movement's "sign on the campuses" (Howe & Ahlum, 1973, p. 93). Women's Studies programs are usually located within humanities or social science faculties and teach mainly undergraduates. Whilst there is obviously much feminist teaching taking place in various ways across tertiary institutions and within non-formal education, we wish to confine our attention here primarily to the teaching occurring within discrete programs of Women's Studies within tertiary education.

It is of interest to us that as the practitioners of Women's Studies are not located within schools of education, their employment is not contingent upon their being up-to-date with educational theory. Hence there are gaps and silences, as well as inappropriate claims, in their work—especially their work on pedagogy—which may be serving to weaken its otherwise splendid potential, either by alienating or simply failing to engage those who might be expected to be interested in pedagogical work arising out of such an arena. One example of an inappropriate claim made on behalf of Women's Studies is the statement of Tobias that Women's Studies is "the educational arm of the women's liberation movement" (Tobias, 1978, cited in Klein, 1987). That this is simply not true has, we trust, been amply demonstrated in our discussion of the gender and schooling debate. The great array of educators the world over who see themselves to be working in education because of their commitment to the liberation of women would doubtless share our concern about Tobias' claim. However, our work on this chapter has reinforced our awareness that Women's Studies teachers often draw from more radical and recent feminisms than do school teachers, curriculum developers, policy makers, and feminist educational researchers, and that they draw on less radical and recent educational theories than do some feminists who theorize and research education in schools.

How can we describe the project of Women's Studies? Suffice it here to offer the following comment on Women's Studies as set forth in the Charter document of the National Women's Studies Association (USA):

> Women's Studies, diverse as its components are, has at its best shared a vision of a world free not only from sexism but also from racism, class-bias, agism, heterosexual bias—from all the ideologies and institutions that have consciously or unconsciously oppressed and exploited some for the advantage of others. . . . The uniqueness of Women's Studies has been its refusal to accept sterile divisions between academy and community, between intellect and passion, between the individual and society. Women's Studies . . . is equipping women . . . to transform [society] (NWSA, 1977).

Statements such as this suggest just how ambitious and diverse the curriculum of Women's Studies needs to be. Renate Klein has helpfully sketched the components of Women's Studies curriculum under three headings: firstly, re-action and re-vision, as women confront the androcentric worldview; secondly, action and vision, as women assess women's experience from within a gynocentric perspective; and thirdly, a combination of these approaches that fuses critique and new vision (Klein, 1986, p. 39–49).

While it has been convenient for us to analyse the gender and schooling debate in this chapter in terms which link the work to Lusted's conceptualization of pedagogy, Women's Studies work on pedagogy does not lend itself so readily to this kind of analysis, largely because the focus of Women's Studies writers on pedagogy has been on issues of process and of classroom interactions, and very much less on curriculum. We realize that to say this runs the risk of appearing not to recognize that what Women's Studies practitioners call "feminist process" *is*, to quite an important extent, the curriculum of Women's Studies. That is, students in Women's Studies learn to confront and transform the apparent "givens" of patriarchy through coming to understand that "malestream" ways of teaching and learning serve to ensure the perpetuation of patriarchal hegemony, whereas consensual, collaborative, non-hierarchical processes of learning/teaching can help to change what is known as well as to create growth-enhancing classrooms. But even if these interactions were the entire content of Women's Studies, the under-theorization by Women's Studies practitioners of the ways in which such content/knowledge is mediated in the classroom would still remain a significant problem. This is a point to which we shall return.

Theorizations of pedagogy within Women's Studies

Women's Studies pedagogy clearly has its roots in a number of emancipatory movements and liberatory impulses in recent times. In making this point we note a recent comment by Jesse Goodman (1988) who felt able to say that "recent expressions that schools should promote the democratic empowerment of teachers and students have not emerged from educational or social movements. Rather their roots are found in scholarly criticism". Following Maher (1987) we discern two distinct styles of pedagogical theorizing within Women's Studies. The two models to which we shall refer are, first, that which in effect equates pedagogy with classroom processes, and second, that which is essentially Freirean/liberatory. We do not, however, see these as mutually exclusive or claim epistemological superiority for one or other of them.

Frances Maher (1987) in a useful article, "Toward a richer theory of feminist pedagogy", proposes calling these two models the "gender" and "liberation" models. Our decision to call the former the "classroom process" model does not indicate radical disagreement with Maher's categories but serves merely to situate the model within educational discourse in a way that is appropriate to the purposes of this chapter. That any sort of categorizing is problematical is evident in the fact that the article by Nancy Schniedewind to which we shall refer, "Feminist values: Guidelines for a teaching methodology in women's studies" has been anthologized in a book on "feminist education" (Bunch & Pollack, 1983) *and* in Ira Shor's *Freire for the Classroom* (1987).

Pedagogy as classroom process

This approach is exemplified in the approaches of Klein (1987) and Schniedewind (1987). What these writers have in common is a concern with the women's movement project to focus attention on "sisterhood, anti-elitism, leaderless consciousness-raising groups and the power of collective decision-making and activity" (Howe & Ahlum, 1973, p. 404). To Klein, the pivotal concern of Women's Studies "gynagogy"—a term she prefers to the male-derived "pedagogy"—is consciousness-raising. She discusses consciousness-raising as "method" and subordinates to it the following concerns: "interactive teaching and learning" (which she borrows quite uncritically from Schniedewind); being "Other" (Black, gay, etc.) in the Women's Studies classroom; and the issue of power (asymmetrical teacher-student relations, and the matter of the authority of the teacher) (Klein, 1987, pp. 189–98). Klein's argument about what feminist pedagogy is, hinges upon a very strong defense of consciousness-raising. However, despite the fact that consciousness-raising processes must introduce and mediate content in powerful ways—indeed, they are clearly seen by Klein as the chief means whereby women make the personal political—Klein's theorizing does not address what it is that happens when Women's Studies classes engage in con-sciousness-raising; one infers that for Women's Studies practitioners the what, how and why of consciousness-raising are "common sense" knowledge.

The particular article by Schniedewind that we refer to here is frequently cited and as we noted above, has been anthologized. The fact that this article first appeared in *Radical Teacher*, no. 8 (n.d.) is an indication of its acceptability within socialist feminism, just as its inclusion in the Shor collection is an indi-cation of its acceptability within socialism more generally. This would lead the reader to expect from its author a systematic treatment of praxis. This is not provided, despite Schniedewind's obvious and acknowledged epistemological debt to Freire. Schniedewind puts forward a fivefold "process goals" approach to pedagogy: (1) development of an atmosphere of mutual respect, trust and com-munity in the classroom; (2) shared leadership; (3) cooperative structures; (4) integration of cognitive and affective learning, and (5) action. Although Schniedewind acknowledges the difficulty of incorporating "field-based action" into her course, further description/analysis of how such action projects contrib-ute to the learning of feminist values would have made this article more compel-ling. Schniedewind is well aware of the need for process and content to be con-gruent if education is to be growthful and democratic. Whilst we would agree with her, we are not at all sure that her claim that her five goals are simply "fem-inist" is appropriate. We shall make further reference to this point when we dis-cuss the more general question of the intersection of feminist pedagogical theo-rizing with broader educational theories.

Also of concern to us in the work of both Klein and Schniedewind is their use of the term "hidden curriculum". Both imply that this consists in classroom dy-namics. We find this to be a very narrow and limited perception of the concept of hidden curriculum, an idea which has been far more robustly theorized by edu-cationalists (see, for example, Seddon, 1981).

Freirean/liberatory pedagogy

The pedagogy frequently termed Freirean/liberatory, whilst it might be seen as "standing on the shoulders" of educators such as John Dewey, has developed mainly in recent liberation movements and revolutionary movements—and in the case of Freire's work, owes much to the theology of liberation emerging out of such places as South America.

Examples of this pedagogy applied to Women's Studies may be found in the contributions by Maher and by Bonder in the anthology *Gendered Subjects* (Cul-ley & Portuges, 1985). (The irony of women's finding so much of value in the work of an educator who comes out of a strongly patriarchal culture and who certainly has not himself theorized gender is noted by Maher).

Maher, in "Classroom pedagogy and the new scholarship on women", builds quite explicitly on aspects of Freire's work, making clear her own political and epistemological frameworks. This helps to some extent to separate her work from that of the "classroom processes" group notwithstanding her decision to bracket "curricular choices" out of the article. Maher consistently applies Freirean categories in her analysis of such things as classroom and course structure and the roles of teacher and student. For example, she makes specific reference to "banking education" and is sensitive to the ramifications of what Freire has called the "culture of silence" of oppressed peoples. We do have some concerns about her extensive use of the expression "interactive pedagogy" in a way that focuses constantly on classroom activities and does not pay nearly enough attention to the articulation of pedagogy with social transformation that is so crucial to Freire's praxis (Maher, 1985).

We note in passing the work of another feminist writer in the Freirean mould, Kathy Higgins. Although Higgins (1982) writes about adult education, which is outside the scope of this chapter, she, too draws on Freire in a way that raises questions for us. Her reading of Freire appears to us to be flawed by its relatively superficial approach to the highly problematical Freirean notion of "dialogue" and her collapsing of "conscientization" into consciousness-raising.

Another Freirean/liberatory style of pedagogy is presented by Bonder (1985), who writes in a way that suggests awareness of the sort of theorizing that informs Lusted's work on pedagogy. Bonder presents a very well-theorized approach to the social-structural change imperatives of so-called consciousness-raising. Bonder and her colleagues discuss a pedagogy which they call "education-formation" and which has a conception of consciousness-raising which stresses its transformative responsibilities.

Recurrent themes in Women's Studies pedagogy

Although Women's Studies teachers theorize pedagogy in somewhat different ways, there is much evidence in Women's Studies literature to suggest that these teachers have many common concerns. These include the idea of the teacher as mother; the issue of authority and its corollary, the grading system; and the problematical notion of consciousness-raising.

The idea of the Women's Studies teacher as nurturer/mother is a significant theme in, for example, the collection *Gendered Subjects* (Culley & Portuges, 1985) and is connected to discussions about "passionate teaching" and the "problem of authority" for women. Several other major works in feminist theory contribute to this debate about nurture: see, for example, Noddings (1984) and Belenky et al. (1986). This literature also draws heavily upon recent psychoanalytic theorizing within feminism. Leck (1987) in a review of *Gendered Subjects*, notes that:

> The authors examine some of the classroom dynamics that might be expected as students recognize a "teacher as a woman". They conclude that power relationships between students and teachers are influenced when they see the

"teacher as a woman" betraying her "mothering" role when engaged in a class-room as a "father" authority; or when they expect her to nurture (stay in her role) and she doesn't; or when they fear maternal power and mistrust paternal authority (Leck, 1987, p. 348).

It is interesting to note a very different point of view coming out of feminist *adult* education. As Hughes and Kennedy (1985) put it: "We have to learn to trust adult students more, and 'mother' them less" (p. 168).

In our view, this concern with mothering is problematic for various reasons. Nurturing qualities have always been assumed to be female traits. However Martin (1985) argues that both sexes are capable of the "generative love of parents" which is increasingly recognized as vital to the survival of society. She refers to what have been described as "nurturing capacities" or "an ethics of care" and their importance to educational philosophy (Martin, 1985, p. 77). Martin argues for the incorporation into education of both the values traditionally associated with women in a positive sense, and those of men: "the three Cs of caring, concern and connection" can become goals of any subject, and need to be linked, she says, to goals reflecting views about the qualities of men: rationality and independent judgment.

The general problem to be solved is that of uniting thought and action, reason and emotion, self and other. . . . This can only be achieved if 'the reproductive processes' . . . (are given) their due (Martin, 1985, pp. 82–3).

This approach suggests a project for education that would rescue it from essentialism and from a simplistic and stereotyped approach to gender-related qualities. It also recognises that mothering is *not* necessarily a wholly benign affair—mothers, like fathers, *can* be very negative if not downright dangerous for their offspring, and Martin refers to statistics on child abuse to help make this point.

For Women's Studies teachers, the problem of authority is connected to women's internalized assumptions about their lack of a right to, or even capacity for, the exercise of authority. It is also related to a desire to foster "horizontal" power relations with their students and not replicate the disempowering hierarchical authority relations found in most educational settings. The dilemma of training students by using a "power with" model of teaching in a "power over" society presents Women's Studies practitioners with some interesting problems; this dilemma has been noted by Maher (1987). Klein (1987) discusses these problems in a most helpful way through reference to various writers on power in the feminist classroom. It is apparent that there is enormous diversity among such writers regarding the ways in which female authority is viewed as problematic. Women's Studies practitioners' desire to model appropriate use of power is especially relevant, given their recognition that most members of Women's Studies classrooms experience life in a female body, and that to an important extent no one woman's experience in that regard should be seen as better than any other woman's experience. Whilst the Women's Studies emphasis on experientially-based learning/ teaching modes may serve to blur the asymmetrical relations of *expertise,* the real issue is, as Misgeld points out:

> . . . not the fact of expertise but how the teacher handles it. Expertise is special knowledge of some field of activity that can be entered into the common knowledge of a cultural group under two conditions: the appropriate vehicles of translation and interpretation must be available (here one might consider supplementing Freire's account with hermeneutical reflections on the transmission of culture and cultural meaning), and those possessing special knowledge must be accountable to the cultural group with which they work (Misgeld, 1985, p. 107).

The interrelated issues of standards and grades in Women's Studies work are corollaries of the authority question. Adrienne Rich, whose famous paper "Taking women students seriously" (1980a) is perhaps the most frequently cited item in works on feminist pedagogy that we have read, argues convincingly that a feminist education is not incompatible with demanding activities and tasks:

> We can refuse to accept passive, obedient learning and insist upon critical thinking. . . . We need to keep our standards very high . . . because self-respect often comes only when exacting standards have been met. . . . A romantic sloppiness, an inspired lack of rigor, a self-indulgent incoherence, are symptoms of female self-depreciation (Rich, 1980a, p. 244).

Grading is certainly a problem for educators who see part of their mission to be the complete transformation of androcentric education systems, which are hierarchical and based on competition and credentialing. Yet to refuse to award quantitative grades may weaken Women's Studies' legitimacy within these structures—quite a dilemma, as Klein (1987) points out. The issue becomes one of exploring styles and modes of assessment rather than refusing to assess.

A somewhat more permissive/laissez faire view on this matter is expressed by Hughes and Kennedy in a discussion of *adult* education:

> Of course, there are tensions over the problem of making feminist research and the teaching of their findings academically acceptable. This, combined with the demands of academic institutions for measurable standards and formal examinations, conflicts with the spontaneity of the women's liberation movement at the grass roots. (The contradiction of how can you examine or grade what the experience of a woman is like!) (sic) (Hughes & Kennedy, 1985, p. 29).

In our view, it is this sort of laissez faire thinking that can run the danger of leading teachers to accept "the inspired lack of rigor" which Adrienne Rich warns of.

We find the feminist pedagogy literature to be most unclear on the question of grades. In this they are not alone: Ira Shor, whose by now justly celebrated book *Critical Thinking and Everyday Life* (1980) is something of a classic, does not grapple with the issue of grades, and does not appear to see that for the teacher with a liberatory project, the grading question is indeed "the $64,000 question" (see Kavaloski, n.d., for comment on this point). The liberatory teacher can *not* "wither away" while she/he remains firmly in control of assessment of student work. Like Shor, Schniedewind poses problems for us in this regard. Schniedewind (1987) is quite clearly in favour of egalitarian processes, yet apparently has no difficulty in suggesting that students who do not wish to engage in the processes she suggests, withdraw from her courses. Consistent, dialogical negotiation over classroom processes and modes of assessment are not in evidence, though Schniedewind states that she has made occasional adjustments e.g., deleting a journal in some courses if students felt they had already had "an overdose of journals in Women's Studies" (pp. 172–73). While strategies such as contracting between teacher and student are recognized within the Women's Studies pedagogy literature, the discussions remain under-theorized. There is by now a large body of research, and classroom experience, with various forms of negotiated assessment, and serious engagement with this work by Women's Studies practitioners, and indeed all feminist teachers, is urgently needed.

It seems important to us that Women's Studies teachers consider the ways in which the almost stereotypical dichotomizing of "passion" and "reason" along gender lines impacts on questions of authority and standards. Cocks (1985) illuminates these problems in an insightful essay on teaching feminist theory, in the *Gendered Subjects* collection. She identifies factors within contemporary feminism that encourage what she terms "a staunch anti-theoreticism" on the part of women in the women's movement and not just women in Women's Studies classrooms. These factors include the sheer immediacy of studying sex-gender relations, the tendency for many feminist women to identify reason with men, and contemporary feminism's "ideological prejudice against power . . . the tendency . . . to portray men as the active agents and women as the passive victims of history, culture and society". In relation to this last point Cocks observes that "the feminist teacher . . . will have to address a host of difficult questions to do with intentionality, agency and responsibility in sex/gender relations" (Cocks, 1985, p. 182).

In this section of our paper we have made several references to the matter of consciousness-raising, pointing out some of the more problematical ways in which it has been used in Women's Studies theorizing of pedagogy. We shall now look at this issue in greater depth.

Consciousness-raising is a direct and inevitable outcome of Women's Studies' origins in the women's liberation movement, as we have seen. If experiential education has refocused educators' attention on the centrality of students' and teachers' experience as both a condition for and content matter of learning, feminist education has argued for the necessary centrality of *women's* experience to *women's* learning. It is certainly true that as "feminism . . . is the theory of women's point of view . . . consciousness-raising is its quintessential expression" (MacKinnon, 1982, p. 535).

What we want to argue here is that there is an urgent need for far more rigorous theorizing of consciousness-raising by Women's Studies practitioners than that which we see at present. The work of Bonder, referred to above, is suggestive of possible directions. Women's Studies practitioners certainly seem to be recognising consciousness-raising as fundamental to the need for "naming" of oppression, which Freire and other liberatory theorists rightly valorize. However, naming is not nearly enough, and for Freire it was only the *beginning* of his process of "conscientizacao" (see Freire, 1972).

We see much discussion of consciousness-raising in Women's Studies work, and almost none on conscientization (Freire's "conscientizacao"). We are concerned about feminist educators' over-valorization of consciousness-raising: there is a world of difference between consciousness-raising and the development of *critical consciousness* inherent in the notion of conscientization. Consciousness-raising, though many would claim that it has been powerful and of lasting value to them, can be engaged in a way that is not articulated with action: after all, one might very well develop a heightened awareness of pain and contradiction but may still feel powerless to resolve problems. Awareness that "the personal is political"—a catch-phrase of some consciousness-raising movements—does not automatically produce appropriate programs for action. In other words, consciousness-raising can so easily become the reflection without action which Freire calls wishful thinking. On the other hand, critical consciousness facilitates analysis of the context of problem situations for the purpose of enabling people together to transform their reality, rather than merely understand it or adapt to it with less discomfort.

Conscientization is not a static concept: as Mackie points out, conscientization in the Freirean context "corresponds to highly permeable, interrogative, restless and dialogical forms of life" (Mackie, 1980, p. 96). For Freire, conscientization is the goal of a dialogical praxis which embodies a developmentally-sequenced problem-posing education, in which students and teachers move from magical through naive to critical consciousness, avoiding the pitfalls of fanaticism and irrationality (see Smith, 1976). Our suggestion that those feminist educators who are interested in Freire seriously engage Freirean scholarship, and resist the temptation to consider their under-theorized notions of consciousness-raising as if they were the same as Freirean praxis, is prompted in part by an awareness of the ease with which powerful ideas can be "co-opted" (Kidd & Kumar, 1981, p. 28).

Another point over which we wish to offer a challenge to so-called Freirean educators among Women's Studies practitioners is their silence about *critiques* of Freire. Whilst many feminist educators whom we have referred to here (e.g. Maher, 1985; Leck, 1987) demonstrate awareness of the problems *for feminists* inherent in taking on a pedagogy which does *not* problematize gender or even mention it, they simply do not demonstrate awareness of the by now considerable literature which exists which points out the inconsistencies, gaps and silences in Freire's own work. Blanca Facundo, a Puerto Rican educator who now seems to have been politely squeezed out of the Freirean fraternity for her analysis of the problems encountered by Latino/Latina educators doing Freirean work in the United States, has this to say:

> Early in the seventies, William Griffith warned that a logical conclusion of Freire's theory was that, after the triumph of a 'revolution', there would be no freedom to disagree with the new ruling group. Those of us who saw in Freire an inspiration were angered. Yet, as of 1984, and analyzing Freire's writings, talks and actions since the *Pedagogy of the Oppressed,* I am more and more inclined to agree with Griffith. . . . If we find that we are or were unclear about the meaning and objectives of the theory upon which our educational activities were or are being based, and have accepted it as inherently relevant to our work, what kind of clarity can we have when evaluating the process and outcomes of our programs? Particularly when we are supposed to be acting and *critically* reflecting upon our actions! (Facundo, 1984, p. 29).

Another woman educator, Linda Harasim (1983), whose doctoral thesis was based on her investigations of what Freire did in Guinea-Bissau, seems also, from what we have heard, to have become persona non grata. Yet it is interesting that in a recent book written in collaboration with Macedo, Freire has taken a great deal of trouble to respond to the substance, if not the letter, of the criticisms that many educators, including women such as Facundo and Harasim, have been raising (Freire & Macedo, 1987).

Such criticism does not, of course, come only from women. Male educators, such as the Australian James Walker (1980) have also—albeit from a different perspective, that of the academic philosopher/activist—taken Freire to task for the perceived potential for manipulativeness inherent in his work. We urge feminist educators to take the trouble to look at the whole variety of points of view on and analyses of Freire's work. At the moment it looks very much as if Freirean idolatry is taking the place of the development of critical consciousness *in the very project of liberatory education itself.*

We would also like to ask Women's Studies teachers working with consciousness-raising methods, "How do you know what is happening?" The immediacy and excitement of the feminist classroom are surely great plusses in feminist education, yet we say to those teachers who may be in danger of over-valuing the passionate classrooms of consciousness-raising, in words that paraphrase Shor—"Are you merely drawn to liveliness or is this dynamism as transformative as it feels?" Women's Studies practitioners write as if it was the women's movement which in fact *invented* consciousness-raising. One of the things missing from feminist educators' accounts of consciousness-raising is the awareness that, as

Smith et al., point out, "consciousness-raising has been as ill-defined as it has been essential in all liberation movements" (Smith et al., 1975, p. 13).

This leads to the last element of our critique of Women's Studies pedagogy—an element which is related to all the others—and that is our wish to highlight the implications for Women's Studies practitioners of insufficient engagement with educational discourses. Not only does their unfamiliarity with these discourses lead them to make inappropriate claims about the inventiveness of Women's Studies pedagogy, but it robs them of powerful support for their own work. Pedagogy itself (or perhaps we should say "teaching practices" for reasons alluded to above) is a case in point. Despite the references in some feminist pedagogy literature (Culley & Portuges, 1985) which acknowledge its heritage in recent radical education movements, we find that conceptual schemes that would be at home within properly-theorized discourses on confluent education or humanistic education abound in Women's Studies work but are not connected to such discourses. Compare, for example, Schniedewind's "feminist values in teaching" and Weinstein's conceptualization of humanistic education. Weinstein (1975) states that humanistic education (i) has as its central data source for decision-making the needs of the individuals involved; (ii) increases the options of the learners; (iii) gives at least as much priority to personal knowledge as to public knowledge; (iv) does not foster any one individual's growth at the expense of someone else's; (v) is conducted through programs all of whose elements contribute to a sense of significance, value and worth for each person involved. A quite similar schedule of concerns to Weinstein's is presented in a recent article by Roy and Schen in an issue of *Women's Studies Quarterly* devoted to feminist pedagogy. This article, through its failure to reference or mention any work that would indicate recognition of its connection to well-established educational traditions, in effect sells its readers short (Roy and Schen, 1987).

In similar fashion, there are problems with such catch-all phrases as "interactive teaching and learning". It is clear to us that most of the agenda of radical education in the last thirty years has involved emphasis on the agency of both teacher and student (Rich, 1980b, p. 231) and a focus on collaboration rather than competition (Maher, 1985, p. 38) that are key features of what these feminist teachers call "interactive learning and teaching" (see Weinstein (1975) for the example from humanistic education; Chickering (1977) on experiential learning; George Brown (1971) on confluent education).

Of course the issue remains—and it is a vital one for educational theorists as well as for Women's Studies practitioners—liberatory/radical educators have *not* adequately theorized gender, and neither have the writers on humanistic and confluent education. But what significance does this have? Leck (1987) poses the following questions:

> Would such a perspective alter an educational theory in any fundamental way?
> Is a heightened consciousness of gender an add-on to an established educa-

tional theory, is it a re-working of the precepts of an existent liberationist theory such as Paulo Freire's, or is it a uniquely different educational theory? (Leck, 1987, pp. 347–8).

Leck's best hope is that "feminist pedagogy may be able to move liberationist theorists to a full recognition of their own risk . . ." However the question here of who is going to "move" whom is crucial. Leck's strategy sounds dangerously like the perennial expectation that it is women who must take responsibility for men's growth. The kinds of dialogue that are long overdue between feminist teachers and "critical pedagogues" need to be predicated upon much more symmetrical notions of responsibility.

Conclusion

We have shown here first that feminist pedagogy has no clear and readily agreed upon connotations amongst feminist educators, and second, that it is not a unitary or static discourse. Although we identified and discussed two primary strands within the field, we also pointed to the different feminisms operating within each strand. In focusing on both the gender and schooling and the Women's Studies literature, what emerged quite markedly is the different ways in which the two parties address the matter of feminist pedagogy. These seem to arise in large part from the dissimilar material conditions in which they work.

The feminist pedagogy about which Women's Studies practitioners write occurs largely, although not exclusively, in single-sex classes in tertiary institutions. The knowledge which is taught is usually some form of either ideology critique of malestream thought, or knowledge produced for, by and about women. Women's Studies teachers thus confront pedagogical and espistemological issues which differ significantly from those of concern to feminists who teach (or research) in co-educational classes of students whose ages ranges from four to seventeen and whose social and educational biographies are much more varied than those in tertiary classes (no matter how open). Further, while Women's Studies may have found a place in some rare school syllabi, most feminist school teachers teach the dominant curricula and seek ways of making these "gender inclusive".

As we implied, the term "feminist pedagogy" is not popular amongst those who are concerned about gender and schooling, but is much used by Women's Studies teachers. Again, this may be explained by the different material and ideological conditions in which the different groups work. Women's Studies teachers are employed as *feminist* academics. Their theoretical frameworks, and indeed their institutional existence, demand not only that they are visibly identified as feminist (and this includes being well-versed in recent feminist theory) but that they offer an education which is critical of and proclaims its difference from the institutional mainstream/malestream. The Women's Studies teacher must be extremely sensitive to any gaps between her theory and her pedagogical practice. She is thus obliged to search for "feminist" alternatives to the educational practices which she associates with males' power and women's oppression. However, given her institutional and, in many instances, deliberately separate location, it is not surprising that her characterization of mainstream educational practice is naive. As we have shown, the Women's Studies literature demonstrates little sense either of the humanist, progressive and critical challenges to the mainstream by educators, male, female and feminist—or of the critical interaction between these fields and the progress made because of this. Their educational critique and theorizing thus often lacks an adequate base in educational theory, and is ahistorical. In our view, a related problem is that the rigorous feminist theory, which one might expect from Women's Studies teachers, is insufficiently brought to bear on the education discourses mentioned above. This is clearly necessary for the purpose of moving us all through and beyond them.

In contrast, as we have shown, those concerned with gender and schooling have a vastly different, and in many ways more difficult, educational project than that for which Women's Studies takes responsibility. Engaging in theoretical debate with "the converted" is an occasional luxury, subsumed within the wider task of constructing a discourse with sufficient ideological power to change the practice of teachers and policy makers—most of whom are not feminists. For this audience "gender" must largely be presented as an educational rather than a feminist or a political issue, and the case, it seems, is best argued in the language of teachers rather than that of academics. Thus, discussions center on "curriculum" rather than "pedagogy", even though the terms may have the same meaning.

While we can strongly identify with the all-consuming dimensions that such a project assumes, we nonetheless wish to reassert the point that gender workers in and for schools have largely failed to come to grips with the pedagogical implications of the notion of praxis. Too often there is an uncritical, oversimplified and unproblematic transfer and application of feminist theories to the classroom or school. There is, then, a subsequent failure to critically reflect on their implications in practice and so to revise theory and practice according to the specificities of the educational setting. A siege mentality is often associated with the community of gender workers in schools and this, in turn, leads to a certain defensiveness. There is a clear and urgent need for the appropriate conditions to be created whereby this may be transformed into supportively critical self and community reflexivity.

The overall implications of our discussion are, firstly, that if feminist and other liberatory pedagogies are to develop their best potential, then more learning must occur between them. Our second implication is that if feminism cannot criticize itself, it cannot "serve as the bearer of emancipatory possibilities that can never be fixed and defined once and for all" (Elshtain, 1982, p. 136).

Postscript

There are many impulses behind our will to write a postscript. Most arise from the distances we have travelled and the places we have stopped at since the original paper was written early in 1989. Some arise from a sense that in this collection, our chapter will have a new and wider audience than that which we anticipated for the original piece. With this different audience in mind we feel we want to allude to different things, make certain qualifications, shift the emphasis and tone, develop certain points, fill some gaps, change the language. However, as postscripts are inevitably short, all impulses can not be satisfied. We have therefore chosen to mention those matters which we believe help move the paper beyond itself, and so, it is hoped, raise further issues for the field.

Our paper arose, in part, from some frustrations we experienced with the ways in which feminist pedagogy is characterized in much of the academic literature. From such literature, one gains the impression that feminist pedagogy is something that happens almost exclusively in Women's Studies classrooms in the tertiary sector of education. In discussing feminist pedagogy in and for schools, and in highlighting the different perspectives which exist within school-based and Women's Studies-based work, we sought to offer two main messages. One was that a diversity of voices and practices make up the project of feminist pedagogy and that it exists in a wide variety of educational settings and modes. Coeducational classes in universities, nonformal adult education, distance education, and the technical and further education sector are all sites where feminists are developing alternative curricula and teaching/learning practices. The second message was that communication between these pedagogical sites and perspectives seems rather limited and that while each must attend to its own specificities, much is to be gained through a better knowledge of the work of others. For instance, those in schools who are struggling against various forms of resistance to gender-inclusive curriculum, will find in the tertiary education literature some theoretical frameworks that are particularly helpful in explaining the sources of such resistance. This is not a call for unproblematical borrowing by one field from another within or beyond the field of feminist educational thought. Clearly a number of us are becoming increasingly uncomfortable with some of the wild eclecticism of our past.

In looking back on our paper we were struck by our preoccupation with Paulo Freire. To spend so much time on someone who doesn't theorize gender! However, as feminist pedagogy has been deeply influenced by Freirean thought, we need to point out that the borrowings that have been made have often been perilously uncritical in some of the Women's Studies theorizing. For the many years Freire's work has been central to the thought of most critical educators, we have seen it within the broader context of work on pedagogy and have struggled with its problematic elements. We want to acknowledge how generative Freire's work has been for us, and accept responsibility for going a lot further than he.

Also, our recognition of our own privileged positioning vis-á-vis educational discourses brings us to observe that we were too quick to criticise Women's Studies practitioners for problems that we as educationalists can see in their educational theorizing. These problems are perfectly understandable, given that most such teachers have come from disciplines other than education. In fact, they have been pioneers, struggling to articulate a theory of education without access to all the theoretical tools one needs for such work.

Researching and theorizing our own educational practice and sharing our knowledge is one way of moving the field forward. Lusted's definition of pedagogy is pertinent to such an enterprise because it emphasizes the ways in which meanings are made in the educational process. It urges us to attend both to the sense students make of what we are doing and to the range of factors which influence their sense-making. How do they receive and replay the main message systems which we create for them and, for better or worse, what part do they play in shaping and reshaping them? Why is it that some students are more positively responsive to feminist pedagogy than others? Indeed, which feminist pedagogies attract more favorable responses and why? Is phase theory (see Anderson, 1988) a helpful way of thinking about students' developing responses or is it too linear? What are the range of implications of feminist pedagogy for students' lives? Should such implications be taken into account in teaching? If so, how? We acknowledge that these sorts of questions are not new to the field. Indeed, the Women's Studies literature includes many descriptive accounts of the pedagogical moment. Absent, however, is a serious and sustained attempt at theory building. In our view the work of Lather, Lewis and Ellsworth in this volume and elsewhere is immensely suggestive for the sort of practice-based theorizing which is necessary in order that our pedagogical imperatives don't congeal into truths fixed for one and all, once and for all.

Our reflections since 1989 lead us to return briefly to two key issues in the paper: those of female authority and dialogue in the feminist classroom. We have always been a bit sceptical about women's concerns about exercising power in the classroom; we could have attended to this with greater effect had we quoted from Janice Raymond's wonderful book on female friendships (Raymond, 1986). Raymond presents convincing arguments against women's preference for subordinating their personal power to the group, and she does this in a way that does not imply a return to highly individualized, "upwardly mobile" feminism. Raymond clearly hopes that women will achieve their true potential. Non-hierarchical practices, she argues, can prevent women from discovering and using their own individual strength and can also encourage them to endeavor to achieve their goals through the exercise of indirect power or even manipulation within a group. As Raymond says, "no real power emerges from a group that silences its best and brightest voices for a false sense of group equality. And certainly no strong friendships can be formed among women who have no power of being" (p. 197). This problem is directly related to our concern about the way

Women's Studies writers have so often spoken of elements of group process in the feminist classroom as if they were always present or always possible of achievement—things such as "trust", "community", "dialogue" and so forth. Maybe Women's Studies classes are far more homogeneous in terms of members' power, race, class, voice, ability and so forth than other classes where a feminist practice is struggled for, but we doubt it, and in the last couple of years educators such as Lather, Lewis and Ellsworth have shown us that given the differences between and among students and teachers, dialogue is far more difficult to foster than feminist educators (or the critical pedagogy fraternity) ever imagined. Perhaps we would do better to understand dialogue as the goal of pedagogy and not a condition for it (see further, Modra, 1991).

Clearly power, truth and authority have long been matters of concern for feminist pedagogy. However, the postmodern turn in much feminist thinking and theorizing asks us to re-think such concepts. Indeed, postmodern feminisms hold views on power, politics, truth, human nature and emancipation which are significantly different from the views which have provided the momentum for the development of much feminist pedagogy to date. Their challenges are fundamental—both promising and dangerous (see Nicholson, 1990)—and far too complex to even touch on here. Some difficult conceptual work is ahead of us, and those with a particular concern for praxis can expect to face conditions of radical uncertainty for some time.

References

Anderson, M. L. (1988) Changing the curriculum in higher education. In E. Minnich, J. O'Bair & R. Rosenfeld (Eds.), *Reconstructing the academy: Women's education and women's studies* (pp. 36–39). Chicago: University of Chicago Press.

Belenky, M., Clinchy, B., Goldberger, N. & Tarule, J. (1986) *Women's ways of knowing: The development of self, voice and mind.* New York: Basic Books.

Blackburn, J. (1982) Becoming equally human: Girls and the secondary curriculum. *VISE News,* July/August, 16–22.

Bonder, G. (1985) The educational process of women's studies in Argentina: Reflections on theory and technique. In M. Culley & C. Portuges (Eds.), *Gendered subjects* (64–77). Boston: Routledge & Kegan Paul.

Boomer, G. (Ed.). (1982) *Negotiating the curriculum.* Sydney: Ashton Scholastic.

Brown, G. (1971) *Human teaching for human learning: An introduction to confluent education.* New York: Viking Press.

Bunch, C. & Pollack, S. (Eds.). (1983) *Learning our way: Essays in feminist education.* Trumansburg, NY: Crossing Press.

Chickering, A. (1977) *Experience and learning: An introduction to experiential learning.* New York: Change Magazine Press.

Chodorow, N. (1978) *The reproduction of mothering.* Berkeley, California: University of California Press.

Clark, M. (1989) *The great divide: The construction of gender in the primary school.* Canberra: Curriculum Development Center.

Cocks, J. (1984) Workless emotions: Some critical reflections on radical feminism. *Politics & Society, 13*(11), 1–26.

Cocks, J. (1985) Suspicious pleasures: On teaching feminist theory. In M. Culley & C. Portuges (Eds.), *Gendered subjects* (pp. 171–182). Boston: Routledge & Kegan Paul.

Connell, R. W. (1985) *Teachers' work.* Sydney: Allen & Unwin.

Culley, M. & Portuges, C. (Eds.). (1985) *Gendered subjects.* Boston: Routledge & Kegan Paul.

Davies, B. (1987, August) *The sense children make of feminist fairy stories.* Paper presented to the South World Congress of Applied Linguistics, University of Sydney, Sydney, NSW.

Elshtain, J. (1982) Feminist discourse and its discontents: Language, power and meaning. In N. Keohare, M. Rosaedo & B. Gelpi (Eds.), *Feminist theory: A critique of ideology* (pp. 127–145). Sussex: Harvester Press.

Facundo, B. (1984) *Issues for an evaluation of Freire: Inspired programs in the United States and Puerto Rico.* Rio Pedro, Puerto Rico, Alternatives (ERIC ED 243 998).

Fowler, R. (1984) HSC, STC: A strategy for equal outcomes for girls. In P. Cole (Ed.), *Curriculum issues* (pp. 42–44). Melbourne: Victorian Institute of Secondary Education, Schools' Curriculum Unit.

Freire, P. (1972) *Pedagogy of the oppressed.* Harmondsworth, Middlesex: Penguin.

Freire, P. & Macedo, D. (1987) *Literacy: Reading the word and the world.* London: Routledge & Kegan Paul.

Gill, J. & Dyer, M. (1987) Out of order: Rethinking the rules of classroom talk. *Curriculum Perspectives, 7*(1), 61–64.

Gilligan, C. (1982) *In a different voice: A study of women's construction and resolution of moral problems.* Cambridge, MA: Harvard University Press.

Goodman, J. (1988) *Democratic empowerment and elementary curriculum: A case study.* Paper presented at the American Educational Research Association, New Orleans.

Harasim, L. (1983) Literacy and national construction in Guinea-Bissau: A critique of the Freirean Literacy Campaign. Unpublished Ph.D. Dissertation, University of Toronto. Cited in B. Facundo (1984), *Issues for an evaluation of Freire—Inspired programs in the United States and Puerto Rico,* Rio Pedro, Puerto Rico, Alternativas. (ERIC ED 243 998).

Harding, J. (1985a) *Switched off: The science education for girls.* London: Longmans.

Harding, J. (1985b) *Values, cognitive styles and the curriculum.* Paper delivered to GASAT Conference, England.

Higgins, K. (1982) Making it your own world: Women's studies and Freire. *Women's Studies International Forum, 51*(1), 87–98.

Howe, F. & Ahlum, C. (1973) Women's studies and social change. In A. Rossi & A. Calderwood (Eds.), *Academic women on the move* (pp. 393–423). New York: Sage.

Hughes, M. & Kennedy, M. (1985) *New futures: Changing women's education.* London: Routledge & Kegan Paul.

Jonas, P. (1990) Improving self esteem: A whole school approach. In J. Kenway & S. Willis (Eds.), *Hearts and minds: Self esteem and the schooling of girls.* London: Falmer Press.

Jones, C. (1985) Sexual tyranny: Male violence in a mixed secondary school. In G. Weiner (Ed.), *Just a bunch of girls* (pp. 26–40). Milton Keynes: Open University Press.

Kavaloski, V. (n.d.) Freedom and necessity (Review of I. Shor (1980): *Critical teaching in everyday life*), *Madison Review of Books.*

Kenway, J. & Willis, S. (1990) *Hearts and minds: Self esteem and the schooling of girls.* London: Falmer Press.

Kidd, R. & Kumar, K. (1981) Co-opting Freire: A critical analysis of pseudo-Freirean adult education. *Economic and Political Weekly, 16*(1 & 2), January 3–10, 27–36.

Klein, R. (1986) *The dynamics of women's studies: An exploratory study of its international ideas and practices in higher education.* Unpublished doctoral thesis, University of London, Institute of Education, London.

Klein, R. (1987) The dynamics of the women's studies classroom: A review essay of the teaching practice of women's studies in higher education. *Women's Studies International Forum, 10*(2), 187–206.

Lather, P. (1984) Critical theory, curricular transformation and feminist mainstreaming. *Journal of Education, 166*(1), 49–62.

Leck, G. (1987) Review article: Feminist pedagogy, liberation theory, and the traditional schooling paradigm. *Educational Theory, 37*(3), 343–354.

Lusted, D. (1986) Why pedagogy? *Screen, 27*(5), 2–14.

Mackie, R. (Ed.) (1980) *Literacy and revolution: The pedagogy of Paulo Freire.* London: Pluto Press.

MacKinnon, C. (1982) Feminism, Marxism, method and the state: An agenda for theory. *Signs, 7*(3), 515–544.

Maher, F. (1985) Classroom pedagogy and the new scholarship on women. In M. Culley & C. Portuges (Eds.), *Gendered subjects* (pp. 29–48). Boston: Routledge & Kegan Paul.

Maher, F. (1987) Toward a richer theory of feminist pedagogy: A comparison of "liberation' and "gender' models for teaching and learning. *Journal of Education, 169*(3), 91–100.

Mahony, P. (1985) *Schools for the boys? Co-education reassessed.* London: Hutchinson.

Martin, J. (1985) Becoming educated: A journey of alienation or integration. *Journal of Education, 167*(3), 71–84.

Misgeld, D. (1985) Education and cultural invasion. In J. Foster (Ed.), *Critical theory and public life* (pp. 77–118). Cambridge, MA: M.I.T. Press.

Modra, H. (1991) On the possibility of dialogue in distance education: A dialogue. In B. King, H. Modra & D. Nation, *Independence, autonomy and dialogue in distance education* (pp. 10–32). Geelong, Victoria: Deakin University Press/University of South Australia.

Nicholson, L. (1990) *Feminism/postmodernism.* New York: Routledge.

Noddings, N. (1984) *Caring: A feminine approach to ethics and moral education.* Berkeley, California: University of California Press.

NWSA (1977) *Founding constitution.* San Francisco.

O'Brien, M. (1984) The commatization of women: Patriarchal fetishism in the sociology of education. *Interchange, 15,* 43–60.

Raymond, J. (1986) *A passion for friends: Toward a philosophy of female affection.* Boston: Beacon Press.

Rich, A. (1980a) Taking women students seriously. In A. Rich (Ed.), *On lies, secrets and silence* (pp. 237–245). London: Virago.

Rich, A. (1980b) Claiming an education. In A. Rich (Ed.), *On lies, secrets and silence* (pp. 231–235). London: Virago.

Rowbotham, S. (1980) The trouble with patriarchy. In Feminist Anthology Collective (Ed.), *No turning back: Writing from the women's liberation movement* (pp. 72–79). London: Women's Press.

Roy, P. & Schen, M. (1987) Feminist pedagogy: Transforming the high school classroom. *Women's Studies Quarterly, 15* (Fall/Winter), 110–115.

Schniedewind, N. (1987) Feminist values: Guidelines for a teaching methodology in women's studies. In I. Shore (Ed.), *Freire for the classroom* (pp. 170–179). New Hampshire: Boynton & Cook.

Schools Commission (1987) *The National Policy for the Education of Girls in Australian Schools.* Canberra: AGPS.

Seddon, T. (1981) The hidden curriculum: An overview. *Curriculum Perspectives, 3*(1), 1–6.

Shor, I. (1980) *Critical teaching and everyday life.* Boston: South End Press.

Shor, I. (1987) *Freire for the classroom.* New Hampshire: Boynton & Cook.

Simon, R. (1988) For a pedagogy of possibility. *Critical Pedagogy Networker, 1*(1).

Smith, W. (1976) *The meaning of conscientizacao: The goal of Paulo Freire's Pedagogy.* Amherst, MA: Center for International Education, University of Massachusetts.

Smith, W., Alschuler, A., Moreno, C. & Tasiquano, E. (1975) Critical consciousness. *Meforum: Journal of Educational Diversity and Innovation* (Spring), 69–74.

Suggett, D. (1987) Inclusive curriculum: A gain or loss for girls? *Curriculum Perspectives, 7*(1), 69–74.

Tobias, S. (1978) Women's studies: Its origins, its organisation, and its prospects. *Women's studies International Quarterly, 1*(1), 85–97, cited in R. Klein (1987).

Tong, R. (1990) *Feminist thought: A comprehensive introduction.* London: Unwin Hyman.

Walden, R. & Walkerdine, V. (1985) *Girls and mathematics: From primary to secondary schooling.* London: Institute of Education, University of London.

Walker, J. (1980) The end of dialogue: Paulo Freire on politics and education. In R. Mackie (Ed.), *Literacy and revolution* (pp. 120–150). London: Pluto Press.

Walkerdine, V. (1981) Sex, power and pedagogy. *Screen Education, 38* (Spring), 14–24.

Walkerdine, V. (1984) Developmental psychology and child centered pedagogy: The insertion of Piaget into early education. In J. Henriques, C. Urwin, C. Venn & V. Walkerdine (Eds.), *Changing the subject* (pp. 153–202). London: Methuen.

Walkerdine, V. (1985) On the regulation of speaking and silence: Subjectivity, class and gender in contemporary schooling. In C. Steedman, C. Unwin & V. Walkerdine (Eds.), *Language, gender and childhood* (pp. 203–242). London, Routledge & Kegan Paul.

Weedon, C. (1987) *Feminist practice and post-structuralist theory.* London: Basil Blackwell.

Weiler, K. (1988) *Women teaching for change: Gender, class and power.* Massachusetts: Bergin & Garvey.

Weiner, G. (1988) *Just a bunch of girls.* Milton Keynes: Open University Press.

Weinstein, G. (1975) Humanistic education: What it is and what it isn't. *Meforum: Journal of Educational Diversity and Innovation* (Spring), 8–11.

Whyte, J., Deem, R., Kant. L. & Cruickshank, A. (Eds.) (1985) *Girl friendly schooling.* London: Methuen.

Willis, S. & Kenway, J. (1986) On overcoming sexism in schooling: To marginalize or mainstream. *Australian Journal of Education, 30*(2), 132–149.

Wyn, J. (1990) Working class girls and educational outcomes: Is self esteem an issue? In J. Kenway & S. Willis (Eds.), *Hearts and minds: Self esteem and the schooling of girls* (pp. 199–231). London: Falmer Press.

Yates, L. (1985) Curriculum becomes our way of contradicting biology and culture: An outline of some dilemmas for non-sexist education. *The Australian Journal of Education, 29*(1), 3–17.

Yates, L. (forthcoming) Some dimensions of the practice of theory and the development of theory for practice in relation to gender and education. In J. Blackmore & J. Kenway (Eds.), *Gender issues in educational administration and policy.* London: Falmer Press.

9

Interrupting Patriarchy: Politics, Resistance and Transformation in the Feminist Classroom

Magda Lewis

In Canada, the fall of 1989 marked a particularly hostile environment for women on university campuses.[1] On my own campus the events surrounding our "NO MEANS NO" campaign drew national attention. "NO MEANS NO" was an educational campaign organized by the Gender Issues Committee of the undergraduate student government (Alma Mater Society), aimed at alerting young women, particularly first-year students, to the forms and expressions of date rape. The reaction of a faction of the male students was to respond with a "sign campaign" that made explicit their belief that women's refusal of male sexual demands could appropriately be countered with violence ("No means tie me up") or with their own definitions of women's sexual deviance ("No means dyke"). To the extent that the signs were accompanied by active verbal threats and physical intimidation, many women experienced the threatening atmosphere as misogyny.

My campus was not the only one experiencing what appeared to be an increasing backlash to a feminist presence inside the academy. As women academics across and between campuses shared stories of violation, more and more examples of misogyny surfaced. Our isolation and small numbers (women still comprise a very small fraction of academic faculty) precluded any possibility of collective action (Brodribb, 1987; McCormack, 1987). In the face of an academic community complicit in its complacency, and unwilling to acknowledge its oppressive practices born of the sexual subordination of women, we were atomized and held inside the private spaces of our own violations. And yet, despite the isolation of our struggles, we worked with our students to create an intellectually and emotionally supportive environment for them (Lewis, 1990a).

It was within this context that we witnessed with horror the spiraling momentum of woman-hating explode, in the early evening of December sixth, with the massacre of fourteen women at the Université de Montréal by a gun-wielding young man who had convinced himself that women, transposed in his own sad head into the phrase "you bunch of feminists," were the cause of his own personal misery.

This incident focused, on several levels, my concerns about teaching and learning as a feminist in the academy. The historical context of our individual and collective experiences as intellectual women enabled me to see that what the media identified as the "idiosyncratic" madness of this young man actually reflected infinitely receding images of male power transformed into violence—a polished surface facing the mirror of masculine privilege. Because of our identification with a politic that makes explicit our critique of women's subordination as a function of masculine privilege, my students' and my own safety were in question. This was not the single act of a deranged mind, nor the outcome of peculiar conditions on that specific campus. That the events at the Université de Montréal could have happened on any campus in this country—indeed, any campus on this continent—became a tangible reality (Malette & Chalouh, 1990).

I am haunted by the image of young women—not unlike the women I teach—lined up against the wall, while their perplexed, perhaps helpless, male colleagues and male instructor vacated the classroom. I am haunted, too, by the words (reported in the media) of that young woman whose vain efforts to save herself and her women classmates were captured when she screamed at the gunman: "You have the wrong women; we are not feminists!"

The words "you have the wrong women; we are not feminists" provides a backdrop for the question I raise: How might we bring about the social changes we desire without negating women's perspective on our reality, or turning it, yet one more time, into a self-perpetuated liability? More specifically, how might I create a feminist pedagogy that supports women's desire to wish well for ourselves, when for many women the "good news" of the transformative powers of feminist consciousness turns into the "bad news" of social inequality and, therefore, a perspective and politics they want to resist? More than resistance, which, drawing on Willis (1977), I characterize as the struggles against social forms that are experienced as oppressive, transformation is the fusion of political perspective and practice. Transformation is the development of a critical perspective through which individuals can begin to see how social practices are organized to support certain interests. It is also the process whereby this understanding is used as the basis for active political intervention directed toward social change, with the intent to disempower relations of inequality.

In short, my agenda in this paper is to understand the basis from which I might fashion a viable feminist pedagogy of transformation out of student resistance—not to patriarchic meaning-making, but to feminist politics.

Using my experiences in Foundations 490, in this article I continue to raise the dilemmas I face as a feminist teacher. I explore the possibilities and limits of feminist teaching and learning in the academy under conditions that directly contradict its intent (Lewis & Simon, 1986; Lewis, 1988a, 1989, 1990a). Foundations 490 is a Sociology of Education course I teach in the faculty of education at Queen's University. While it is not one of the core Women's Studies courses, it is cross-listed in the Women's Studies Program Calendar. For this reason, the course often draws students from a wide range of disciplines. The specific title of the course, "Seminar in Social Class, Gender and Race in Education," is explicitly descriptive of the course focus. In the course outline, I tell students that the theoretical framework we are using draws on critical and feminist theory and method. More specifically, the course proposes to "examine and develop a critical understanding of the implications for children's educational experiences of the effects of social class background, sex/gender differences and racial background." It also proposes to "locate school practices as part of the larger social context within which schools exist." The course format is a seminar which incorporates class discussion around assigned readings and student presentations. The class presentation component requires students to articulate the social meaning of a cultural artifact or practice of their choice. Students examine how the artifact or practice reflects the social/cultural context out of which it has arisen. The purpose of the assignment is to help students develop their skills in raising questions about our culture about practices that they had previously taken as given. My intention is also that, through the exercise, they might see differently how sexism, racism, class differentiation, homophobia, and so on, are embedded in concrete cultural products and social practices.

I begin the course with an introductory lecture that outlines to the students what I intend that we take up during the coming term and the perspective from which my analysis proceeds. By doing this, I attempt to incorporate many aspects of women's lives articulated within feminist politics.

The course is attended by both female and male students, although women tend to outnumber the men four to one. This, in part, is accounted for by the fact that student enrollment in faculties of education is still largely skewed in favor of women, who comprise approximately 70 to 75 percent of the undergraduate teacher education complement. Because the majority of students in Foundations 490 are women, in this paper I use the general designation "student" to refer to women or to the students in general. When I refer to the men in the classroom I shall use the qualifier "male".

While in this paper I explore the context of my teaching practice and the politics of the classroom, it is not my intention to offer prescriptive and generic feminist teaching strategies abstracted from the particular situations of feminist classrooms. Although it might be possible to employ suggestive approaches, we cannot artificially construct pedagogical moments in the classroom to serve as moments of transformation toward a critical political perspective. Nor can we predict how such moments will be responded to when they arise in particular situations given the personal histories of the students and instructors involved.

Rather, I believe questions about the politics of feminist teaching have most specifically to do with how we identify those pedagogical moments whose transformative power lies precisely in the understandings we bring to the gendered context of the classroom. Ruth Pierson (1987) provides a clear and comprehensive definition of feminism, which frames the intent of my own teaching from a feminist perspective:

> One identifiable characteristic of feminism across an entire spectrum of varieties has been the pursuit of autonomy for women. Integral to this feminist pursuit of independent personhood is the critical awareness of a sex/gender system that relegates power and autonomy to men and dependence and subordination to women. Feminists start from an insistence on the importance of women and women's experience, but a woman-centered perspective alone does not constitute feminism. Before a woman-centered perspective becomes a feminist perspective, it has to have been politicized by the experience of women in pursuit of self-determination coming into conflict with a sex-gender system of male dominance. From a feminist perspective the sex/gender system appears to be a fundamental organizing principle of society and for that reason it becomes a primary object of analysis. (p. 203)

From this perspective I raise the psychological, social and sexual dynamics of the feminist classroom as a site where, I believe, the political struggle over meaning must be seen as the focus of our pedagogical project. It is a context in which a serious intrusion of *feminist pedagogy* must concern itself, as Rachel Blau DuPlessis (1985) suggests, not with urging our women students to "resent the treatment of [their] sex and plead for its rights" (p. 33)—a project that acts to reaffirm women's subordination and encourage our exploitation—but to self-consciously examine and question the conditions of our own meaning-making and to use it as the place from which to begin to work toward change.

In taking up the psychological, social and sexual dynamics of the feminist classroom, in this paper I propose to examine the violence/negotiation dichotomy environment as a feature of women's educational experience. In this context, I share the strategies I employ in specific instances as a feminist teacher to subvert the status quo of classroom interaction between women and men. Finally, in the conclusion I suggest a specific framework that articulates the terms of feminist teaching.

Theoretical framework

In the largely unchallenged practices of the school setting marked by patriarchic privilege (Corrigan, 1987), for women, the dynamics of contestation born of knowledge are more complex than is often implied in the resistance literature. By paying close attention to practices in the classroom, forms of discourse, directions taken in discussion, the subtleties of body language, and so on, it is clear that, for women, a dichotomy between desire and threat is reproduced and experienced inside the classroom itself.

The salience of this dichotomy for women is suggested by Kathleen Rockhill

(1987b), in her powerful and moving article, "Literacy as Threat/Desire: Longing to be SOMEBODY," in which she articulates women's contradictory reality as an educational dilemma. For the women in Rockhill's study, the knowledge and power made potentially available through becoming literate contradictorily also repositioned them in such a way that it threatened familial, conjugal, and ultimately economic relations.

Rockhill explains:

> It is common today for education to be ideologically dressed as the pathway to a new kind of romance for women, the romance of a "career," a profession, a middle-class way of life; the image is one of a well-dressed woman doing "clean" work, important work. As such, it feeds her yearning, her desire, for a way out of the "working class" life she has known (Steedman, 1986). It is precisely because education holds out this promise for women that it also poses a threat to them in their everyday lives. This is especially true for women in heterosexual relationships when their men feel threatened by the images of power (independence and success) attached to education. (p. 315)

In the feminist classroom, the contradiction that women experience is compounded by the way in which feminist politics challenges the everyday lives they have learned to negotiate.

The complexities of student resistance to the intentions of schooling have been documented before, and indeed such accounts provide much of the data for the theoretical framework of critical pedagogy. Paul Willis's classic work, *Learning to Labour* (1977), influenced by the theoretical work of Bowles and Gintis, Althusser, Bourdieu and Passeron, and Gramsci, was one of the first. Willis's study dealt exclusively with the experiences of male students. He included women only in their relations as girlfriends and mothers. In this context, it is interesting to note the irony of the title of the more recent book by Dale Spender and Elizabeth Sarah, *Learning to Lose* (1980), a study of the experiences of girls in school.

In its classic form, critical pedagogy emphasizes that student resistance to the experiences of institutionalized education is forged from the contradictions perceived between the dominant discourse of school knowledge on the one hand and students' own lived experiences of subordination and violation on the other. According to resistance theory, students struggle to mark themselves off against the dominant discourse of the school through the enactment of practices that reaffirm and validate their subjectivities as specifically classed, raced, and gendered social actors.

It is my explicit intent in the classroom to raise with students issues of social relations from a critical perspective. But I am also a feminist who has worked for many years in feminist politics across a variety of sites. My family life, my involvement with grassroots community organizations, and my intellectual work are informed in concrete ways by the politics of feminist analysis. By extension, the politics that informs my everyday life infuses my relations with students, generates the readings for the course, and suggests my classroom teaching style and practice. Yet my frustrations as a feminist teacher arise significantly from the extent to which critical thinking on transformative pedagogical practices fails to address the specifics of women's education as simultaneously a site of desire and threat.

Based on my own experiences, I know that a feminist perspective could offer understandings the students might develop and bring to bear on their own experiences (Lather, 1988). Yet I also realize that attending to feminist politics and cultural critique in the classroom requires difficult emotional work from them and from me. I know that new understandings are often experienced painfully, and that lives are transformed.

All of this has happened in Foundations 490. Yet, the forms through which such transformations have taken place are not those that I anticipated—or perhaps hoped for. As a teacher and a feminist I share the hope for the promise of education as a political project: that through the offer of a theoretical framework—analysis and critique—students would eagerly join in my enthusiasm to work for social change in their personal and public lives. Clearly there are times when women immediately embrace the intentions of feminist teaching because it helps them make a different sense of their experiences. But just as often, students struggle with these new understandings as they explore the space between the public and theoretical agenda of the course and the privacy of their everyday lives, where complex negotiations across gender often take their most salient form.

In the academy, women find themselves inside institutions whose practices and intentions are historically designed to keep them outside its concrete and theoretical frames. For women students, negotiating masculine content and practices often means that they have to absorb as well as struggle to survive the violations of their subordination. My students often find more simple and, therefore, more powerful words through which to express my meaning. The legacy of the violations women experience in the academy are apparent in the following conversations:

—I don't speak in class anymore. All this professor ever talked about was men, what they do, what they say, always just what's important to men. He, he, he is all I ever heard in class. He wasn't speaking my language. And whenever I tried to speak about what was important to me, whenever I tried to ask questions about how women fit into his scheme all I got was a negative response. I always felt I was speaking from inside brackets, like walls I couldn't be heard past. I got tired of not being heard so I stopped speaking altogether.

—I often tried to bring up examples of famous women in class because I thought it was important that people should acknowledge that women had done some things too. But no one ever knew who I was talking about. There was this assumption that if someone was a woman she couldn't possibly have done anything famous. The most important thing that happened to me in high school was that one of my history teachers had a picture of Agnes Mcphail pinned above the blackboard in the classroom. We never talked about it directly but for me that became a symbol of a woman. Sometimes I got really disgusted in some of my classes but I would think of that picture in that history class and that helped me to feel less alienated.

—In history we never talked about what women did; in geography it was always what was important to men. The same in our English class, we hardly ever studied women authors. I won't even talk about math and science . . . I always felt that I didn't belong . . . Sometimes the boys would make jokes about girls doing science experiments. They always thought they were going to do it better and it made me really nervous. Sometimes I didn't even try to do an experiment because I knew they would laugh if I got it wrong. Now I just *deaden* myself against it, so I don't hear it anymore. But I feel really alienated. My experience now is one of total silence. Sometimes I even wish I didn't know what I know.

For me, as a feminist teacher, such statements are not only painful but revealing. The remarks suggest that the politics of my teaching should focus not on teaching women what we already know, but on finding ways of helping all of us articulate the knowledge we gain from our experience.

As a beginning point I agree with the claim of Giroux and Simon (1988):

We are not concerned with simply motivating students to learn, but rather *establishing the conditions of learning* that enable them to locate themselves in history and to interrogate the adequacy of that location as both a pedagogical and political question. (p. 3, emphasis added)

Yet a feminist pedagogy cannot stop here. For women, the cultural, political, and ultimately historical discourse of the everyday, the present, and the immediate are conditions of learning marked by the varied forms of patriarchic violence (Brookes, 1992; Belenky, Clinchy, Goldberger & Tarule, 1986; McMahon, 1986). Pedagogy, even radical pedagogy, does not easily translate into an education that includes women if we do not address the threat to women's survival and livelihood that a critique of patriarchy in its varied manifestations confronts.

The dynamics of the classroom context when students engage a feminist analysis presents the most challenging aspects of feminist teaching (Lewis, 1988a). In what follows I explore the psychological, social, and sexual aspects of this context.

Psychological dynamics in the feminist classroom

For women, tension in the feminist classroom is often organized around our historically produced nurturing capacity as a feature of our psychologically internalized role as caretakers (Lewis, 1988b). The following example is a case in point. Recently, in reference to a set of class readings dealing with peace education, my introductory presentation spoke to the connections between patriarchy, violence, and political economy. As I finished, one of the first students to speak was a young woman. She said, "As you were speaking I was wondering and worrying about how the men in the room were feeling. What you said made sense to me, but I felt uncomfortable about how the men took it." A couple of other women nodded their agreement. Such a protective posture on the part of women on behalf of men is a common drama played out in many classrooms.

Similar responses to feminist critique are not specific to mixed-gender classrooms. The absence of men in the classroom does not significantly diminish the psychological investment women are required to make in the emotional well-being of men—an investment that goes well beyond the classroom into the private spaces of women's lives, which cannot easily be left at the classroom door. The response women bring to feminist politics/analyses arises from women's social/political location within patriarchic forms, which requires that men be the focus of women's attentions. Examples range from general claims that men are also isolated and contained by patriarchy in what is required of them within the terms of masculinity, to more specific references to personal family relations aimed at exempting intimate male relations from the general population of men. The sharing of household duties is often used as an example, although the articulation of details of this shared housework is often vague. Young women growing up in physically violent and sexually violating homes know a more brutal side of the caretaking imperative.[2]

Whether or not men are physically present in the classroom, women carry the parameters of patriarchic meaning-making as a frame from within which we struggle to articulate our own interests. How women live this experience is not specific to mixed-gender classrooms. While it is my observation that the practice of a woman-as-caretaker ideology is more obvious in the presence of men, this ideology holds sway whether or not men are present, as long as women believe their interests to be served by maintaining existing relations.

This formulation is not intended to subsume the experiences of all women and men under seamless, hegemonic constructs articulated through dominant expressions of femininity/masculinity. I use Alison Jaggar's (1983) formulation of Gramsci's notion of hegemony: a concept

> designed to explain how a dominant class maintains control by projecting its own particular way of seeing social reality so successfully that its view is accepted as common sense and as part of the natural order by those who in fact are subordinated to it (p. 151).

In this respect, hegemony is accomplished through an ongoing struggle over meaning not only against, but for the maintenance of, power. Lesbians and gay men experience the social constructs of femininity/masculinity differently than women and men whose emotional and psychic investment is in heterosexual relationships. However, especially in professional schools, where students' aspirations for future employment often govern their willingness to challenge the status quo, pressures to conform to the dominant social text are shared by lesbians and heterosexual women alike (Khayatt, 1987). Because lesbians and gay men often remain voiceless within such classroom dynamics, the relations between the women and men in the classroom remains a site that supports only practices that construct women's social acceptability as caretakers of men.

In the mixed-gender classroom, much of the caretaking takes the form of hard-to-describe body language displayed as a barely perceptible "moving toward"; a not-quite-visible extending of the hand; a protective stance accomplished through eye contact. However, as the young woman's question of concern has shown, just as often it is explicitly articulated. In the feminist classroom, such caretaking responses on the part of women toward men are ones that, as feminist teachers, we easily recognize and anticipate. We must choose words carefully and negotiate our analyses with the women students in ways that will not turn them away from the knowledge they carry in their experiences.

Following the young woman's comments, many of the men seemed to feel that what she said vindicated their feelings of discomfort with the way in which I was formulating the issues. Some of the men expressed this through verbal support of the woman's concern over their emotional well-being. They showed a strong inclination to redirect the discussion toward notions of world violence as a *human* and not a gendered problem. By doing so, the men attempted to reappropriate a speaking space for themselves, which they saw to be threatened by my analysis. Even more troublesome for me was the pleasure some of the men seemed to take in encouraging women to take up the caretaking on their behalf, and in how the women seemed to be brought up against one another in the debate that followed. The question of whether or not feminist critique constituted a confrontational stance by women against men was the substance of the debate between the women and the men and among the women. Some of the men offered verbal support for women who agreed with them and a rebuttal of those who did not. However, the more subtle forms of pleasure-taking are difficult to describe. We do not have language that can adequately express the social meaning of the practice of relaxing back into one's chair, with a barely-there smile on one's face while eyes are fixed on the object of negation. One of the reasons feminist films are a source of exceptionally powerful critique is because they can display how violation works at the level of the non-verbal (Lewis, 1990b). Yet such practices are unmistakable in their intent. The non-verbal is a social language that women—and all culturally marginal groups—have learned to read well and that does its sad work on women's emotions.

That such a dynamic should develop among the students was not a surprise. I know that, within the terms of patriarchy, women have had no choice but to care about the feelings of men. Women know that, historically, not caring has cost us our lives: intellectually, emotionally, socially, psychologically, and physically. I see this played out over and over again in my classes, and in every case it makes women recoil from saying what they really want to say and simultaneously leaves men reassured about their right to speak on behalf of us all.

For me, this dynamic presented a pedagogical dilemma. How could I question particularities of our present social organization, which requires women to work as caretakers of men not only in economic/material relations, but in emotional/ psychological ones as well? Furthermore, how was I to do this in ways that did not reproduce the women's strong inclination to protect the men for what was *felt* to be an indictment of men in general and the men in the classroom in particular? Specifically, how could I help them focus on social organizational practices, rather than on the man sitting next to them in the classroom?

I asked them to think of instances when we might expect men to reciprocate for women the kind of caretaking practices and ego support that women are expected to extend on behalf of men. Most specifically, I asked the women if they had ever been in the company of a male friend/partner/family member/stranger who, upon seeing our discomfort at the common public display of misogyny in such examples as billboards, had ever offered support for how uncomfortable and violated such displays must make us feel. By asking students to focus on the personal, I felt that it might be possible to reposition the women and men in a social configuration that did not take a gendered hierarchy and its attendant practices for granted. Not only the women, but the men as well, admitted that they had never had such an experience. More to the point, there was general agreement that the possibility had never even occurred to them.

Through our discussion, it became clear that as a collective social practice, for men, attentiveness to other than one's self is largely a matter of choice, whereas for women, it has been a socially and historically mandated condition of our acceptability as women. This provided, for some of the students in the class, a moment of critical reflection and transformation. It also offered a framework from which to envision a set of social relations not based fundamentally on inequality. For men such transformation often appears as a willingness to listen. Less eager to talk, they sometimes acknowledge that they can see themselves on the privileged side of the gender divide and admit that they had not previously given it a lot of thought. These acknowledgements are often fairly brief and to the point: "I had never thought of it that way" is a common response. Whether or not men carry their new understanding into their public and private lives outside the classroom is unclear. If they do, they have not shared it with me. For women, transformation often means a more active process. At times, younger women have asked to bring male friends to the class with them. More frequently, students have reported that they have asked their male friends or partners to read some of the course material. And some women have reported major changes in their family life, either in terms of renegotiated practices—mostly pertaining to household responsibilities—or in a decision to end a relationship. I do not want to suggest that every student in every class experiences these transformations. Progress is slow, and often tentative, as students struggle with the implications of their new understanding.

By shifting our focus from the topic of discussion—the political economy and masculine forms of world violence—and refocusing on the dynamics in the classroom at that moment, we made it possible to ask what cultural/political forms might articulate caretaking as a reciprocal process between women and men. This teaching strategy is central to my pedagogical agenda: identifying the moment when students might be most receptive to uncovering how they are invested in their own meaning-making practices.

Social dynamics in the feminist classroom

For many students, the social context of the feminist classroom is another sphere of tension. For the women students, the content and processes of feminist curricula and teaching can result in the classic version of consciousness raising. "Feminist method," says Catharine MacKinnon (1983), "is consciousness raising:"

> . . . the collective critical reconstitution of the meaning of women's social experience, as women live through it. . . . Consciousness raising . . . inquires into an intrinsically social situation, into that mixture of thought and materiality which is women's sexuality in the most generic sense. It approaches its world through a process that shares its determination: women's consciousness, not as individual or subjective ideas, but as a collective social being. . . . The process is transformative as well as perceptive, since thought and thing are inextricable and reciprocally constituting the women's oppression, just as the state as coercion and the state as legitimizing ideology are indistinguishable, and for the same reason. The pursuit of consciousness becomes a form of political practice. (p. 225)

Reading Catharine MacKinnon has convinced me that the politic of consciousness raising has earned a bad name precisely because it is a profoundly effective practice. There is a long history to the fear of women coming together and, in that space, sharing the personal stories that become metaphorical bases for generating a theory of women's subordination (Daly, 1978). The dominant forms of discourse are aimed hegemonically at preventing women from engaging in discussions that lead toward consciousness raising; the threat of social sanctions defuses the vitality of storytelling. Telling our stories of violation and subordination in the presence of those whose advantages are highlighted and challenged by such sharing, or doing so in the presence of those who hold the discursive power to subvert the act of consciousness raising as a feminist method, is for many women a contradictory outcome of their experiences in the feminist classroom.

I believe the following exchange demonstrates this point well. Recently, a student was making a class presentation on the topic of violence against women. A few minutes after the beginning of her presentation, a frustrated young man demanded to know why we had to talk about women and men all the time, and why the presenter did not offer "the other side of the story." This example confirms other experiences indicating that students, particularly those who benefit from the present social arrangements, often find it difficult to engage in the self-reflection required to question the unequal and violent social relations in which we ourselves are social actors.

As a feature of classroom dynamics, the unpacking and uncovering of deeply submerged social practices of domination/entitlement experienced by the "Other" as subordination/oppression, which we carry in and on our gendered bodies, in our verbal expressions, in the privilege (or lack of it) of having choice, can itself become another source for experiences of oppression. For women, as for other subordinate groups, it is the fact of "knowing" that is seen to be an act of insubordination; exposing that knowledge, speaking it in public space, claiming language through which to articulate our knowledge, and refusing to believe that the dominant discourse speaks for all, as it speaks on behalf of patriarchic interests, is used as the justification for continued violation.

In part, patriarchy disempowers women by marginalizing our experiences of violation in an ongoing discourse that legitimates only those ways of making sense or the telling of only those kinds of stories that do not make men "look bad" (MacKinnon, 1987, p. 154). The use of language, for example, which exchanges "wife-battering" with "family violence," as a way to redirect our focus away from masculine practices is a case in point.

One way male students sometimes wish to displace the sense women make of our experience is to refocus the discussion in directions that are less disquieting for them. In the instance mentioned above, I understood the young man's demand—the tone of his voice left no doubt that it was a demand—to be an attempt to redirect the discussion away from his own social identity as a male who, whether he acknowledges it or not, benefits from the culturally, legally, and politically encoded social relations of patriarchy (MacKinnon, 1987). Yet men can no more deny the embodiment of their masculine privilege than any of us can deny the embodiment of our entitlement if we are white, economically advantaged, heterosexual, able-bodied, and carrying the valued assets of the privilege of Euro-American culture. As is suggested by Biddy Martin and Chandra Mohanty (1986):

> the claim to a lack of identity or positionality is itself based on privilege, on a refusal to accept responsibility for one's implication in actual historical or social relations, on a denial that postionalities exist or that they matter, the denial of one's own personal history and the claim to a total separation from it (p. 208).

Furthermore, to the extent that sexism, racism, and social class inequalities represent social systems within which we either appropriate or struggle against particular personal relations, those who embody positions of privilege are often not attracted to an articulation of their interests in the terms required by self-reflexivity.

On this occasion, I judged that, by providing for the possibility of self-reflexive critique, I might avert the tendency of such debates to degenerate into expressions of guilt and victimization which would destroy the creative potential of a feminist political discourse that speaks not only to women but to men as well. I also felt that how I presented my response was crucial. Whatever my response was, it had to be possible for women to see it as a model for how they might also take up similar challenges to their own meaning-making in ways other than to demand their right to do so—precisely the point of debate. My challenge was to create the possibility for students to be self-reflexive.

The young man's demand for the "other side" of the story about men's violence against women created the space I was looking for. In classrooms, as in other social/political spaces, women and men come together unequally (Lewis & Simon, 1986). In such a context, a pedagogical approach that fails to acknowledge how such inequality silences serves to reinforces the powerlessness of the powerless. I knew from my own experience that under such circumstances, asking women to "speak up" and intervene on their own behalf would have reproduced exactly that marginalization that the young man's demand was intended to create. Clearly, I needed to employ another strategy.

The power of teaching as dramatic performance cannot be discounted on this particular occasion. Following the question, I allowed a few moments of silence. In these few moments, as the question and the dynamics of the situation settled into our consciousness, the social history of the world was relived in the bodies of the women and men around the table. What is the "other side of the story" about violence against women! What could the women say? Faced with the demand to articulate their *reality in terms not of their own making*, the women visibly shrank into their chairs; their breathing became invisible (Rockhill, 1987a). In contrast, whether I imagined it or not, it seemed to me that the men sat more upright and "leaned into" the response that began to formulate in my head. It seemed clear to me that the young man's objections to the woman's presentation constructed women as objects of practices which were experienced by him as umproblematic; the threat of physical violence is not one which most men experience on a daily basis. By objectifying women through his question, he reinforced male privilege. I needed to find a way of repositioning us—women and men—in such a way that the young man had no options but to face his own social location as problematic.

The stage was set for dramatic performance. Reassuring the young man that indeed he was right—that "other sides" of issues need to be considered whenever possible—I wondered if *he* would perhaps be the one who could tell us about the "other side" of violence against women. My memory of this moment again focuses on the breath: the men's as it escaped their bodies, and the women's as it replenished theirs.

Turning the question away from the women in the class created the self-reflexive space that I believed could truly challenge the men in the class to take up not women's subordination, but their own positions of privilege. Given the social realities of violence against women, the student was no more able to answer his own question than it might have been possible for the women to do so. At the same time, it remained for him to tell us why he couldn't answer his own question. He found himself speechless. This time, the silence that followed reversed the order of privilege to name the social realities we live. The young man's failure to find a salient way of taking up the issue he had raised made it possible for the young woman to continue with her presentation without challenge to her fundamental right to do so.

The incident ended at this point, and the class presentation proceeded. Reflecting on my own practice in this instance, I cannot deny that my politics embraced and supported the struggle for women's autonomy and self-determination. Working with women to create the space for our voice is fundamental to this politic. Whether the young man experienced transformation, or was simply intimidated into silence, was something that required sorting out. I was willing to let him undertake the hard work of doing so for himself. If I had silenced him, I could only hope that perhaps the experience would provide him with a deeper understanding of an experience women encounter every day. That the incident was experienced by the women in ways that signalled a moment of possibility for them is captured by the reaction of one young woman, who came over to where I was distractedly picking up my papers after the long three-hour class and lightened the load of my exhaustion with the announcement that she wanted to be a sociologist and a feminist and would I tell her "how to become it." Both her naiveté and mine embarrassed us into shared laughter; but such fleeting moments of embrace are sometimes all we have, it seems to me, to collect ourselves and move on. Such experiences reveal the feminist classroom as profoundly relevant to women's lives.

Sexual dynamics in the feminist classroom

Finally, the sexual dynamics of mixed-gender classrooms are complex and often contradictory. Particularly for younger women, at times still caught in the glare of sexual exploration and identification, the feminist classroom can feel threatening. The following example is a case in point.

Recently, during the introductory lecture I use as a way of framing the seminar session, I was addressing the educational concerns over the low number of women in mathematics and science programs. On this occasion, trying to concretize the issues for the students, I asked them to indicate, by a show of hands, which of them were preparing to be math and science teachers. A number of students raised their hands. As might be expected, many of those who raised their hands were men. However, a number of women also raised their hands. A "guffawed" and embarrassed laughter rose from the back corner of the room after a young man whispered a comment to a young woman who had raised her hand.

I do not generally make use of or support embarrassment as a pedagogical strategy. In this instance, however, I felt certain that I knew what the laughter was about and wanted to capture the moment as a concrete example of exactly the issues I was raising. I requested that the young man tell us what he had said. He resisted; I insisted. The use of institutional power, I believe, should not always be viewed as counterproductive to our politics. Feminism is a politic that is both historical and contingent on existing social relations. I had no problem justifying the use of my institutional power to create the possibility for privilege to face itself and own its violation publicly. Using power to subjugate is quite different from using power to liberate. The young man complied. He told us that he had whispered to the young woman that perhaps she had had a sex change.

The assumed prerogative to pass such commentary on women's choices of career and life possibilities is not, of course, new to any of us. However, in the feminist classroom, such commentary and attendant laughter become overtly political issues that can be taken up as instances of gender politics. I used the incident as an example of the kind of academic environment created for women when such interactions are not treated as problematic. In doing so, I was aware that both the women and the men experienced various degrees of discomfort. Many of the men and some of the women insisted that I was making too much of an innocent joke, while many of the women and none of the men, as far as I could tell, sat quietly with faces flushed. In thinking about how I approach my teaching, I can recall the salient details of this example to understand how gender politics can be transformed into sexual dynamics in the classroom. Not only gender, but sexuality, is a deeply present organizing principle in the classroom, and one which enters into the dynamics of how we come together as women and men in pursuit of shared meaning.

The production of shared meaning is one of the ways we experience deeply felt moments of psycho sexual pleasure, whether across or within gender. Yet, in a patriarchic culture, women and men can find the articulation of shared meaning profoundly elusive, and the desire for pleasure in conflict with mutual understanding.

While women have always found support in separate women's communities, education cells, political movements, work, and so on, these sites of solidarity have usually existed outside of the dominant male culture—a culture of which, we cannot forget, women are also an integral part. Social, political, and economic relations are articulated through the personal/collective experience we have of the world. Feminist politics insist on using these experiences as the lens through which to look at the barely perceptible, yet tenacious, threads that hold the social forms and forces in place. For women who refuse subordination, who refuse to pretend that we don't know, standing against these social forces has not only economic and political consequences but psycho/sexual ones as well. bell hooks (1989) comments:

> Sexism is unique. It is unlike other forms of domination—racism or classism—where the exploited and oppressed do not live in large numbers inti-

mately with their oppressors or develop their primary love relationships (familial and/or romantic) with the individuals who oppress and dominate or share in
the privileges attained by domination. . . . (For women) the context of these
intimate relationships is also the site of domination and oppression. (p. 130)

This dynamic is seldom, if ever, talked about in the feminist classroom, and yet,
it explains the conflicting emotional and analytic responses women have to the
content of the course.

Exploring the sexual parameters of the conditions under which women are
required to undertake their intellectual work is crucial. Finding examples is not
hard; relating them is. It is with difficulty that I cite specific examples, and then
only briefly, because of my own complex emotions associated with writing these
words and having them stand starkly, darkly on the page to be read and reread;
knowing that stories of violation violate at each retelling. These stories are not
lightly told nor lightly received; they are often related in the privacy of my office.
One woman's books disappeared (an event reminiscent of the one related in Janice Radway's *Reading the Romance*, 1984); another, alerted by the words,
"maybe you should be reading this instead," had a copy of a pornographic magazine flung at her as she sat reading her course material; and yet another was told,
as a "joke" at a social gathering, that to "celebrate" the completion of the course
she would be "rewarded" by being "raped" so she could "get it out of her system"
and return to her "old self." The monitoring and banning of what women read is
shown in these examples to be closely associated with demands for women to
conform to a particular version of male-defined sexuality. While the above may
represent especially harsh examples, the antagonistic relationship drawn between
women's desire for knowledge and our embodiment as sexually desirable human
beings is an issue that lies always just below the surface in the classroom.

For many women, a feminist worldview is deeply incorporated at the level of
everyday practice. Yet, we need to be aware that by requiring women to challenge masculine constructs—as I had done in the classroom example cited
above—we also require them to break with the dominant phallocentric culture.
While as feminist teachers we might believe that such a break may offer the only
possibilities for the resolution of this conflict, we must be aware that for many
women the concrete possibility of doing so is difficult to contemplate. As Claire
Duchen, quoted in Rowbotham (1989), suggests, "the tailoring of desire to the
logic of politics is not always possible or acceptable" (p. 85).

Feminist critique of phallocentric culture is at once fundamentally necessary
for and profoundly disruptive of the possibilities for shared meaning across gender, leaving women vulnerable to what Sheila Radford-Hill (1986) has analyzed
as the potential "betrayal" and "psychosexual rejection" of women by men (pp.
168–169), attended by more or less severe economic and political consequences.
None of this dynamic escapes women's awareness. "The personal is political" is
not just a useful organizing concept, it is also a set of material enactments that
display and reflect back how the political is personal.

As Susan Griffin (1981) suggests, a woman knows that "over and over again culture tells her that men abandon women who speak too loudly, or who are too *present*" (p. 211). Coupled with the strong cultural message that "her survival in the world depends on her being able to find a man to marry" (p. 211), many young women in the feminist classroom find themselves caught in the double bind of needing to speak and to remain silent at the same time in order to guarantee some measure of survival. While the salience of this politic is more immediately obvious in the case of heterosexual women, woman-identified (Rich, 1986, p. 57) women who do not comply, at least minimally, with acceptable forms of sexual self-presentation do not escape the consequences of marginalization and exclusion. For all women in professional schools specifically, compliance with particular displays of femininity can mean the difference between having or not having a job. (Britzman, 1991).

As women and men struggle over establishing and articulating shared meanings, we need to notice the reality that, for many women, such struggles often take place in the context of deeply felt commitments reverberating with emotional psycho sexual chords and attended by the material conditions of unequal power. While perhaps these relations are lived most deeply not in the classroom itself, but in those private spaces lived out between women and men beyond the classroom, for women, course content can be instrumental in raising these relations as questions.

The following is an example of how one woman took up these struggles in her private life. After a particular encounter in the classroom regarding the issue of voice/discourse, discussed in the context of who has the right to name whether or not a joke is funny, she wrote me the following note:

> The articles at this point in the course . . . have plunged me into the next phase of my feminist awareness, which is characterized by anger and a pervading sense of injustice. . . . The "feminist" anger that I feel is self-perpetuating. I get angry at the discrimination and stereotyping I run up against so I blame the patriarchal society I live in in particular, and men in general. Then I think about women who feel that feminism is unnecessary or obsolete and I get angry at that subset of women. Then I think about the good guys like Mike and Cam and I get angry because the patriarchal society biases the way I think about these men, simply because they're members of a particular gender (sex class?). Then I think about men who stereotype and discriminate against women and criticize us for being "overly sensitive" when we get uptight or even just point out or suggest humanistic egalitarian changes that are good and smart and I get REALLY angry because I realize that they're all a bunch of (expletives deleted) [sic]. . . . One of the most difficult aspects of this anger is that I become frustrated and impatient with people who can't see the problems or don't see the urgent need for solutions. (I am writing) a lot during this time because I often can't communicate orally with people who don't at least respect my feminist views.

hooks states that

feminist works that focus on strategies women can use to speak to males about male domination and changes are not readily available, if they exist at all. Yet women have a deep longing to share feminist consciousness with the men in their lives (the "good guys"), and together work at transforming their relationships.

hooks goes on to say that "concern for this basic struggle should motivate feminist thinkers to talk and write more about how we relate to men and how we change and transform relationships with men characterized by domination" (p. 130).

Yet despite their desire to genuinely share the meanings they have drawn from their experiences, for young women in the feminist classrooms, phallocentric myth-making often collides with the theoretical agenda of the course. Phallocentric myths are those beliefs that continue to marginalize women through the process of naturalizing politically created gender inequalities: "Women are not in positions of decision and policy-making because they don't want to be"; "Everybody has equal opportunity to become school principal. Women choose not to be because they like teaching better"; "If abused and battered women don't leave their partners it is because they have deviant personalities"; "Women who are raped did something wrong"; "Boys are better at math, girls are better at reading"; "women who do math are not really women"; "Jokes, sexually offensive to women, are funny"; "There are no women in history because they didn't do anything"; "Women like staying home with children"; "Men share equally in housework"; and so on. I have heard some version of all of these statements in the classroom. While the men might express a comfortable indignation at such beliefs, they don't often understand what practices are required of them to change how they live their lives. For example, one man recently told the class that he supports his wife's career by "baby-sitting" the children while she goes to work. It is precisely this imbalance of power that constructs the women's silence, suppressed behind embarrassed laughter.

The pedagogical implications of such gender relations in the feminist classroom must be taken seriously if we are to understand how and why women students might wish both to appropriate and yet resist feminist theoretical and political positions that aim to uncover the roots of our deeply misogynist culture and give legitimacy to women's desires and dreams of possibility. As feminist teachers we need to look closely at the psychosexual context within which we propose the feminist alternative and consider the substance of why women may genuinely wish to turn away from the possibilities it offers.

Women know through experience that the threat to our sexuality is a way of controlling our political activities. In her review of Spender (1982), Pierson (1983) points out that there is a long history to the process of displacing women's legitimate political and intellectual critique and struggles into distorted evaluations of women's sexuality as a form of social control hammered into place by the material conditions of women's lives. The meaning that patriarchy has assigned to the term "lesbian" has resulted in its use as a pejorative term to undermine the serious political work in which women as women have been engaged in resistance to a set of social relations marked by patriarchic domination. The misogyny of such a designation violates all women at all points of the heterosexual/lesbian continuum (Rich, 1986). Clearly "the regulation of speaking and silence" (Walkerdine, 1985) is not just achieved through concrete regulatory practices, but also through the emotional, psychic, and sexual sphere—articulated through the practices of patriarchic myth-making—that combine in our hearts and heads to silence us from within. Given the terms of such social conditions, it would be a surprise, indeed, if women did not feel the constraints of contradictory choices and conflicting interests.

The power of patriarchic social controls on women's sexuality does not escape even (or perhaps especially) very young women. For example, within a recent three-week period, two separate groups of elementary and high school students were invited to participate in different events sponsored by the faculty where I teach. The first was a forum on women and education, attended by 150 students, at which the guest speaker, Dale Spender, presented an address entitled "Young Women in Education: What Happens to Girls in Classrooms." Three weeks later, a dramatic presentation by a feminist acting troupe, The Company of Sirens[3] presented an upbeat production called *The Working People's Picture Show,* dealing with such issues as women in the work force, day care, unionism, and sexual harassment. The question period that followed each event was telling. In each case the young women's concerns were well demonstrated by the almost identically phrased question aimed at the program presenters, individuals who were seen as the embodiment of feminist critique: "Are you married and do you have children?" I don't believe this was a theoretical question. For many young women the concern about the compatibility of feminist politics with marriage and family is the concrete realization that making public what our feminist consciousness reveals about women's experiences of patriarchy can result in potential limits on desire. The extent to which any woman who displays autonomy and independent personhood is seen as a threat to male power and therefore subjected to male violence was reaffirmed by the massacre at the Université de Montréal. Such events are not lost on young women.

My response to the sexual dynamics in the classroom is to create a context that offers "space" and "safety", particularly to women students. Men in the feminist classroom often state that the course readings and class discussions feel threatening and that they experience various degrees of discomfort. I would like to understand more about these feelings of threat and discomfort—what do they find discomforting: what is the basis of their disease, what do they fear? I am concerned that all students—women and men—have access to the analyses we take up in the class. I am also concerned that all students feel equally validated in doing the hard work toward a transformed consciousness. However, this work is different for women than it is for men. Women need space and safety so that they are free to speak in order to better understand and act against the violations they have experienced in a social/cultural setting that subordinates them in hurtful and violent ways. The consciousness around which men need to do hard work is the pain of their complicity in benefitting from the rewards of this same culture. I support men in doing this hard work. Personally, I have not seen many of them try. Those who have are strong and welcome allies.

The language of "space" and "safety" is not new to discussions of feminist teaching. However, I believe that it is not always clear what practices attend these abstractions. I believe, first, that women don't need to be taught what we already know: fundamentally, that women are exempted from a culture to which our productive and reproductive labor is essential. The power of phallocentrism may undermine our initiative, it may shake the foundations of our self-respect and self-worth, it may even force us into complicity with its violence. But it cannot prevent us from knowing. Nor do women need to be taught the language through which to speak what we know.

Rather, the challenge of feminist teaching is in finding ways to make speakable and legitimate the personal/political *investments* we all make in the meanings we ascribe to our historically contingent experiences. In this context, I raise with students the contradictory reality of women's lives, wherein one's interests, at the level of practice, lie both with the dominant group and against it. Through such discussion emerges the deeply paradoxical nature of the conditions of the subordinate in a hierarchical culture marked by gender, class, and race inequalities. Approaching women's lives from this perspective means that practices previously understood by students to be a function of choice can be seen as the result of a need to secure some measure of emotional, intellectual, and quite often physical survival (Wolfe, 1986, p. 58).

Pedagogy that is grounded in simple notions of false consciousness that articulates teaching as mediation or, worse, as a charitable act, does not support knowledge invested with the meanings students ascribe to their own experiences. This not only buries the complexity of human choices in an unproblematized notion of self-interest but, further, can only offer validating or supplementary educational options without transforming the conditions under which we learn (Lewis, 1989). By fusing women's emotional and concrete lives through feminist critique, it is possible to make problematic the conditions under which women learn, and perhaps to make a feminist political agenda viable in women's own lives wherein they can transcend the split between personal experience and social form.

Conclusion

What are the possibilities of doing feminist politics/pedagogy in the classroom? In answering this question, I want to examine the potential for feminist teaching that does more than address the concerns of the already initiated. For me, the urgency of this issue arises from my own teaching. On one hand, the often chilling stories women students share with me and each other in the context of classroom relations point to their clear understanding of the politics of gender subordination. Within the confines of traditional academic practices, the politics of personal experience are often seen to be irrelevant. In contrast, the feminist classroom can be a deeply emotional experience for many women, offering the opportunity to claim relevance for the lives they live as the source of legitimate knowledge.

On the other hand, I also hear the young woman who speaks to me in anger, who derides me for being the bearer of "bad news," and who wants to believe that our oppression/subordination is something we create in our own heads. Given the context of violence within which students are being asked to embrace a feminist politic, their concerns about their emotional, intellectual, and, quite obviously, physical safety have to be recognized as crucial. For women, overt acts of violence, like the one that occurred at the Université de Montréal, are merely an extension of their daily experiences in the psychological/social/sexual spaces of the academy. Resistance to the emancipatory potential of a liberating politic indicates the extent of women's subordination. Thus, we cannot expect that students will readily appropriate a political stance that is truly counter-hegemonic, unless we also acknowledge the ways in which our feminist practice/politics *creates,* rather than ameliorates, a feeling of threat: the threat of abandonment; the threat of having to struggle within unequal power relations; the threat of psychological/social/sexual, as well as economic and political marginality; the threat of retributive violence—threats lived in concrete embodied ways. Is it any wonder that many women desire to disassociate from "those" women whose critique of our social/cultural world seems to focus and condense male violence?

The challenge of feminist teaching lies for me in the specifics of how I approach the classroom. By reflecting on my own teaching, I fuse content and practice, politicizing them both through feminist theory and living them both concretely rather than treating them abstractly. To elaborate: as I reflect on my teaching, it is clear from the detailing of the examples I provide above that feminist teaching practices cannot be separated from the content of the curriculum. Specific political moments arise exactly because of the content of the course. As is suggested by Gayle MacDonald (1989), "the process by which teaching occurs in a feminist classroom is one which is very difrrent from technique/pedagogy used in other settings" (p. 147). I want to extend this idea by suggesting that the "difference" MacDonald identifies in the feminist classroom is that, as students articulate their interests and investments through particular social practices, a dialectic develops between students and the curriculum in such a way that the classroom dynamics created by the topic of discussion reflect the social organization of gender inequality. Indeed, the irony is that feminist critique of social relations reproduces exactly the practices we are critiquing. When these practices are reproduced, so are the attendant violations, marginalizations, struggles, and transformation which again lend themselves to be revisited by the critique of feminist politics.

An interesting case in point is the experience I have had on various occasions when I have presented some version of this argument at academic conferences. On each occasion, in responding to my presentation, some members of the audience tended to reproduce to some extent the practices that I take such great pains to critique in the text. The caretaking practices, the concern that men not feel unfairly marginalized or attacked, the willingness of men in the audience to speak unproblematically on behalf of women, and the dynamics of sexual marginalization have all played a part in the reception of my article-in-progress. My purpose here is not to suggest that every instance of critique of feminist social/cultural analysis is a display of phallocentric power or male privilege. Indeed, as feminist scholars we put our work forward in good faith, and both invite and welcome articulate and substantive engagement of it (Ellsworth, this volume). My point is, rather, that responses to feminist critique often take forms that reproduce the gendered practices that I have described in this paper.

The strategies I have employed in the classroom have been directed toward politicizing not only what we take up in the class as course content, but also the classroom dynamics that are generated by our topic and subsequent discussion. These practices included: shifting our focus from larger social issues to the dynamics in the classroom so that we might explore the relationship between the two; legitimating the meanings women bring to their experiences by turning challenges to these articulated meanings back on the questioner, thereby requiring the questioner to make different meanings sensible; disrupting the order of hierarchy regarding who can speak and on whose behalf; requiring that men in the class own their social location by exploring the parameters of their own privilege, rather than the limits on women of their oppression; providing opportunities for self-reflexive critique of unequal power relations; staying attentive to the political context of women's lives—those seemingly unconnected experiences made to seem livable by the tumble of daily life—in order to offer a vision of a future that women might embrace; attending to the ways in which women have been required historically to invest in particular and often contradictory practices in order to secure their own survival; and, finally, treating women's resistance to feminism as an active discourse of struggle derived from a complex set of meanings in which women's practices are invested.

The above suggestions are intended to be neither exhaustive nor prescriptive. Pedagogical moments arise in specific contexts: the social location of the teacher and students; the geographic and historical location of the institution in which they come together; the political climate within which they work; the personalities and personal profiles of the individuals in the classroom; the readings selected for the course; and the academic background of the students all come together in ways that create the specifics of the moment. It is not appropriate to think of what I have presented here as a "model" for feminist teaching. "Models," can only be restrictive and reductive because they cannot predict and thus cannot take into account the complexity of contingent and material realities. My intent, rather, has been to articulate how, at particular moments in my teaching, I made sense of those classroom dynamics that seemed to divide women and men across their inequalities in ways that reaffirmed women's subordination, and how making sense of those moments as politically rich allowed me to develop an interpretive framework for creating a counter-hegemony from my teaching practice. My hope is that through such shared struggles in the classroom women might embrace for themselves the politics of autonomy and self determination rather than reject it as a liability.

Notes

1. This article is dedicated to the fourteen women massacred at the Université de Montréal on December 6, 1989: Genevieve Bergeron, Helene Colgan, Nathalie Croteau, Barbara Diagneault, Anne-Marie Edward, Maud Haveirnick, Barbara Maria Klueznick, Maryse Laganiere, Maryse Leclair, Anne-Marie Lemay, Sonia Pelletier, Michele Richard, Annie St-Arneault, and Annie Turcotte.
2. I thank Barbara McDonald for providing me with a deeper understanding of this reality through the work we share.
3. The Company of Sirens, 176 Robert Street, Toronto, Ontario Canada, M5S 2K3.

References

Belenky, M. F., Clinchy, B. M., Goldberger, N. R., Tarule, J. M. (1986). *Women's Ways of Knowing: The Development of Self, Voice and Mind.* New York: Basic Books Inc.

Britzman, D. (1991). *Practice Makes Practice: A Critical Study of Learning to Teach.* New York: SUNY Press.

Brodribb, S. (1987). Women's Studies in Canada. [Special Issue]. *Resources for Feminist Research.*

Brookes, A-L. (1992). *Feminist Pedagogy: An Autobiographical Approach.* Halifax: Fernwood Books Ltd.

Childers, M. (1984). Women's Studies: Sinking and Swimming in the Mainstream. *Women's Studies International Forum, 7,* (3), 161–166.

Corrigan, P. (1987). In/Forming Schooling. In D. Livingston and contributors, *Critical Pedagogy and Cultural Power.* Toronto: Garamond Press, 17–40.

Daly, M. (1978). *Gyn/Ecology: The Metaethics of Radical Feminism.* Boston: Beacon Press.

DuPlessis, R. B. (1985). *Writing Beyond the Ending: Narrative Strategies of Twentieth-Century Women Writers.* Bloomington: Indiana University Press.

Giroux, H. and Simon, R. (1988). *Critical Pedagogy and the Politics of Popular Culture.* Unpublished manuscript.

Griffin, S. (1981). *Pornography and Silence: Culture's Revenge Against Nature.* New York: Harper and Row.

hooks, b. (1989). *Talking Back: Thinking Feminist, Thinking Black.* Boston: South End Press.

Jagger, A. (1983). *Feminist Politics and Human Nature.* Sussex: The Harvest Press.

Khayatt, D. M. (1987). *Gender Role Conformity in Women Teachers.* Unpublished Ph.D. dissertation, University of Toronto.

Lather, P. (1988). Feminist Perspectives on Emancipatory Research Methodologies. *Women's Studies International Forum,* 11, (6), 569–581.

Lewis, M. and Simon, R. I. (1986). A Discourse Not Intended for Her: Learning and Teaching Within Patriarchy. *Harvard Educational Review, 56,* (4), 457–472.

Lewis, M. (1988a). *Without a Word: Sources and Themes for a Feminist Pedagogy.* Ph.D. dissertation. University of Toronto.

Lewis, M. (1988b). The Construction of Femininity Embraced in the Work of Caring for Children— Caught Between Aspirations and Reality. *Journal of Educational Thought, 22,* (2A), 259–268.

Lewis, M. (1989). The Challenge of Feminist Pedagogy. *Queen's Quarterly, 96,* (1), 117–130.

Lewis, M. (1990a). Solidarity Work and Feminist Practice. Paper presented at the American Educational Research Association annual meeting. Boston, Massachusetts.

Lewis, M. (1990b). Framing: Women and Silence Disrupting the Hierarchy of Discursive Practices. Paper presented at the American Educational Research Association annual meeting. Boston, Massachusetts.

MacDonald, G. (1989). Feminist Teaching Techniques for the Committed but Exhausted. *Atlantis, 15,* (1), 145–152.

MacKinnon, C. A. (1983). Feminism, Marxism, Method and the State: An Agenda for Theory. In E. Abel and E. Abel (Eds.) *The Signs Reader: Women, Gender and Scholarship.* Chicago: University of Chicago Press, 227–256.

MacKinnon, C. (1987). *Feminism Unmodified: Discourses of Life and Law.* Cambridge: Harvard University Press.

Malette, L. and M. Chalouh. (Eds.). (1990). *Polytechnique, 6 Décembre.* Montreal: Les Editions du remue-menage.

Martin, B. and Mohanty, C. T. (1986). Feminist Politics: What's Home Got To Do With It? In T. de Lauretis (Ed.) *Feminist Studies/Critical Studies.* Bloomington: Indiana University Press, 191–212.

McCormack, T. (1987). Feminism, Women's Studies and the New Academic Freedom. In J. Gaskell and A. McLaren (Eds.) *Women and Education: A Canadian Perspective.* Calgary: Detselig Enterprises Limited, 289–303.

McMahon, M. (1986). *A Circuitous Quest: Things That Haunt Me When I Write.* Unpublished Manuscript.

Pierson, R. R. (1983). Review of Women of Ideas and What Men Have Done to Them. *Resources for Feminist Research, 12,* (2), July, pp. 17–18.

Pierson, R. R. (1987). Two Marys and a Virginia: Historical Moments in the Development of a Feminist Perspective on Education. In J. Gaskell and A. McLaren (Eds.) *Women and Education: A Canadian Perspective.* Calgary: Detselig Enterprises Ltd., 203–222.

Radford-Hill, S. (1986). Considering Feminism as a Model for Social Change. In T. de Lauretis (Ed.) *Feminist Studies/Critical Studies.* Bloomington: Indiana University Press, 157–172.

Radway, J. (1984). *Reading The Romance: Women, Patriarchy and Popular Literature.* Chapel Hill: University of North Carolina Press.

Rich, A. (1986). *Blood, Bread and Poetry.* New York: W. W. Norton and Co.

Rockhill, K. (1987a). The Chaos of Subjectivity in the Ordered Halls of Academe. *Canadian Women Studies, 8,* (4), (n.p.).

Rockhill, K. (1987b). Literacy as Threat/Desire: Longing to be SOMEBODY. In J. Gaskell and A. McLaren (Eds.) *Women and Education: A Canadian Perspective.* Calgary: Detselig Enterprises Ltd., 315–331.

Rowbotham, S. (1989). To Be Or Not To Be: The Dilemmas of Mothering. *Feminist Review, 31,* 82–93.

Spender, D. (1982). *Women of Ideas and What Men Have Done To Them.* London: Routledge and Kegan Paul.

Spender, D. and Sarah, E. (Eds.) (1980). *Learning to Lose: Sexism and Education.* London: The Women's Press.

Walkerdine, V. (1985). On the Regulation of Speaking and Silence: Subjectivity, Class and Gender in Contemporary Schooling. In C. Steedman, C. Urwin and V. Walkerdine, (Eds.) *Language, Gender and Childhood.* London: Routledge and Kegan Paul, 203–241.

Willis, P. (1977). *Learning to Labour: How Working Class Kids Get Working Class Jobs.* New York: Columbia University Press.

Wolfe, A. (1986). Inauthentic Democracy: A Critique of Public Life in Modern Liberal Society. *Studies in Political Economy, 21,* 57–81.

I wish to thank Gayle MacDonald, Barbara McDonald, Elizabeth Ellsworth and Roberta Lamb for making helpful comments on earlier drafts of this paper.

10

Women in the Academy:
Strategy, Struggle, Survival

Carmen Luke and Jennifer Gore

This chapter reflects on our contributors', colleagues' and our own experiences as women in the university. The discussion focuses on the politics of knowledge and feminine identity in the academy as they are structured in what Elizabeth Grosz (1988) calls sexist, patriarchal, and phallocentric knowledge systems. It is along these axes, none of which functions independent of support from the others, that academic feminist "in(ter)ventions" are located. In our work as feminist theorists, researchers, and educators we daily contest power-knowledge relations at all three levels as they permeate social and intellectual life in the university. The turn, in this chapter, to the phenomenology of experience aims to emphasize the embodied situatedness of women—the gender politics of local sites—in what Foucault (1980, p. 93) terms the "capillary" network of power in knowledge regimes.

Feminist theory and classroom practice

Educational and pedagogical concerns, as the preceding chapters have shown, are as integral to universities as they are to schools. Such concerns emerge not only from the research, teaching, and theorizing of those in Education (and related) faculties, but also in scholarship and teaching across disciplines. Generations of academics—small in number but committed nonetheless—have advocated educational reform aimed at improving conditions, access and outcomes for those students (people of color, physically and cognitively challenged students, women, the poor, lesbian and gay, and mature aged students) who, historically, have suffered in traditional and progressive schooling structures and practices. Such calls for reform have taken various forms including research on marginalized groups, arguments for culture and gender inclusive curricula and policy provisions, and attempts to theorize difference as foundational to pedagogical practice. Despite the widespread rhetoric in support of social justice in and through education—or, what in the U.S. is more commonly considered the liberal agenda of equal opportunity—much of this work and many of its advocates continue to be marginalized.

Of particular concern to many feminist educators who take seriously the plight of 'women and girls in schooling' is the ongoing opposition to and undermining of feminist work through sexist, patriarchal and phallocentric knowledge systems which militate against women in the academy. It is these oppositions to and subversions of feminist work that are the focus of this chapter. Although much of the focus in this volume has been on the discourses of critical pedagogy, the essays have also shown some of the problems women and feminist perspectives encounter in educational theory and practice. We maintain that educational reforms which are to prove significant for girls and women cannot forge ahead without feminist women at the political forefront. Recall that, historically, men have not been at the forefront of contesting sexism, just as Anglo-Europeans have not generally united in solidarity against the racism of their discourses. Feminist intellectual work has been central in making public and finding solutions to the problems girls and women encounter in schooling contexts.

Some might argue, however, that feminist intellectual work on education, such as that contained in this volume, does not directly benefit girls and women or their teachers. Others might ask what do feminist theorists such as Donna Haraway, Luce Irigaray, Carol Gilligan, Andrea Nye or Sandra Harding have to do with gender issues in educational institutions? And what practical relevance can postmodernist or poststructuralist theories possibly have for the everyday practices of schooling? We would claim in response that classroom practice is ultimately linked to theories of the subject, the social, learning and teaching. Teacher education is all about linking theoretical positions to practical application. Feminist theories are centrally concerned with the social and educational experiences of girls and women. But the differences, for instance, between an essentialist and constructivist theory of gendered subjectivity have significant implications for the ways pedagogical relations can be conceptualized. In that regard, theoretical choice does have important consequences for practice. And what some might call the more esoteric concerns of poststructuralist feminisms form the very work which has opened up questions of representation, of voice, difference, power, and authorship-authority which are central to the politics of classroom practice. The theoretical position educators take on the subject, on voice or on power ultimately has significant political and ethical consequences for how teachers treat students, and how educational policy defines the pedagogical subject. Feminist theory, therefore, is vital not only to effect political change for girls and women in schooling at both theoretical and practical levels, but is also important in formulating an agenda for change with relevance for groups that have been contained and subjugated in discourses that mark their differences as negative.

We wish to make the point, then, that how feminists and their work fare in academe has a lot to do with gender issues and feminist practices in public school and university classrooms. Theorizing social subjects and practice is no less "work" (and for feminists it is political work) than the work teachers do in schools. Moreover, our work is not of some mystical higher order of abstract intellectual labor. There are "diva girls" (hooks, 1990) in all disciplines and these we do not discount. But we speak here of the women represented in this volume. Through a theoretical framing of the experiences we have encountered as feminists in the academy, we aim to show the following. First, women's intellectual work in the university *is* of a different order than that of our Anglo-European male colleagues. Women, it still seems, are treading on foreign and often hostile territory of male domains, and therefore are caught up in political struggles which are quite different in kind from those men engage in among each other. Second, knowledge productions always occur in specific sites, historical trajectories and socio-cultural contexts. Unlike many of the (rationalist, objectivist, positivist) master discourses, feminist epistemology sees knowledge as contextual and political. We therefore consider it important not to divorce "experience" from theoretical knowledge, but to foreground the conditions and relations of production within which feminist work is generated. Third, we consider it vital to demystify our textual identities as feminist signifiers. The women in this volume should not be read as hallowed authors, as an intellectual feminist elite but, rather, as women hard at work. Our work—our pedagogical and textual practice—is eminently tied to the conditions and relations of production in which we work. It makes sense, therefore, to analyze how power and knowledge relations are structured in the university by looking at how we live them and how they inform and politicize our work.

Feminist interventions

In *Unsettling relations: The University as a site of feminist struggle* (1991), Himani Bannerji, Linda Carty, Kari Dehli, Susan Heald and Kate McKenna write:

> The way relations of power and knowledge are organized in and through the university make it possible to live these relations without reflecting on them. . . . This "not seeing" participates in the ruling practices which regulate the social relations in which we live. Historically, universities have been, and continue to be, central to the production and reproduction of such practices" (pp. 7–9)

The suggestion here is two-fold. First, given the relative legitimacy Women's Studies has attained in universities, a certain measure of structurally accorded 'success' and security for some women means that they are more reticent to take on the very power relations which inhere in their "success"—they no longer or refuse "to see". Second—and this more closely reflects the contexts from which the experiences documented in this chapter derive—women's more tenuous structural positions in the academy limit the extent to which they can speak about what they "see". In other words, our training has taught us that our public speech via the book or article must confine itself to the measured discourse befitting academic protocol. We are taught to maintain a scholarly separation of academic knowledge from the actual people who are engaged in the production of such knowledges: in short, airing dirty laundry is not the way to get tenure. The silences, then, on the institutional contexts and personal relations that are the ground for feminist scholarship gloss over a complex realm of struggle that is profoundly political and personal. Remaining silent or breaking the silence, moreover, are equally difficult and fraught with anxiety, self-doubt, and uncertainty over whether one has done the right thing.

Finally, the contradictory locations feminists occupy in the university often makes it difficult "to see" where and how our politics are co-opted by our institutional signification, where and how our power and privilege become transformed within the bureaucratic web into potentially disabling political effects on others and ourselves. The issues we contest, the various fronts on which we struggle, and the political strategies we use are often loaded with contradictory meanings and effects. If we act one way, it may have repercussions on another level; if we get outraged over one issue, we will make enemies in one camp but form alliances in another; if we speak and behave unbefitting the feminine academic image, we may lose the attention of those men whose attention we need in order to get our agenda on board. In short, in all that we do as women, we are always already marked as other. Susan Heald (1991, p. 142) explains:

> Those of us who bring to academia any difference from the norm are faced with the work of combining those discourses and managing the contradictions among them. The struggle to fit into the definitions of "normal" are different for differently-located people, although they share some commonalities. It is possible to resist fitting in, but this brings its own set of problems. That these struggles are difficult—maybe impossible—and usually crazy-making is not the concern of those who "author/ize" the discourses.

The power-knowledge relations of gendered academic discourse are inscribed on the academic experiences of all the women in this book. We have different experiences, but they reflect a pattern of remarkable similarity. In order to conceptualize the logic of divide and rule underneath the variations of experience, we have found Elizabeth Grosz's (1988) three-tiered model of "feminist in(ter)ventions" most useful. This framework, we believe, helps clarify and organize understanding of how our everyday "work" encounters are mediated through the social and epistemic relations of the culture of institutionalized scholarship.

Grosz (1988, p. 93) explains that in the "kinds of relations feminist scholars have adopted in their various encounters with mainstream knowledges, three levels or types of intellectual misogyny can be distinguished for the purposes of analysis": sexist, patriarchal, and phallocentric. She goes on to explain that women's oppression encoded in these levels of knowledge also give rise to feminist resistance to and critiques of those knowledges at the corresponding levels. Since the university is an institution that specializes in intellectual knowledge (re)production, feminist academics in particular live and experience the misogynist deployments of masculinist rule—epistemically and procedurally. Sexist knowledge, according to Grosz (p. 93) "consists in a series of specifically determinable 'acts of discrimination' privileging men and depriving women. By 'acts' here I mean propositions, arguments, assertions, methodologies". This level refers to identifiably sexist practices and commentary. Patriarchal knowledge is the scaffold which supports the structural organization and differential valuation of women and men; it serves to validate sexist knowledges. Institutionalized gender inequalities marked by the differential valuation of women and men's work, speech, and power reflect patriarchal knowledges. The discursive and social connection between sexist and patriarchal knowledges suggests that differentiation between them is not always analytically clear-cut: some of the sexist encounters we discuss below clearly are also instances of institutionalized patriarchal discourse of the academy. At the level of phallocentric knowledge, "women are construed on the model of the masculine, whether in terms of sameness/identity, opposition/distinction, or complementarity. Women and the feminine function as silent supports for all modes of male theory" (pp. 94–95). This is the level of the great master narratives of science and philosophy where ostensibly androcentric Human Nature, Truth, Reason and Impartiality marks difference (from the masculine) as fundamentally Other. Phallocentric knowledge forms the epistemic horizon for patriarchal and sexist knowledges. Feminist work in the academy is structured by and contests all three levels of containment and opposition on a daily basis. The work of feminist educators and scholars reflects the interrogations and interventions of those entrenched knowledges and practices that disavow women, their knowledges and intellectual labor.

Sexist discourse

The politics of difference rationalized by the western phallocentric order subjugates not only women in general as well as women marked by particular differences, but men outside the normative (white heterosexual) representation of "inside". The vision of the normative human subject has authorized not only sexist discourses and practices, but extends its rule across multiple dimensions of difference that cut across gender difference: from race, ethnicity, sexuality to religion, nationality, ability, and so forth. The exclusions and subjugations women experience under patriarchal and sexist discourses are in many ways not that dissimilar from the personal and structural discrimination many men of color or gay men experience within that same regime (cf. Bartky, 1990).

To get ahead in industry, business, or the academy has always meant for

Anglo-European men that they learn the codes with which to gain entry into the "old boys club". In the university, the sponsorship model is still the most powerful relationship that enables entry into the inner circles. To gain entry means that a male graduate student, for instance, might have to prove his character in the weekly pub sessions or basketball games with the professor. Over and above learning what kind of wine the professor likes, what his favorite political columnist, herbs, ice cream, and football team are, the grad student will have to learn the "in" intellectual jokes and witticisms, and rattle off the appropriate authors of a given corpus in conversation and on the essay or thesis. It is the insider knowledge both on and off "court" that male academics share with their Anglo male graduate students to which women and, often, men of color are commonly not privy. Insider codes are not only facility with the dominant language and symbolics but with an "anti-language" as well. It is not only learning the rules of the game to "do academics" well but learning also how, when, and who can speak the anti-academy subtext. This subtext goes beyond the standard intellectual critique of schools of thought or key thinkers. It includes the "appropriate" ironies, parodies, witticisms, and sardonic and sexist jokes about the very rules of the game. A good example is the reverence and importance accorded to the conference circuit the subtext of which is that it is a careers market where suits do business. The conference suit market is where young turks network their insider knowledge: an intellectually sharp paper, the nimble distribution of calling cards, dinner, drinks, and academic "in" jokes with the target academic or group are all part of the sales pitch to land a job. Women's access to the discourse of networking these sites is in many cases reduced to a female huddle in some corner of a room, the only place where they are not ignored or rudely dismissed. As one of our contributors reports: "As I was leaving the room after a protracted and heated discussion with a man at AERA in 1991 about program decisions, he said to his male buddies 'She thought I couldn't get my dick up!' " Part of the insider codes are a rampant sexism which women continually put up with and which, for untenured women, is virtually impossible to contest.

Yet, women among women in the academy have their own secret stock of insider knowledge. In addition to a corpus of feminist knowledges, insider jokes, witticisms, and an anti-language which serve as survival strategies, what is common knowledge among junior and senior female academics is that we have to work much harder to get the recognition that men do. When it comes to getting ahead, women find that it often pays to modify one's vita so that it doesn't signal 'FEMINIST' in red flashing lights. Women have told of doctoring their vita when going for promotion or a job by deleting publications in feminist journals, omitting published articles with obvious feminist titles, or ensuring that their referee list is not exclusively female but includes at least one senior male in the field. In interviews, unless the position is in a Women's Studies program, feminist women tend to focus their intellectual qualifications on a mainstream disciplinary area, rather than foreground their research and theoretical orientation as feminist first and sociological, anthropological, or psychological second. At a recent sociological conference an untenured woman from a Florida university spoke of having published the obligatory number of refereed articles in key sociological journals, all of which intentionally excluded feminist references or a feminist theoretical orientation which she clearly held. She spoke of her frustration at having to write and publish text that was at odds with her politics and theoretical perspective. And despite playing the rules of the game in print, she commented that her feminist position had already been detected and opposed by her male colleagues and that tenure was probably not forthcoming. She was considering looking for work in the public service sector.

As we discussed in the introduction, our schooling as girls and our induction into the academy as undergraduate and graduate students, trained us well as daughters to the masters: as reciters not makers of knowledge. Andrea Nye (1990), in her feminist rereading of analytic logic, puts it well: "We have read what men said, studied their words, heard the ambivalence and confusion in what they say no matter how univocal and logical" (p. 184). But as students, our critiques of male confusion, contradiction, omission, or impaired vision afforded by perspectiveless objectivity were always articulated within the parameters of logical argumentation. We read and learned to speak the script of the masters. Some of us encountered women teachers who showed us other texts and other ways of speaking. Yet we also encountered women teachers who ruled our voices out, who taught us the statistical significance of gendered differences, and who showed us that some women academics are much harder on female than on male students. Elizabeth Grosz (1988) comments on such women who "dutifully serve their masters, using the work of their masters to chastise wayward women for going beyond the acceptable limits of their various disciplines" (p. 96).

When we returned to the university as teachers (often on non-tenurable contract appointments) we felt ready to embark on our mission: ready to do the right thing and make a difference for our students and ourselves. What we had not anticipated was the powerful entrenchment of what Foucault (1980, pp. 135–144) calls the "juridico-discursive" power of law that rules the social organization of academic life: the "insistence on the rule", a "logic of censorship", a "cycle of prohibition" and a "uniformity" of application that structures social and knowledge relations at different levels. Nor had we anticipated that the gains of our feminist predecessors would so quickly erode in a new wave of violence against women: in conservative political regimes that no longer repressively tolerate women but actively repress them, or in the resurgence of fraternities (and sororities) in which large numbers of the next generation develops its politics.

So, for instance, we found and continue to find ourselves battling sexism in the classroom and among some of our colleagues. Contesting sexist, racist, and homophobic remarks among students too often leads to comments that pejoratively label us "feminist" and thereby as too sensitive, unable to take a joke, and locked into a dated position of a generation ago (cf. Lather, 1991). When we take up what we read as sexist terms of endearment from male colleagues—when we ask them to call us by our names rather than "love", "dear", or "girl"—we are told that we take ourselves too seriously, that nothing is meant by those terms, that we are trying to censor language, and that our strident feminism locates us outside "normal" social conventions that even the office secretaries accept.

For women to challenge sexism in the classroom is difficult enough, given that many younger female and male students bring very conservative positions to classroom encounters which show in disinterest in and often refusal to debate issues of racism or sexism. When women teach about "gender issues", students dismiss them in course evaluations by accusing them of "putting in too much of her own opinion", of being "too subjective". Yet when our pro-feminist male colleagues give lectures on gender, their objectivity and authority on the subject go unchallenged (cf. Heald, 1991; Kramer & Martin, 1988). For women to challenge sexism and harassment among male colleagues invites a very different exchange, one which puts a woman on trial by forcing her to confess to her reading of social behaviors by men as sexually and ethically offensive. Here is one such incident experienced by one of our contributors.

I work with two senior male colleagues who use every opportunity to put their hands on me: in the hallway, at meetings, in front of students, in the office. It is often just a hand on the shoulder or arm or a "collegial" lock around the waist; nonetheless, it is unwanted touching and especially paralyzing when done in front of students. One calls me "darling", "dear", "pet" (an intentional "tease" because he knows I hate it), and not too long ago used my return from leave to plant a "collegial kiss" on me with a "welcome back" in front of staff. The other staff members used the occasion of my birthday to sneak into my office, grab me ("collegially") from behind while I was talking on the phone and plant a birthday kiss on my cheek. Before I could even respond, this colleague left the office with what he clearly thought was funny: "Happy Birthday! I'd stay for more, but I've got to run". When people run into each other in the general office or hallway, one commonly says "sorry", or "excuse me"; for years, such commonplaces from me had always elicited "joking" comments from him such as: "That's ok, I'm not sorry". Verbal reprimands on my part had never worked, and as temporary contract staff, I felt it unwise to take it up along more formal channels. But it was the "birthday kiss" that ended my tolerance of this constant violation. I agonized for days over how to deal with this. I was furious at having to deal with someone else's pathology; furious at having been made angry and furious at having to figure out a way to deal with a situation not of my own making. I set a meeting with him and our department head, and felt embarrassed, angry, and thoroughly disempowered at having to front up to two males over something which I suspected both would see as a relatively "harmless" and friendly gesture.

I began the meeting by explaining my reading of the event, how it had made me feel, and why I considered such behavior unprofessional and unethical. My birthday, or my open office door gives no person the right to invade my space without invitation, let alone touch or kiss me. When I told both men that they would not kiss each other on the occasion of a birthday, or any other occasion, nor would men call each other "pet" or "darling", the gendered dimension of professional banter, finally sunk in. He responded with appeals to innocence: an innocent and friendly gesture among colleagues, nothing was meant by it. The absurdity of having to explain the boundaries of my space and body while two men listened and looked on threw me into a schizoid tension between a very rational and contained response of emotion and anger, and the irrationality of having to formulate my position in the rationalist discourse appropriate to the context in which I was speaking. The culprit in this scenario did apologize but not without letting me know that my reaction was atypical, picky, over-sensitive, and would certainly change our interactions in the future. I had hoped so.

After the meeting, I felt like I had been the little girl called into the princi-pal's office: I had been to the confessional to talk to two men about my own sexuality by exposing my sexualized reading of and reaction to the kind of subjugating gendered behaviors many men engage in as a matter of course. I felt vindicated but, for all the wrong reasons, I also felt somewhat silly. I felt silly because I knew both men considered the incident relatively harmless, and because in some ways it was indeed relatively harmless: after all, this man did not wrestle me to the floor. The ambiguity of these emotions, my inability to feel completely right about my actions, bothered me for a long time despite my theoretical understanding of how my gendered body is positioned in discourse.

It is this kind body inscription of knowledge which constitutes part of the hidden gender curriculum of the university. As Magda Lewis puts it, "my knowledge of it comes more directly through the body—my body—overtly contained within the academy by the ideological frame of allowable knowledge" (In press, 1991). The constant pressure of having to take a position in someone else's discourse generates for many women a constant and profound disempowerment.

And it is not only the few men who harass women at work. We have put up with an offensive male gaze since we were girls. We have been whistled, shouted and stared at, we have heard and seen the verbal and gestural obscenities, anon-ymous hands in the crowd have pinched and grabbed us. Women silently put up with a lot of this kind of harassment, since the barrage of sexual violence cannot be countered in every instance. The "Look" structures the cartography of wom-en's daily lives in sometimes violent and often imperceptible ways. The follow-ing example from one of our contributors is a familiar one:

For months now, building construction has been going on between my office and the main building (largely the domain of senior male academics). Often workers are standing around leaning against the posts of either side of the only direct path between the two buildings. It is disturbing that I even have to give thought to alternative paths. But I think about the fact that if I walk straight along the path, I have to deal with "The Look". I have to walk the narrow space between groups of men whose talk ceases as I approach and whose comments follow me through the door. If, on the other hand, I walk around this group of men, taking a curved path, they would know that it was because of them. So I put up my inner defenses, focus my eyes on my destination and brave the direct route. It's a trivial incident, but descriptive of one of the many ways in which my intellectual or pedagogical work is interrupted by negotiating the gendered terrain of the academy.

The "Look" follows us everywhere. It is a map that structures our everyday: the clothes that we wear, the places we go, where and when we need accompaniment. At work, we then are expected to smile with understanding as men fire off sexist comments, always with a glance in our direction and the knowing nod that is supposed to signal the proverbial quotation marks around what for them is an ironic metacommentary on sexism. Women cannot speak up or walk out in protest at every faculty meeting when misogynist slander, even its quotationed form, permeates public and rational discussion. A strategy of consistent vigilance and protestation seems to result in men shutting out women completely whereas a selectively strategy of struggle seems to have more political force. But with every sexist comment or bad joke in quotation marks directed at the "resident feminist" who does not speak up, we sanction and institutionalize the discursive violence against ourselves and against all women. So some of us protest selectively: we target some issues and let others pass. We work hard to provide the evidence and arguments for the big issues such as improved campus safety for women, timetabling to cater for mothers, and so forth. The downside of such a selective politics is that, in order to be heard on what counts as important for women as a group, individual women remain silent on many personal affronts.

Sexist knowledges, then, are not only the kinds of sexist encounters illustrated above, but include the interminable references to the male subject in speech and text across the university. University documents for the most part have re-addressed the subject as "his/her" but this textual reference continues to signify the male. In most classrooms, in faculty meetings, in curriculum or policy discussions, the subject of choice remains male. When women academics speak, men may listen but they don't hear and they don't take up what women say. One of our contributors puts it this way:

> Women's struggle for equality and inclusion, and our attempts to gain public acknowledgment of our violation and marginalization are countered by claims of reverse sexism, preferential treatment of women and the silencing and intimidation of those who have never known what it means to be truly without voice, as women are, not because we cannot speak but because we are not heard and not being heard we cease to speak. Women repeatedly tell me of their conscious decision to stop speaking in classrooms where sexism is a non-negotiable dynamic of the curriculum and classroom practice. Some women tell me of not having spoken in class for years. Women speak of unconscionable sexism while those in power co-opt the language of the powerless. The

stories my students tell me about their educational experience are not unlike those I already know all too well.

In class or exam timetabling the particular circumstances of women (e.g., those with children) remain ignored. Reading lists in most courses do not include feminist works. The greatest percentage of sexual harassment complaints continue to be lodged by female students. Campus security is a real need for women and this too continues to be underfunded and, in many universities, wholly inadequate. Not all academic women, but certainly many feminist academics continue to fight for basic recognition of and provision for women's need in the university. The strategies for struggle against structural sexism are complex. If we speak up too often about the same old problems, men stop listening. Vocal feminist academics tend to get labeled feminist battle axes with a gender agenda. In coalition, our demands acquire more force but as some women have found, group solidarity can pose a greater threat than individual voices of resistance.

Patriarchal discourse

At the level of patriarchal knowledges, Grosz suggests that institutional structures organize and regulate women and men in "places of different value and differential access to self-determination. Patriarchal oppression provides a context, structure, support and legitimation for the various sexist acts of discrimination" (1988, p. 94). In other words, even if the liberal agenda of equal numbers, access, opportunity, and outcomes were implemented, and even if men and women "behaved in identical ways, their behaviors would still not have the same social meaning and value" (p. 94). At the level of patriarchal structure (institutional and discursive), women's struggle against strategies of oppression, marginalization and exclusion takes on a different form from contestations against sexist encounters. Few other places of work exemplify patriarchal rule better than the university, from the bureaucratic distribution of power to the Foucauldian "network of writing" (1979) rationalized in the rule system of the form and memo that administer procedure, persons and knowledge. Despite significant gains in the last two decades, women continue to be grossly underrepresented in senior positions and remain locked into the contract mill of the junior ghetto (cf. Slater & Glazer, 1989). Journal and book publishing editorial boards are dominated by males, promotion committees are stocked by suits, and department, faculty and school chairs remain the seats of male control. There is nothing hidden about this structural distribution of power. They are the visible sites from which the vocabularies and interpretations that underwrite oppositional gender politics emanate, and yet they are also obvious targets for Affirmative Action interventions. And, indeed, the liberal agenda has relocated women into some of these positions and has legislated spaces for women and women's issues.

Positions and unequal representation in the academy can be contested. What is much more difficult to identify and contest are the subterranean politics that bind some men together against women. We refer here to the "backroom deals" male academics are still entitled to make over women's theoretical and research contributions when it concerns women's application for research funds, their promotions or hiring. It concerns the impenetrability of the male network on non-feminist journal editorial boards who decide what counts as publishable: which works pose a threat to established male discourse, and what counts as "acceptable" feminist work to fit into male defined parameters of feminist critique. In the early years of academic feminism, the political agenda of claiming voice urged us to spell out our full names on manuscript title pages. It was imperative that we name ourselves. Two decades later and many women across the disciplines are substituting a first name initial for a full first name to preclude evoking a "feminist reading" on the part of referees. Why are women doing this, if not in reaction to the gendered political relations that continue to oversee academic knowledge production? On one hand, women's maneuvers in the business of academics suggests that feminist readings of that which is, remain threatening subversions of the canon (both of the Left and Right). On the other hand, the tremendous efforts women expend on achieving the academic rewards Anglo-European men can take for granted, and the emergent strategies of exscription of our feminine identities (and "feminist" publications) suggests a renewed colonization of and siege mentality among academic women. Further, the backward slide of the momentum the feminist movement had gained in the 1970s and part of the 1980s, has redirected many women's focus on issues that require recuperation. In other words, instead of moving forward, we seem to be expending a lot of energy in attempts to maintain and even recuperate the political gains achieved some time ago.

At the level of patriarchal knowledges and relations, then, women in the academy continue to struggle for equality: of rights (to speak and be heard), access (to positions of power, resources), and representation (on boards, committees, etc.). Beyond these visible targets for contestation, women also struggle with the more invisible relations of ruling. And these, as the following examples illustrate, are not only struggles with the conservative opposition, but are struggles within the terrain of the pro-feminist left. Perhaps this should not be a surprise. Historically, it is the liberal Left that has been the most vocal in its pro-feminist support (and pro all other marginalized causes and peoples), and which throughout the 1970s and 1980s has helped clear a space for Women's Studies, women's issues, and the hiring of female academics. On our reading, many of our male colleagues on the sympathetic Left have changed their discourse and have indeed been working on their public "attitudes". However, these "self-reflexive" moves do not automatically translate into giving up male privilege and power. Male academics on the ideological Right and Left hold fast to authoritarian rule over knowledge through strategies of exploitation and domination. Friendly fire is often indistinguishable from enemy fire.

Many of our male colleagues have been very supportive of our work. Others, by contrast, especially some who are at the center of radical pedagogy discourse, have gone to inordinate lengths to silence our work. Two of the papers in this volume have traveled through various reviewer networks only to be rejected through the political networking among those whose work they argued against. Much as the politicking among males remains a "boys only" information network, so too does an information network bind groups of academic women working on particular topics in specific disciplinary areas. It is through this network that information about active resistance to and interference with our work by our male colleagues came to light. One of the papers received an urgent invitation for submission to a leading educational journal. Shortly after submission, the paper ended up in the hands of one of the persons whose work was the object of the paper's critique; he denounced the paper in front of her colleague, who also happened to be her personal friend. This is her account:

> I could not understand the audacity of this person in denouncing my paper to my friend. I also became suspicious of how this paper ended up in his hands, given that I had submitted that particular version only to the journal. Knowing the connections this person had to the journal's editorial board, I was not surprised to hear within weeks that my paper was rejected. Months later a senior academic told me that this same person had asked him how and why he would let me get away with writing and trying to publish that kind of work. This kind of talk among men confirmed for me the continuing politics of subjugation and silencing that our colleagues on the "left" are engaged in; it also made me realize once again how tenuous our position is given that our work remains under overt and implicit control of men. In my case, a supportive departmental head counteracted the discursive violence which, under other circumstances, may have had more serious effects on my position and work. More importantly, this and similar encounters made me see clearly the duplicitous politics at work in a discourse that insists on the political importance of centering marginalized voices, of emancipation, freedom, and political solidarity.

The misogynist politics underlying what for many readers of the radical pedagogy literature appears as a liberatory, pro-feminist discourse of social justice are usually not challenged publicly. Many women work and live with and around such abuses.

Many women do not have the security of tenured positions to protest—verbally or in print—their continuing colonization. Pressured by the mandate to publish or perish, many women not uncommonly take second or third authorship on work that was clearly theirs. As graduate students, some of us gave up our work to supervising or senior professors who, after having taken first authorship, would guarantee us a publication. As women academics, some of our work is still being raided and our identities colonized in self-serving moves by our male colleagues "in the alliance" who claim first authorship and authority over "postmodernist pedagogies of liberation". These territorial politics are familiar to women throughout the academy and have a long-entrenched history (cf. Bannerji et al., 1991; Sherif, 1987). Academic debate, fine-tuning theory, and attempts to get right the political fallout of our theorizing towards a non-coercive pedagogy (see Orner, Chapter 5), should not in principle lead to the kinds of hostilities some of us have endured as a consequence of speaking out.

As, for instance, Hartsock (1987) and Lloyd (1986) have pointed out, masculinist epistemology and ways of doing business—whether in global politics, academic or office politics—is competitive, oppositional, and at its most rudimentary, it is war. The war of words in academic discourse is best exemplified by the subtext of "rejoinders". The "avant-garde" and "border pedagogy" agenda of counterdominant practice, one that exhorts us to work in collective struggle against oppressive structures and knowledges, realizes its transformative praxis in the strategy and tactics of war. As with most other disciplinary discourses, one is either "in" or "out" of the dominant camp. Feminist critiques of master discourses are by historical definition "out". In this divide and rule relation, academic debate is deferred as other (critical) voices are quickly positioned as opposing, contesting, and destructive forces which need to be silenced and put in their place by a verbal dressing down in the textual space of the rational counter-argument: the endless rejoinder. Women, of course, are not exempt from this format of contestation, since academic protocol demands that we rise to the challenge; if we don't, we are seen as not having what it takes by not having the theoretical backbone to fight a good fight. But this is not how feminist practice envisions its politics of knowledge building, intellectual debate, critique, and theorizing.

Nor should women of any color, or persons of any differences, constantly be positioned in confrontational relations. Why do women feel as though they are going to war when they face the opposition in hiring or promotions panels? Why is the de rigeur suit of armor—the mountain of "relevant" publications, the appropriate scholarly discourse, dress, and self-presentation—still insufficient for many women who come out of hiring or promotions interviews completely embattled? One of our Australian colleagues, a senior and extensively published academic, recently had a job interview with an all-male panel at one of Australia's "status" universities. She was told in no uncertain terms early in the interview that anyone who uses too many "isms"—as in feminism, poststructuralism, postmodernism, Marxism, etc.—is "feebleminded". As she explained it, despite her understanding of the pathology underlying such a statement, the discursive violence of the one-hour interview was a shattering experience. This encounter illustrates the powerful interconnections between phallocentric epistemology mirrored in patriarchal rule and valuation, and underscored with outrageous sexism.

Other women engage in war more publicly. One colleague, after a nine-year stint on the contract treadmill during which time an army of junior males moved effortlessly up the ranks, took her university to court on a sexual discrimination charge and was granted her tenure through legal interventions. The shame and humiliation of having to prove academic worth in the public discourse of the courts, of having to prove that feminist research and publications are of legitimate disciplinary caliber, are not the kind of confessional encounters academic men experience. This woman's battle with the procedure and structure of institutionalized patriarchy is part of a much larger war zone so many women are engaged in—a war not of their own making.

Differential valuations of women and men concern not only intellectual or disciplinary orientations but are centrally implicated in women's bodies in ways that they aren't for men. Women's sexualities—in its manifestation in dress, appearance/appeal, "looks", age, bodily habitus—continue to be read by many men as signposts of women's worth. Women positioned outside the normative representational order—that is, those discursively marked as "old", "larger", "physically impaired" or "lesbian", etc.—often comment on (in)visible slights they endure which are nothing short of devaluations of embodiment. There is no doubt that some hiring, promotion and funding decisions take women's sexuality and bodies into account in ways that they don't for men. Indeed, both of us have been in academic interviews where our sexuality seemed more important to some panel members than what we had to say. For some, sexuality continues to be a means by which a few women maneuver up through the academic ranks. But for many others it seems a weapon too often used against them.

Women's work in the academy, then, is not only about fighting for equal access, places, rewards, and representation. Our research, teaching, and careers require commitment not only to our personal and theoretical politics, but require also that we work within and according to the rules laid down and maintained by those whose interests those rules serve. In Grosz's (1988) view, patriarchy has to do with the underlying structures and processes that regulate and organize women and men in different locations and value systems. So while it is indeed patriarchy that has "granted" women places in the public, some even of equal formal status to men, our academic titles and positions do not guarantee immunity from the politics of domination and exploitation that continue to have a profound influence on our lives and our work. No university calendar, job description or contract explains the rules of the game. The unspoken rules and unspeakable application of those rules are the subtext of many women's academic experiences which hover between the lines of much of women's writing. For all of us, the personal that generally is invisible to readers of our texts but which profoundly influences our work as teachers, researchers and theorists, is eminently political.

Phallocentric discourse

Our struggles against incorporation and domination at the levels of sexist and patriarchal knowledges coalesce in our resistance to what Grosz (1988) calls "phallocentric knowledges". She writes (p. 94):

Phallocentrism . . . is a discursive or representational form of women's oppression. Phallocentrism conflates the two (autonomous) sexes into a singular "universal" model which, however, is congruent only with the masculine. Whenever the two sexes are represented in a single, so-called "human" model, the female or feminine is always represented in male or masculine terms. Phallocentrism is the abstracting, universalising and generalising of masculine attributes so that women's or femininity's concrete specificity and potential for autonomous definition are covered over.

It is the logic of phallocentric knowledges and the socio-cultural relations and structures that express and justify those knowledges which enable the differential valuation of women and men at the levels of patriarchal and sexist discourse. The master narratives that have written Truth, Logic, Reason, History, and the Individual to the center of Meaning and the Real, have been constitutive of Anglo-European male experience and "consciousness" at the expense of constructing and positioning negative identities outside the masculine positivity. The constitutive "human subject" exists only on the basis of numerous oppositional others and the disavowal of other ways of knowing, being, speaking. In phallocentric knowledges the universal (male) subject and his characteristics and values subsume the feminine; feminine and masculine principles, women and men assume an identity of the same. And because the feminine is all that which the universal human subject is not, she serves as the silent other support for all that which is universally human (and male). Universal "man" is a rational impassionate thinker, a builder of civilizations and military strategist, an objective lawmaker and observer, a writer and speaker of doctrine and truth. Women, historically, are none of these—either in historical practice or discourse. Her difference, then, in andro- and phallocentric discourse, is actualized in her differential valuation at the levels of patriarchal and sexist knowledge. Because she is not that which universally human and male, her lack and Otherness at the level of theory—philosophical, political, social, etc.—translates at the level of social practice into her exclusion, subjugation and inferiority. Political theory denies her political participation and education; philosophy denies her an analytic and logical mind; theory denies her the right to speak and interpret doctrine. The "logical" transfer, then, from her non-being in androcentric discourse to patriarchal and sexist discourse means that this is where her lesser positioning takes on its "natural" expression.

As we noted in the introduction, feminists in the academy have been hard at work the past two decades in contesting phallocentrism across disciplinary knowledges. The great volume of theoretically sophisticated feminist scholarship that has tackled the misogyny and Euro-centrism of grand narratives in the social and natural sciences, in literary studies, philosophy and history, has no contemporary parallel. Grosz (1988, p. 94) points out that phallocentrism is much harder to locate because "it is a theoretical bedrock of shared assumptions that is so pervasive that it is no longer recognized". As historians, scientists, philosophers, literary and social theorists, women may well salute each other for having produced the scholarly goods which have exposed the misogynist and some of the racist fictions of the fathers. However, a critical analytic re-reading of the Great Texts is much easier than contesting the pervasive, naturalized shared assumptions which those texts have justified for so long and on which so much of contemporary social organization and relations are founded. Hence, women's struggle against sexist and patriarchal containments is always also a struggle against phallocentric regimes.

We are able to reverse the masculinist order of things in our own classrooms by selecting readings for students that are not derivative of masculinist epistemology. We conduct our research and construct our theoretical base on feminist epistemologies; our citations therefore disrupt the reproduction of phallocentric knowledges. But these subversions in our own authorized spaces tend to remain a network of writing by women and for women. For the most part, the rule of the masculinist signifier remains intact in mainstream disciplines. In sociology, for instance, introductory undergraduate courses continue to recirculate the "greats"—Marx, Weber, Durkheim, Giddens—not as historical texts, but as valid theoretical frameworks for interpreting the present. In fact, the "crisis in sociology" has led to a reinstatement of the old masters (Archer, 1990; Himmelstrand, 1986). Feminist sociologists (e.g., Dorothy Smith, Ruth Wallace, Joan Acker) remain on reading lists in women's studies courses and specialty electives on "feminism" within sociology departments. In the natural sciences, in philosophy and political science, the feminist challenge of phallocentric discourse is an even greater struggle, as Harding, Haraway, Nye, Pateman and others have shown. In education, the current, predominantly male-authored "back-to-basics" and cultural literacy discourses, pose a significant challenge to all feminist and non-feminist educators and scholars who have a political stake in fighting on behalf of persons of difference against yet another move of incorporation into a re-emergent canon. And while a new generation of male theorists, often self-professed postmodernists, argue forcefully for the rejection of Enlightenment narratives, for a skepticism of all totalizing narratives, and for the celebration of a fragmented decentered subject, such discursive gestures belie a subtle reproduction of the same old epistemic assumptions and textual strategies which account for the fantasies of "women in the beehive" (Derrida), the rugged individualism of a Jack Kerouac nomad and observer of cultural authenticity (Baudrillard), or the story of grand systems theory revisited (Lyotard). These contemporary master visions are no less phallocentric, no less a spectacle of the male image that narrates once again its vision of itself, than those master narratives now accused of Enlightenment humanism and positivism. Theorists of the contemporary may well defer on linguistic essentialism, but it *is* the textuality of postmodernist theoretical discourse that is rewriting the subject, the social, and social criticism. And as Fraser and Nicholson (1988) have eloquently argued, the new narratives are potentially as theoretically and politically dangerous to others of difference as the old narratives.

Feminist resistance against phallocentric discourse, then, operates on the terrain of both conservative narratives of old and neo-conservative narratives of the new avant-garde. The counterpractices we target at phallocentric knowledges are our textual productions and selections: our research and writings, and reading lists. Our struggles against patriarchy and sexism are waged on the terrain of the classroom, the faculty and committee meeting, the office and staff lounge. The women in this volume are by now well familiar with the politics of academic practice; we have paid our dues and we *are* collectively making a difference for some women, in some locations, some of the time. What we have tried to show in this chapter is that feminist theory and practice is fundamentally grounded in the daily routines of women's work as university teachers. Our students in our classrooms and those who read our books and articles are generally unaware of the power-knowledge regime that structures our work, subjectivities, and institutional identities. And for every personal narrative documented in this chapter, there are many more which, like women elsewhere, we share. Women discuss these issues a lot, but discuss them in private: in conversation at conferences, through the mail, via fax and on the phone. This is the subtext of feminist women's academic careers which is fundamentally personal and private. We therefore consider it politically essential to make public how some academic feminists experience the myriad refractions of that regime, in order to foreground the hidden dimension of feminist theoretical and pedagogical practice.

References

Archer, M. (1990) Resisting the revival of relativism. In M. Albrow and E. King (Eds.), *Globalization, knowledge and society: Readings from international sociology* (pp. 19–33). London: Sage.

Bannerji, H., Carty, L., Dehli, K., Heald, S. & McKenna, K. (1991) *Unsettling relations: The university as a site of feminist struggles.* Toronto: Women's Press.

Bartky, S. L. (1990) *Femininity and domination.* New York: Routledge.

Fraser, N. & Nicholson, L. (1988) Social criticism without philosophy: An encounter between feminism and postmodernism. *Theory, Culture & Society,* 5(2 & 3), 373–394.

Foucault, M. (1980) *Power/knowledge.* New York: Pantheon.

Foucault, M. (1979) *Discipline and punish.* New York: Vintage Books.

Grosz, E. (1988) The in(ter)vention of feminist knowledges. In B. Caine, E. Grosz & M. de Lepervanche (Eds.), *Crossing boundaries* (pp. 92–106). Sydney: Allen & Unwin.

Hartsock, N. (1987) The feminist standpoint: Developing the ground for a specifically feminist historical materialism. In S. Harding (Ed.), *Feminism & methodology* (pp. 157–180). Bloomington, IA: Indiana University Press.

Heald, S. (1991) Pianos to pedagogy: Pursuing the educational subject. In H. Bannerji, L. Carty, K. Dehli, S. Heald & K. McKenna, *Unsetting relations: The university as a site of feminist struggles* (pp. 129–149). Toronto: Women's Press.

hooks, b. (1990) *Yearning: Race, gender, and cultural politics.* Boston, MA: South End Press.

Himmelstrand, U. (1986) (Ed.) *The social reproduction of organization and culture.* Beverly Hills, CA: Sage.

Kramer, L. & Martin, G. (1988) Mainstreaming gender: Some thoughts for the nonspecialist. *Teaching Sociology,* 16.

Lather, P. (1991) Staying dumb? Student resistance to liberatory curriculum. In P. Lather, *Getting smart: Feminist research and pedagogy with/in the postmodern* (pp. 123–152). New York: Routledge.

Lewis, M. (1991) Power and education: Who decides the forms schools have taken and who should decide? In J. Kincheloe (Ed.), *Thirteen questions: New perspectives on American education.* New York, NY: Peter Lang Inc.

Lloyd, G. (1986) Selfhood, war and masculinity. In C. Pateman & E. Grosz (Eds.), *Feminist challenges: Social and political theory* (pp. 63–76). Sydney: Allen & Unwin.

Nye, A. (1990) *Words of power: A feminist reading of the history of logic.* New York: Routledge.

Sherif, C. (1987) Bias in psychology. In S. Harding (Ed.), *Feminism and methodology* (pp. 37–56). Bloomington, IN. University of Indiana Press.

Slater, M. & Glazer, P. M. (1989) Prescriptions for professional survival. In J. Conway, S. Bourque & J. Scott (Eds.), *Learning about women: Gender, politics & power* (pp. 119–136). Ann Arbor, MI: University of Michigan Press.

Index

Notes on Contributors

Elizabeth Ellsworth is Associate Professor in the Department of Curriculum and Instruction and a member of the Women's Studies Program at the University of Wisconsin-Madison, USA. She teaches graduate courses on the interrelations of media, culture, and curriculum, and has recently taught special topics courses on the intersections of gender, race and class in curriculum and instruction. She is currently co-authoring a book with Mimi Orner on media, power and (re)presentation in education.

Jennifer Gore is Senior Lecturer in the Department of Educational Studies at the University of Newcastle, Australia where she teaches sociology of education and curriculum theory. She has published articles in the areas of teacher education and curriculum studies and is author of *The struggle for pedagogies,* forthcoming from Routledge, Chapman & Hall.

Jane Kenway is Senior Lecturer in Social and Administrative Studies in the School of Education at Deakin University, Australia. Her research is centered on the connections between education and social inequality. She has published widely on this topic. Currently she is involved in a major research project which draws on post-structuralist theory to examine gender reforms in schools.

Helen Modra is a Senior Tutor in the Faculty of Education at Deakin University, Victoria, Australia. Before moving to Deakin in 1988 she worked for over twenty years as a librarian—in State Librarian Services, including consultancy service and in Municipal libraries—and as a lecturer in librarianship. Because of this background, Helen has a strong commitment to and indentification with non-formal community education. She is currently working towards a Ph.D in education at Deakin University.

Patti Lather currently teaches qualitative research and gender and education courses at Ohio State University. Her book, *Getting Smart: Feminist research and pedagogy with/in the postmodern* (Routledge, 1991), explores her interest in the methodological implications of the critical theories of feminism, neo-marxism and poststructuralism. She is a part of the core faculty for the developing Gender and Education doctoral emphasis at Ohio State University, USA.

Magda Lewis earned her Ph.D. at the Ontario Institute for Studies in Education/University of Toronto. As assistant professor she teaches gender and education, sociology and Women's Studies at Queen's University at Kingston, Canada. Presently she is preparing a book for Routledge, Chapman and Hall on the topic of feminist pedagogy.

Carmen Luke is Senior Lecturer in the Department of Social and Cultural Studies, James Cook University in Australia. She is author of *Pedagogy, printing and protestantism: The discourse on childhood* (SUNY, 1989), *Constructing the child viewer* (Praeger, 1990) and co-editor of *Language, authority and criticism* (Falmer Press, 1989).

Mimi Orner is a community video activist and educator, currently finishing her doctoral dissertation at the University of Wisconsin-Madison. Her work combines feminist studies and theories of representation with the de/reconstruction of curriculum. She has worked as a distance education outreach program director and as a university lecturer.

Valerie Walkerdine grew up in Derby, England and like many young working class women of her generation turned to primary school teaching as "a good job for a woman". She went on to study psychology, art and film (in that order). She has been Reader at the University of London, Institute of Education and is currently Professor of Psychology and Communications, University of London, Goldsmiths' College. (She also makes art and films when she has the time!)

Her recent books include: *Democracy in the kitchen* (Virago, 1989); *Counting girls out* (Virago, 1989); *The mastery of reason* (Routledge, 1988/1990); *Schoolgirl fictions* (Verso, 1991).

2748 082